The Novels

ANALYSING TEXTS

General Editor: Nicholas Marsh

Published

Chaucer: The Canterbury Tales *Gail Ashton*

Shakespeare: The Comedies *R. P. Draper*

Charlotte Brontë: The Novels *Mike Edwards*

Shakespeare: The Tragedies *Nicholas Marsh*

Jane Austen: The Novels *Nicholas Marsh*

Emily Brontë: Wuthering Heights *Nicholas Marsh*

Virginia Woolf: The Novels *Nicholas Marsh*

John Donne: The Poems *Joe Nutt*

D. H. Lawrence: The Novels *Nicholas Marsh*

Analysing Texts
Series Standing Order ISBN 0–333–73260–X
(outside North America only)

You can receive future titles in this series as they are published by placing a standing order. Please contact your bookseller or, in case of difficulty, write to us at the address below with your name and address, the title of the series and the ISBN quoted above.

Customer Services Department, Macmillan Distribution Ltd
Houndmills, Basingstoke, Hampshire RG21 6XS, England

D. H. Lawrence: The Novels

NICHOLAS MARSH

First Published 2000 by
MACMILLAN PRESS LTD
Houndmills, Basingstoke, Hampshire RG21 6XS
and London
Companies and representatives
throughout the world

ISBN 0–333–77124-9 hardcover
ISBN 0–333–77125-7 paperback

A catalogue record for this book is available from the British Library.

This book is printed on paper suitable for recycling and made from fully managed and sustained forest sources.

10   9   8   7   6   5   4   3   2   1
09   08   07   06   05   04   03   02   01   00

Printed in China

Published in the United States of America by
ST. MARTIN'S PRESS, LLC.,
Scholarly and Reference Division,
175 Fifth Avenue, New York, N.Y. 10010

ISBN 0–312–23284-5 (cloth)
ISBN 0–312–23286-1 (paper)

For Marianne

Contents

General Editor's Preface

This series is dedicated to one clear belief: that we can all enjoy, understand and analyse literature for ourselves, provided we know how to do it. How can we build on close understanding of a short passage, and develop our insight into the whole work? What features do we expect to find in a text? Why do we study style in so much detail? In demystifying the study of literature, these are only some of the questions the *Analysing Texts* series addresses and answers.

The books in this series will not do all the work for you, but will provide you with the tools, and show you how to use them. Here, you will find samples of close, detailed analysis, with an explanation of the analytical techniques utilised. At the end of each chapter there are useful suggestions for further work you can do to practise, develop and hone the skills demonstrated and build confidence in you own analytical ability.

An author's individuality shows in the way they write: every work they produce bears the hallmark of that writer's personal 'style'. In the main part of each book we concentrate therefore on analysing the particular flavour and concerns of one author's work, and explain the features of their writing in connection with major themes. In Part 2 there are chapters about the author's life and work, assessing their contribution to developments in literature; and a sample of critics' views are summarised and discussed in comparison with each other. Some suggestions for further reading provide a bridge towards further critical research.

Analysing Texts is designed to stimulate and encourage your critical and analytic faculty, to develop your personal insight into the author's work and individual style, and to provide you with the skills and techniques to enjoy at first hand the excitement of discovering the richness of the text.

NICHOLAS MARSH

A Note on Editions

References to *Sons and Lovers*, *The Rainbow* and *Women in Love* are page references to the Penguin Twentieth-Century Classics editions of 1994, 1995 and 1995 respectively. Where it is obvious from the context which novel is being referred to, the page number appears on its own.

PART 1

ANALYSING
D. H. LAWRENCE'S
NOVELS

1

Narrative Texture

D. H. Lawrence provokes strong reactions among his readers. Some are immediately swept up in the enthusiasm, the commitment with which Lawrence battles to express his feelings and his ideas. Others are provoked, irritated and frustrated by the struggles sometimes met with in his style, by being bludgeoned with experiences, and the sudden sweep of a breathtaking generalisation. The professional critics are just the same: they seem to suffer from a 'Lawrence effect' which sows division and discord, so the critical establishment is now shattered into little fissiparous fragments, in their estimations of Lawrence.

We are about to embark on detailed textual study of Lawrence's three most admired, and most established novels. One of the conclusions we will reach at the end of this study is that nothing in these novels is resolved: nothing is finished, and contradictions abound – and readers will then be able to consider for themselves, whether they find these contradictory novels a great achievement or a grand failure.

The present chapter has a limited aim. Here, we simply want to meet Lawrence's writing, in close detail, head on. We start by analysing what his writing does to us as we read, and working out how and why it works on us. This, then, is our first confrontation with the actual texture of his novels, with no other aim than to pin down what that texture is like. Our analysis will therefore aim to discover as much as possible about why Lawrence wrote in the way he did. What effects did he seek? What aims and concerns are revealed by the special flavour of his style?

Since we begin with a practical exploration of the text, no further introduction is needed at this stage. We will go straight to our first passage, an extract from *Sons and Lovers* in which Paul Morel begins to look for work:

> Paul was now fourteen, and was looking for work. He was a rather small and rather finely-made boy, with dark brown hair and light blue eyes. His face had already lost its youthful chubbiness, and was becoming somewhat like William's, rough-featured, almost rugged, and it was extraordinarily mobile. Usually he looked as if he saw things, was full of life, and warm; then his smile, like his mother's, came suddenly and was very lovable; and then, when there was any clog in his soul's quick running, his face went stupid and ugly. He was the sort of boy that becomes a clown and a lout as soon as he is not understood, or feels himself held cheap; and again is adorable at the first touch of warmth.
>
> He suffered very much from the first contact with anything. When he was seven, the starting school had been a nightmare and a torture to him. But afterwards he liked it. And now that he felt he had to go out into life, he went through agonies of shrinking self-consciousness. He was quite a clever painter, for a boy of his years. And he knew some French and German and mathematics, that Mr Heaton had taught him. But nothing he had was of any commercial value. He was not strong enough for heavy manual work, his mother said. He did not care for making things with his hands, preferred racing about, or making excursions into the country, or reading, or painting.
>
> 'What do you want to be?' his mother asked.
>
> He had not the faintest notion. He would have liked to go on painting, but that never occurred to him, since it was impossible. He quite strongly did not want to do anything. But it was urgent now that he should begin to earn. And since he did not feel that he was of high monetary value in the world, and since he knew that at any job a man makes thirty shillings or thirty-five shillings a week, he invariably replied:
>
> 'Anything.'
>
> 'That is no answer,' said Mrs Morel.
>
> But it was quite truthfully the only answer he could give. His ambition, as far as this world's gear went, was quietly to earn his thirty or thirty-five shillings a week, somewhere near home, and then, when his father died, have a cottage with his mother, paint and go out as he

liked, and live happy ever after. That was his programme as far as doing things went. But he was proud within himself, measuring people against himself, and placing them, inexorably. And he thought that *perhaps* he might also make a painter, the real thing. But that he left alone.

'Then,' said his mother, 'you must look in the paper for the advertisements.'

He looked at her. It seemed to him a bitter humiliation and an anguish to go through. But he said nothing. When he got up in the morning, his whole being was knotted up over this one thought:

'I've got to go and look for advertisements for a job.'

It stood in front of the morning, that thought, killing all joy and even life, for him. His heart felt like a tight knot.

And then, at ten o'clock, he set off. He was supposed to be a queer, quiet child. Going up the sunny street of the little town, he felt as if all the folk he met said to themselves: 'He's going to the Co-op Reading Room to look in the papers for a place. He can't get a job. I suppose he's living on his mother.' Then he crept up the stone stairs behind the drapery shop at the Co-op, and peeped in the reading room. Usually one or two men were there, either old useless fellows, or Colliers 'on the club.' So he entered, full of shrinking and suffering when they looked up, seated himself at the table, and pretended to scan the news. He knew they would think, 'What does a lad of thirteen want in a reading room, with a newspaper,' and he suffered.

Then he looked wistfully out of the window. Already he was a prisoner of industrialism. Large sunflowers stared over the old red wall of the garden opposite, looking in their jolly way down on the women who were hurrying with something for dinner. The valley was full of corn, brightening in the sun. Two collieries, among the fields, waved their small white plumes of steam. Far-off on the hills were the woods of Aldersley, dark and fascinating. Already his heart went down. He was being taken into bondage. His freedom in the beloved home valley, was going now.

(*Sons and Lovers*, pp. 113–15)

Let us start by looking at sentences. In this extract there are very short sentences – only four or five words long – and a few sentences which are considerably longer. The longest occurs in the first paragraph, and is 79 words long. It describes Paul's facial expressions, and is in three parts linked by semi-colons. Another long sentence, beginning 'His ambition . . .', describes Paul's vision of his future life. This is a looser sentence, strung together along eight commas, and its effect is easier to describe. Paul's hopes come in short, simple stages ('quietly to earn his thirty or thirty-five shillings a week' and 'have a cottage with his mother') interrupted by simple conditions which will make them possible ('somewhere near home' and 'when his father died'), and the *naïveté* of the boy's ambitions builds in increments to its final cliché phrase 'happy ever after'. The length of this sentence conveys the plain sequence of Paul's plans as life gets better and better in his imagination, ironically including his father's death as a trivial but wished-for event.

The other long sentence describes contrasting moods in Paul: it tells us that he is usually 'full of life, and warm', and the consequence of this is that he looks attractive ('lovable'); sometimes, on the other hand, there is a 'clog in his soul's quick running' and the consequence of this mood is that he looks 'stupid and ugly'. The meaning of this sentence – that two different feelings give him two different expressions – is not difficult to follow, but Lawrence has included one challenging phrase, 'any clog in his soul's quick running', which we find difficult to internalise. What does Lawrence mean by the 'quick running' of the soul? What sort of events in life could be likened to putting a 'clog' in the soul? If we read on, we find that Paul becomes a 'lout' when he is 'not understood', or 'held cheap'; and these two situations seem to explain what can put a 'clog' in his 'soul'. In these two sentences, then, Lawrence has first confronted us with a problematic phrase which combines metaphor and metaphysical concept, which is hard to accept and impossible to define; then he has provided us with two quite practical examples we can all relate to – the situations of being 'not understood' and 'held cheap' – which help us towards understanding what Lawrence might mean by the soul.

This sentence also indirectly makes another important claim: that the inside and outside are organically linked. There is a natural and unavoidable correspondence between the state of Paul's 'soul' and his outward behaviour and appeal. Yet this is not shown logically: Paul does not *say* that his soul is well or ill. Instead, it happens in a way which seems to bypass his head, and the effects of two states of 'soul' are quite surprising. Paul's beauty – his attractiveness – appears and disappears with his mood; and conversely he becomes a 'clown' and 'lout' when his 'soul' is hurt. This sentence, then, implies that a person is an organic 'whole' with inner and outer lives inextricably linked; yet at the same time, this unity of personality appears to happen on a curious and almost metaphorical level, rather than in the more usual spheres of speech and action.

The metaphor contained in the puzzling phrase is also of interest. Paul's soul is seen as a machine, running smoothly, and the image of a clog is one of sabotage. We will return to this idea, as industrial life is a recurrent theme in the whole passage. For the moment, it is enough to notice that Lawrence's image connects mechanisation with a metaphysical concept – the 'soul' – in a surprising conjunction of ideas.

The short sentences in this extract serve two purposes. Some are merely narrative, and we will find that it is characteristic of Lawrence that physical actions are related in a terse, economical manner. For example, in this extract we find 'He looked at her', and 'But he said nothing'. Other short sentences convey mental actions or emotional states. So we find 'But afterwards he liked it', and 'His heart felt like a tight knot'. The shortness of these sentences gives us a sudden impression of changing thoughts and temporary, volatile states of feeling. Again, we will find these short statements of sudden emotion to be typical of Lawrence's writing.

Many of the sentences in this extract begin with the conjunctions 'and' or 'but'. In Lawrence's time, this habit was regarded as bad style, so why does he do it? What effect does he gain from it? Look at the discussion of Paul's ambitions, when we are told that he has low expectations of any career. Lawrence continues 'But he was proud within himself, measuring people against himself, and placing them, inexorably. And he thought that *perhaps* he might also make a painter, the real thing. But that he left alone.' Here we have three successive sentences beginning with conjunctions, and they tell us about the unresolved ends of Paul's hopes and fears. The effect seems to be to give us an impression of what happens in Paul's mind: clearly he enjoys painting, and would like to be an artist, but he has persuaded himself not to think about it seriously because he recognises, realistically, that it is 'impossible'. Each sentence seems to add to or counter the thought contained in the previous sentence: in this way Lawrence conveys the uneasy conflict in Paul's mind. Additionally, the word 'inexorably' stands out as a literary word among plain vocabulary. The effect is difficult to define: it is as if this is Paul's own word, and it stands in the sentence like a mental action. It bolsters Paul's ego, making him sound stricter and more intellectual, before he admits his lack of faith in his painting. An equivalent sense of angry compensation is present in the short dismissive sentence, 'But that he left alone'. Lawrence's language conveys how thinking about an artistic career makes Paul feel uncomfortable with himself.

Turning to the dialogue in the extract, we notice that there is very little of it. Two main characters hold a discussion, yet they say hardly anything. The fact that their communication is inadequate is underlined both by its brevity and by Paul's unexpressed thoughts and feelings which are detailed, in contrast to the one word 'Anything' that he speaks, which his mother further devalues when she says 'That is no answer'. There is a terrible poverty in the dialogue: the characters misunderstand and hurt each other. In this extract we find Paul feeling 'a bitter humiliation and an anguish' as a result of what his mother says, but 'he said nothing'. Such dialogue emphasises the difficulties and failures of communication between people.

A second effect produced by this brevity of dialogue is of the richness of interior life: the unspoken emotional and mental life of the boy is narrated at length. This is the level at which subtlety, sophistication and complexity, change, volatility and development exist. By writing in this way, Lawrence seems to say to us that the important story of a human being takes place inside: the important events for his characters are mental and emotional events, and are never articulated. In relationships, significant changes occur between people, and are sensed, without being expressed or discussed. Here, Mrs Morel has trampled upon her son's artistic ambitions, humiliating him, yet none of this has been mentioned between them.

So far, we have concentrated on the way in which the passage is written. Two further points are worth remarking before we turn to the content.

First, we should notice the number of alternative descriptions we are given. For example, Paul's face is 'rough-featured', then 'almost rugged'. Lawrence seems to be struggling for the right word here: 'rough-featured' represents the author's first attempt at describing what his imagination sees; then 'rugged' is as close as language can get, but it is not quite true, only 'almost' true. Similarly, emotions often provoke a series of attempts at description. At the end of our extract, for example, we read 'Already his heart went down. He was being taken into bondage. His freedom in the beloved home valley, was going now'. The author conveys a single development of feeling when Paul becomes depressed at the prospect of having to work. Three successive short sentences express three aspects of the same feeling, elaborating the simple statement of depression into its contributing overtones of bondage and lost freedom. This technique is characteristic of Lawrence, as we will find: it creates a sense of the author struggling to express things that cannot quite be put into words, things that are in the process of being realised and translated into language, with only limited success.

Secondly, what is the narrative stance? What points of view are represented in the passage? The answer is that several points of view are given at different times, and the reader needs to be alert to this fact.

Much of the time, Lawrence writes as an omniscient author: he tells us the truth and clearly expects us to trust him. So, when the author tells us that Paul 'went through agonies of shrinking self-consciousness', this is a description of Paul's emotion which we accept at face value. Again, when Paul is described as 'a rather small and rather finely-made boy', we can take the author's word for it. However, the authorial voice is not consistent. Sometimes the narrative slips into the thoughts in a character's mind, presenting a kind of interior indirect speech and replacing the detached author. For example, when Paul gives his one-word answer 'Anything', the narrative tells us: 'But it was quite truthfully the only answer he could give'. The phrase 'quite truthfully' sounds like Paul talking to himself in his mind: it smacks of self-justification, self-excuse. We know from the end of the same paragraph that it is not quite the truth, because he still harbours secret ambitions as a painter. So, Paul's understanding is less complete, not as reliable as what Lawrence tells us in the author's own 'voice'. Such modulations of voice can even be confined to a single word, as in the case of 'inexorably' which we discussed above. We must be alert to such subtle shifts, which distinguish Lawrence's authorial voice from the less reliable thoughts of his characters.

Some further points of view appear in this extract, also. The sentence 'He was supposed to be a queer, quiet child' raises the question: who 'supposed' this? Presumably, this is his family's and the local community's opinion. Lawrence has indicated a shift in the point of view, by including 'supposed to be'. Another example is found in the sentence, 'He was not strong enough for heavy manual work, his mother said'. Again, a single phrase – 'his mother said' – changes the viewpoint. In this case, we hear what Mrs Morel says about her son, which Paul accepts; but the author disassociates himself, suggesting that this idea about Paul may not be true. Knowing the Morel family as we do by this stage of the novel, we are prompted to ask: is he *really* not strong enough, or do his mother's middle-class aspirations, and her hatred of her husband, *make him* 'not strong enough'? In this case, the slight shift in viewpoint brings a wide and complex area of family dynamics into play in the reader's mind. We are suddenly reminded that Paul is a product of conflicting forces and pressures: he is not only a person with his own thoughts and feelings, he has also been created by his mother's hopes and his father's nature.

Finally, we should briefly comment on the content of the passage. This is not a dramatic crisis, part of a momentous plot, but an ordinary episode in an ordinary life: after leaving school, a boy begins to look for work. However, Lawrence's theme of restriction, economic limitation and even enslavement is pursued relentlessly throughout the extract. The economic necessity of working is repeatedly emphasised. Paul's education gives him nothing 'of any commercial value', and 'it was urgent now that he should begin to earn' yet he was not of 'high monetary value' and does not expect much from 'this world's gear' because he feels limited to between 'thirty shillings' and 'thirty-five shillings' a week. Paul's response to economic necessity is also strongly and repeatedly expressed: he went through 'agonies' and felt 'shrinking self-consciousness', while in the reading room he is 'full of shrinking and suffering'; having to look in the paper was 'bitter humiliation' and 'an anguish' which made him 'knotted up' so that 'His heart felt like a tight knot'. His fear and misery are conveyed as he 'crept', 'peeped' and 'suffered' until his heart 'went down'.

Lawrence develops unspoiled nature as a contrast to economic necessity. The view from the reading room window, described in the final paragraph, sets the valley 'full of corn, brightening in the sun', and the woods 'dark and fascinating' in contrast to a single word: 'industrialism'. Earlier in the extract, Lawrence prepared for this nature/industrialism contrast, when he described the thought of work as standing 'in front of the morning', and killing 'even life'. Lawrence adds the images 'prisoner' and 'bondage' to define Paul's relationship to the industrial and economic world.

In this extract, then, Lawrence is repeatedly concerned with the conflict between imprisoning and restricting economic necessities, a complete set of circumstances which he calls 'industrialism'; and the individual's desire for freedom and artistic expression, which are associated with childhood, 'joy' and nature. This is our first analysis, and for the present we should be satisfied to have grasped a broad theme about which Lawrence seems to be concerned: conflict between material and economic constraints, and their opposite – as yet ill-defined, but clearly associated with ideals of freedom and nature. However, even from this one short passage, there are two further indications worth remarking before we move on.

First, there are indications that the contrast between industry and nature may not be clear-cut. We were already surprised that Lawrence describes Paul's soul using the metaphor of a 'quick running' machine, because machines and souls seem to be on opposite sides of the industry/nature divide. Notice also the description of collieries in the final paragraph: 'among the fields, [the pits] waved their small white plumes of steam'. Here, to our surprise again, the mines are presented as pretty, and 'small' denies any threat. We can speculate that Paul's view out of the window is, in some way, a nostalgic view from his innocent childhood, before industry began to threaten his happiness. This might explain the clean, pretty 'plumes' of smoke he sees. With regard to his mechanical soul, we may relate this to his naïve and clichéd ambitions which lead to a 'happy ever after'. Lawrence may ironically imply that there is something contemptible and limited in Paul's unthinking happiness at this time: it is a facile dream, and as such it is on a low, mechanical level. However, we would need more evidence to make more than tentative suggestions at this stage.

Secondly, we have noticed that communication between Paul and his mother is very restricted, in contrast to Paul's full inner life. This may remind us of the bondage/freedom conflict we have found elsewhere in the passage, and we wonder whether Lawrence's theme may operate in the same way on different levels. So, is the hurtful relationship between mother and son portrayed as a kind of imprisonment, while an individual's inner life has the potential for freedom and fulfilment?

*   *   *

We have learned a great deal from our first analysis, both about the texture of Lawrence's style, and about a theme which seems to be a major concern in *Sons and Lovers*. We now turn to *The Rainbow*. Our extract comes from the first chapter, and it tells of Tom Brangwen's encounter with a foreigner, and a girl:

> . . . and had gone off with the girl, into the woods, not quite knowing where he was or what he was doing. His heart thumped and he thought it the most glorious adventure, and was mad with desire for the girl.
>
> Afterwards he glowed with pleasure. By Jove, but that was something like! He stayed the afternoon with the girl, and wanted to stay the night. She, however, told him this was impossible: her own man would be back by dark, and she must be with him. He, Brangwen, must not let on that there had been anything between them.
>
> She gave him an intimate smile, which made him feel confused and gratified.
>
> He could not tear himself away, though he had promised not to interfere with the girl. He stayed on at the hôtel over-night. He saw the other fellow at the evening meal; a small, middle-aged man with

iron-grey hair and a curious face, like a monkey's, but interesting, in its way almost beautiful. Brangwen guessed that he was a foreigner. He was in company with another, an Englishman, dry and hard. The four sat at table, two men and two women. Brangwen watched with all his eyes.

He saw how the foreigner treated the women with courteous contempt, as if they were pleasing animals. Brangwen's girl had put on a ladylike manner, but her voice betrayed her. She wanted to win back her man. When dessert came on, however, the little foreigner turned round from his table and calmly surveyed the room, like one unoccupied. Brangwen marvelled over the cold, animal intelligence of the face. The brown eyes were round, showing all the brown pupil, like a monkey's, and just calmly looking, perceiving the other person without referring to him at all. They rested on Brangwen. The latter marvelled at the old face turned round on him, looking at him without considering it necessary to know him at all. The eyebrows of the round, perceiving, but unconcerned eyes were rather high up, with slight wrinkles above them, just as a monkey's had. It was an old, ageless face.

The man was most amazingly a gentleman all the time, an aristocrat. Brangwen stared fascinated. The girl was pushing her crumbs about on the cloth, uneasily, flushed and angry.

As Brangwen sat motionless in the hall afterwards, too much moved and lost to know what to do, the little stranger came up to him with a beautiful smile and manner, offering a cigarette and saying:

'Will you smoke?'

Brangwen never smoked cigarettes, yet he took the one offered, fumbling painfully with thick fingers, blushing to the roots of his hair. Then he looked with his warm blue eyes at the almost sardonic, lidded eyes of the foreigner. The latter sat down beside him, and they began to talk, chiefly of horses.

Brangwen loved the other man for his exquisite graciousness, for his tact and reserve, and for his ageless, monkey-like self-surety. They talked of horses, and of Derbyshire, and of farming. The stranger warmed to the young fellow with real warmth, and Brangwen was excited. He was transported at meeting this odd, middle-aged, dry-skinned man, personally. The talk was pleasant, but that did not matter so much. It was the gracious manner, the fine contact that was all.

They talked a long while together, Brangwen flushing like a girl

when the other did not understand his idiom. Then they said goodnight, and shook hands. Again the foreigner bowed and repeated his
goodnight.

'Goodnight, and *bon voyage*.'

Then he turned to the stairs.

Brangwen went up to his room and lay staring out at the stars of
the summer night, his whole being in a whirl. What was it all? There
was a life so different from what he knew it. What was there outside
his knowledge, how much? What was this that he had touched? What
was he in this new influence? What did everything mean? Where was
life, in that which he knew or all outside him?

He fell asleep, and in the morning had ridden away before any
other visitors were awake. He shrank from seeing any of them again,
in the morning.

His mind was one big excitement. The girl and the foreigner: he
knew neither of their names. Yet they had set fire to the homestead of
his nature, and he would be burned out of cover. Of the two experiences, perhaps the meeting with the foreigner was the more significant. But the girl – he had not settled about the girl.

He did not know. He had to leave it there, as it was. He could not
sum up his experiences.

The result of these encounters was, that he dreamed day and night,
absorbedly, of a voluptuous woman and of the meeting with a small,
withered foreigner of ancient breeding. No sooner was his mind free,
no sooner had he left his own companions, than he began to imagine
an intimacy with fine-textured, subtle-mannered people such as the
foreigner at Matlock, and amidst this subtle intimacy was always the
satisfaction of a voluptuous woman.

                                        (*The Rainbow*, pp. 24–6)

Let us start by looking for the features we noticed in our first extract.
Here is one of the longer sentences from this extract: 'He saw the
other fellow at the evening meal; a small, middle-aged man with
iron-grey hair and a curious face, like a monkey's, but interesting, in
its way almost beautiful'. The texture of this sentence repays close
attention. Notice, for example, that the phrase 'the other fellow'
comes from Brangwen talking to himself in his mind – it is the
hostile phrase of a jealous man because Tom is watching his girl's
man. Notice also how the sentence changes in the middle: there is

matter-of-fact description until Brangwen notices the man's 'curious' face. Suddenly everything changes: the last moments of the sentence bring in the monkey image, and the words 'interesting' and 'beautiful'. The sentence should end after 'face', but Lawrence extends it by three further phrases – just as Brangwen, fascinated, goes on looking at the other man much longer than he expected to.

Again, direct speech is limited to the point of irrelevance: the foreign man says 'Will you smoke?' And 'Good night, and *bon voyage*' – that is all. Yet this extract centres on a conversation, and one which has such a powerful effect that afterwards Brangwen feels 'his whole being in a whirl' and it colours his daydreams 'day and night' for a long time. Lawrence explicitly contrasts the irrelevance of their dialogue against the richness and significance of what they do not say. They talk 'chiefly of horses', and their conversation 'was pleasant, but that did not matter so much'; the excitement of the meeting, on the other hand, is conveyed in powerful language. Brangwen is 'fascinated', he 'loved' the foreigner and was 'transported' because of the 'fine contact' of the encounter. He is 'too much moved and lost to know what to do', then 'blushing to the roots of his hair', and the next morning 'his mind was one big excitement'. Clearly, something very important in Tom Brangwen's life has occurred, which is what Lawrence calls the 'contact' with a foreign man; but the narrative insists that this is on a submerged level beneath their conversation.

What does the passage tell us about what has happened? First, there is considerable descriptive detail about the foreigner, then, the narrative focuses on Brangwen's state of mind after the meeting. The difficulty is that both of these elements in the passage are presented in a way that provokes us to think before we can gain an insight.

Descriptions of the foreigner do not fit together in an obvious way. He is said to be treating women with 'courteous contempt' and he has a 'cold, animal intelligence' with a face 'like a monkey's'. His age is also emphasised: he is said to be 'dry-skinned' and 'withered', and all of these details convey a repulsive impression of low, animal nature. Lawrence undercuts this impression, however, by adding a contrasting strand to the description. The foreigner is 'amazingly a gentleman', an 'aristocrat' who has a 'beautiful' manner with

'exquisite graciousness' and 'tact', a 'gracious manner', and is cultivated enough to make his goodnights with a formal bow. We are
given two distinct impressions of the man, therefore: he is a withered, wrinkled old animal, like a monkey; and at the same time he is
sophisticated, highly cultivated – an aristocrat. Lawrence implies
that it is the combination of these two distinct and opposed character traits that has such a powerful effect: he is like a monkey, and
'amazingly' an aristocrat.

Brangwen's state of mind after their meeting is given as the character's thoughts, in a format we have already met, a kind of indirect
speech of the mind. In this case it appears as a series of questions.
Here – as in our extract from *Sons and Lovers* – the style conveys the
struggle to define and describe, by making several attempts. Tom
Brangwen is trying to understand something 'so different', which is
'outside his knowledge'. He has 'touched' this 'new influence', but
feels that it is 'all outside him'. There is a beating insistence in this
paragraph, with the much repeated question form 'What was . . .?',
the repetition of 'outside', and the repeated phrases for the other
pole of Brangwen's experience: 'what he knew it', 'his knowledge',
'that which he knew'. So, Lawrence creates the sense of Brangwen's
mind bouncing backwards and forwards between two limits – the
known and the unknown – by making his battery of questions do
the same thing.

We have already noticed that the point of view in Lawrence is
shifting and complex. After entering Brangwen's thoughts, the point
of view returns to authorial omniscience and Lawrence provides an
image for what is happening in his character: 'they had set fire to the
homestead of his nature, and he would be burned out of cover'. We
easily understand why Brangwen's nature is compared to a 'homestead', as we know of his primitive life on the isolated Marsh Farm.
The idea of setting fire and burning out of cover, on the other hand,
paints a more confusing picture of the foreigner's role. He is either
an invading warlord, or a hunter – both roles lethal to Tom. Most
strongly this image conveys contempt for Tom, either as peasant or
hunted animal, and the violence of him being forced into the open.

In this passage we are struck by the variety of alternative descriptions given to us, and the variety of means the author uses, in par-

allel, in seeking to convey his meaning. The foreigner appears in a bewildering variety of guises – from monkey to aristocrat to bandit or hunter – and the incident is narrated in constant shifts between a character's stream of consciousness, the author's view, and provocative metaphor. Additionally, each element of the narrative seems to be given to us in alternative forms (see, for example, 'he did not know. He had to leave it there, as it was'.), so that the uncertainty and inadequacy of language is constantly re-emphasised. Lawrence writes in a way which makes us continuously aware of the gulf between actual experience and words, which denies us any illusion of 'final' understanding, or any delusions about 'mastering' his story. Instead, the story seems to be alive – developing, struggling, changing, and with the potential for further change in the future – even as he writes and as we read. Thus we are placed in the same predicament as the character, who 'could not sum up his experiences'.

Finally, let us briefly consider the content of this passage. In our first extract, we found a conflict between 'industrialism' and nature, and we speculated that this conflict between restrictions or 'bondage' and the riches of freedom might operate on the individual level also, within Paul. We can discern a similar pattern in the present extract: there is certainly a combination of opposites in the foreigner's character, which adds to our sense that Lawrence works with 'dialectical' ideas – dualities, tensions, conflicts and what they produce. Our guess that Lawrence is interested in constraints and freedom within the human character seems to be confirmed by the presentation of Tom. Clearly, his encounter with the foreign gentleman acts like opening a door, showing Tom how limited his experience has been and filling him with wonder at 'all outside him' of which he is suddenly newly aware. We can see Tom as trapped in his narrow experience, and liberated in his mind by meeting the foreigner. Only two paragraphs after our extract we find that Tom's day-to-day life is called 'the mean enclosure' and he becomes 'a bull at a gate, refusing to re-enter the well-known pound of his own life'. There can be no question that Lawrence is deeply and consistently concerned about the individual's freedom or imprisonment, both in the physical sense where constraints are imposed by society and economics (these are the circumstances which oppressed Paul Morel), and in the psychological sense where developing character may be stifled by limiting thoughts and habits (these are the constraints from which Tom Brangwen struggles to escape).

Some further ideas about people have been introduced in this extract, however. The man Tom Brangwen meets is called a 'gentleman' and an 'aristocrat', and he is a foreigner. We may think these terms are merely descriptive of one man, at first. However, when Tom daydreams about the stranger later, it is clear that his foreignness and his sophisticated manners are linked, and are significant in his effect on Tom. The phrases 'of ancient breeding', 'fine-textured' and 'subtle-mannered' elaborate the idea of an aristocratic gentleman. Tom is described as 'full of the exquisite pleasure of aristocratic subtlety and grace'. In this case the challenge of new ideas and freedoms comes not merely from beyond Tom's experience, but actually from abroad. We cannot draw firm conclusions for the present, but it seems probable that Lawrence is interested in exploring the qualities of Englishness and foreignness.

With regard to the term 'aristocrat', the present extract gives us help in defining this. It follows a lengthy description of the stranger's eyes, which emphasises that he looked around 'calmly' and 'unconcerned', 'without referring to' other people. He looks at Brangwen 'without considering it necessary to know him at all'. At the same time, the stranger's eyes are twice said to be 'perceiving'. So, Lawrence describes the aristocrat as closely observant, but emphasises his independence – his lack of need for others.

Brangwen's character is set in contrast to this independence: he feels too confused to refuse, so he accepts a cigarette, but is embarrassed by his 'thick fingers' and blushes 'to the roots of his hair'. Brangwen speaks a local dialect, and is embarrassed ('flushing like a girl') when the foreigner does not understand his English. This is a picture of a man constrained and embarrassed by his class and his background, and Lawrence sets him in contrast to the 'aristocrat', who is free from such insecurities, and the self-consciousness they generate. We will return to Lawrence's concept of the 'aristocrat' in our further studies.

Sex is the last thing to notice about this extract. Tom Brangwen and the girl have sexual intercourse in the woods, before Tom meets the foreigner. Lawrence treats this experience with economy and indulgent amusement. Beforehand, Tom's 'heart thumped' and he was 'mad with desire'; afterwards he 'glowed with pleasure' and Lawrence slips into Brangwen's vernacular for his character's approving comment 'By Jove, but that was something like!'. Lawrence and sexuality go hand in hand in the public consciousness, partly because of the famous obscenity trial of *Lady Chatterley's Lover* in 1960. If we are new to Lawrence, we might expect a graphic description of this couple's sexual exploits. In this extract, we get nothing of the kind. Why?

The answer seems to be that this event is simply a chance physical encounter. The sex is purely a physical satisfaction, and no emotional relationship exists between Tom and the girl. Lawrence underlines the *kind* of sex they indulge in, by his precise choice of words afterwards, when he repeatedly tells us that Brangwen's daydreams of a cultured foreigner are associated with 'the satisfaction of a voluptuous woman'. The woman is not 'fascinating', 'charming' or even 'beautiful': she is merely 'voluptuous'. The mere sensuality of Tom's sexual experience here is carefully defined by the author.

We will come across more elaborate and lengthy descriptions of sexual experiences in our next two chapters, and we will find that it is often difficult to work out exactly what has happened, physically, between the characters. For the moment, we note that Tom's and the girl's sexual encounter is portrayed in a matter-of-fact manner, as a relatively uninteresting event; while a conversation about horses with a foreigner is treated as far more significant.

*   *   *

Here is our first extract from *Women in Love*. This novel is a sequel to *The Rainbow*. Ursula, Tom Brangwen's step-grand-daughter, is a teacher; and at the end of the first chapter she and her sister Gudrun watch a wedding taking place at the local church. The bride's brother is Gerald Crich, from a rich mine-owning family; and his friend Rupert Birkin, the school inspector, is another guest at the wedding. At the start of our extract, Ursula is thinking about Rupert Birkin:

. . . He piqued her, attracted her, and annoyed her.

She wanted to know him more. She had spoken with him once or twice, but only in his official capacity as inspector. She thought he seemed to acknowledge some kinship between her and him, a natural, tacit understanding, a using of the same language. But there had been no time for the understanding to develop. And something kept her from him, as well as attracted her to him. There was a certain hostility, a hidden ultimate reserve in him, cold and inaccessible.

Yet she wanted to know him.

'What do you think of Rupert Birkin?' she asked, a little reluctantly, of Gudrun. She did not want to discuss him.

'What do I think of Rupert Birkin?' repeated Gudrun. 'I think he's attractive – decidedly attractive. – What I can't stand about him is his way with other people – his way of treating any little fool as if she were his greatest consideration. – One feels so awfully sold, oneself.'

'Why does he do it?' said Ursula.

'Because he has no real critical faculty – of people, at all events,' said Gudrun. 'I tell you, he treats any little fool as he treats me or you – and it's such an insult.'

'Oh, it is,' said Ursula. 'One must discriminate.'

'One *must* discriminate,' repeated Gudrun. – 'But he's a wonderful chap, in other respects – a marvellous personality. But you can't trust him.'

'Yes,' said Ursula vaguely. She was always forced to assent to Gudrun's pronouncements, even when she was not in accord altogether.

The sisters sat silent, waiting for the wedding-party to come out. Gudrun was impatient of talk. She wanted to think about Gerald Crich. She wanted to see if the strong feeling she had got from him was real. She wanted to have herself ready.

Inside the church, the wedding was going on. Hermione Roddice was thinking only of Birkin. He stood near her. She seemed to gravitate physically towards him. She wanted to stand touching him. She could hardly be sure he was near her, if she did not touch him. Yet she stood subjected through the wedding service.

She had suffered so bitterly when he did not come, that still she was dazed. Still she was gnawed as by a neuralgia, tormented by his potential absence from her. She had awaited him in a faint delirium of nervous torture. As she stood bearing herself pensively, the rapt look on her face, that seemed spiritual, like the angels, but which came from torture, gave her a certain poignancy that tore his heart with pity. He saw her bowed head, her rapt face, the face of an almost demoniacal ecstatic. Feeling him looking, she lifted her face and sought his eyes, her own beautiful grey eyes flaring him a great signal. But he avoided her look, she sank her head in torment and shame, the gnawing at her heart going on. And he too was tortured with shame, and ultimate dislike, and with acute pity for her, because he did not want to meet her eyes, he did not want to receive her flare of recognition.

The bride and bridegroom were married, the party went into the vestry. Hermione crowded involuntarily up against Birkin, to touch him. And he endured it.

Outside, Gudrun and Ursula listened for their father's playing on the organ. He would enjoy playing a wedding march. – Now the married pair were coming! The bells were ringing, making the air shake. Ursula wondered if the trees and the flowers could feel the vibration, and what they thought of it, this strange motion in the air. The bride was quite demure on the arm of the bridegroom, who stared up into the sky before him, shutting and opening his eyes unconsciously, as if he were neither here nor there. He looked rather comical, blinking and trying to be in the scene, when emotionally he was violated by his exposure to a crowd. He looked a typical naval officer, manly, and up to his duty.

Birkin came with Hermione. She had a rapt, triumphant look, like the fallen angels restored, yet still subtly demoniacal, now she held Birkin by the arm. And he was expressionless, neutralised, possessed by her as if it were his fate, without question.

Gerald Crich came, fair, good-looking, healthy, with a great reserve of energy. He was erect and complete, there was a strange stealth glistening through his amiable, almost happy appearance. Gudrun rose sharply and went away. She could not bear it. She wanted to be alone, to know this strange, sharp inoculation that had changed the whole temper of her blood.

(*Women in Love*, pp. 20–2)

We will begin with the dialogue. In our first two extracts, what the characters say to each other is minimal, and it is dismissed as irrelevant to the real story – the story of their thoughts and their emotional reactions to each other. Here, Ursula instigates the dialogue by asking her sister what she thinks of Rupert Birkin. True to form,

Lawrence notes that talking runs counter to her feelings: she asked 'a little reluctantly', and 'she did not want to discuss him'. At the end of their conversation, the same note of silent dissent is repeated. Ursula felt 'forced to assent', but was 'not in accord altogether'.

In between, Ursula's role in the conversation amounts to nothing – she merely feeds what Gudrun says, asking her to carry on and agreeing that 'one must discriminate'. Meanwhile, what does Gudrun say about Rupert? First, she calls him 'decidedly attractive', then she criticises him for treating everybody in the same way. It is interesting that Gudrun's first response to a question about a man is to assess his attractiveness; but the rest of what she says is much more revealing of her than of Birkin. We hear the contemptuous phrase 'any little fool' twice, and Gudrun complains that 'one feels so awfully sold' and 'it's such an insult'. In short, Gudrun reveals her contempt for other people, and her annoyance that Birkin does not recognise her superiority. As a result of these feelings she makes a thoroughly unjustified statement about him: 'you can't trust him'.

Lawrence seems to be using dialogue in a slightly different way from the previous examples in the other two novels. Here the characters do discuss other people and talk analytically, so their conversation is different from the empty banality of Paul and Mrs Morel, or Tom Brangwen.[1] On the other hand, Lawrence still insists that conversation fails to achieve genuine communication between the characters, as it runs counter to the current of emotion; Ursula disagrees but suppresses her opinion. The difference, then, is not that the characters express their feelings in conversational interaction – at least they do not do so directly. Gudrun's 'pronouncements' about Birkin come in the form of an opinion, but they reveal much more about her feelings than she has thought herself. In fact, Lawrence makes sure that the two strongest impressions in what she says are emotional: the snobbish contempt in her repeated 'any little fool', and her petulant annoyance because she is not recognised as superior. The reader is induced to dismiss what she says – that 'you can't

---

[1] In the second half of *Sons and Lovers*, Paul Morel becomes a great talker. His use of speechifying as a means of self-defence is analysed by Diane S. Bonds, one of the critics discussed in Chapter 9, below (see pp. 242–5).

trust' Birkin – because it is drowned out by the emotional noise of her arrogant anger. Dialogue is used slightly differently in this extract, then, but Lawrence's subject remains the same: here, we are treated to a display of Gudrun's attitudes and emotions, that she is not aware of herself. There is an underlying consistency in Lawrence's use of talk, which is highlighted if we make a brief summary of what has happened: the subject of the *conversation* is Birkin, the subject of the *writing* is Gudrun.

By now we can recognise the Lawrentian features of the rest of this passage. There is the author's apparent struggle with words: the habit of extending sentences by adding a comma and a descriptive phrase, then another comma and yet another descriptive phrase, is evident here as well. There are two examples of this in the first paragraph of our extract, in the voice of Ursula's thoughts. First, she struggles to express her feeling that there is a relationship between her and Birkin, even though she hardly knows him. She calls it variously 'some kinship' between them, a 'tacit' and 'natural' understanding, and 'a using of the same language'. Then, Ursula is aware that something keeps them apart at the same time, and she again struggles to define what this is: a 'certain hostility', a 'hidden ultimate reserve' and him being 'cold and inaccessible'.

We have previously commented that this struggling with expression highlights the inadequacy of language. This time further questions arise. Ursula seems to have a particularly hard struggle with her thoughts at these two moments: why? It is quite easy to understand her difficulty with the first problem. She hardly knows Birkin, they have never discussed anything personal, so what she senses – that they share a subterranean 'kinship' – has no social foundation. What is more, she knows him to be Hermione's lover. No wonder she feels hesitant, trying to define what happens on a shadowy emotional level. Ursula's difficulty with the second problem – what keeps them apart – is more interesting and significant.

Remember that we were able to describe the movement of Brangwen's thoughts, swinging between the known and the unknown, because the writing imitates that movement. We can use the same technique to find out more about Ursula. She wants to account for the fact that the relationship with Birkin – which she senses – does not amount to anything yet on the outside. Her first effort excuses them both: 'there had been no time for the understanding to develop'. This does not satisfy her, so she goes further: 'something kept her from him'. This is a neutral remark – the 'something' could be in her or in him or in both of them. Then her mind tries again. First, there is 'a certain hostility', which could again be something neutral between them; next, there is an 'ultimate reserve in him'; and finally he is described as 'cold and inaccessible'. The movement in Ursula's thoughts is obvious: she goes further and further in blaming Birkin until she construes a damning statement about him, that he is 'cold and inaccessible'. At the same time, she moves further and further away from the idea of something in herself which stops the relationship from developing.

We have looked at this minor example in very close detail, because it demonstrates an important principle in analysing Lawrence: we are just as interested in the *movement* of a character's thoughts as in what they think. Putting the *movement* of Ursula's mind together with *what she thinks* shows us how she shies away from questioning herself, and externalises the problem, blaming it on a coldness in Birkin.

There is, then, a dynamic conflict in Ursula's emotions. On the one hand, attraction draws them together; on the other hand, her need to defend herself against the perils of a relationship keeps them separate. We can easily understand this: giving in to attraction lays you open, leaves you vulnerable; and it is hard to overcome a barrier of self-defensive feelings. What Lawrence shows in this paragraph is the hostility generated by attraction's danger, so that Ursula ends by damning Birkin as 'cold and inaccessible'.

Our first two extracts each focused on the character central to the narrative at the time: Paul Morel and Tom Brangwen respectively. The extract from *Women in Love* is different. It is remarkable for the way the narrative dives into several characters in succession. Traditionally, novelists allow one character's point of view to dominate – as happens with Elizabeth Bennet in Jane Austen's *Pride and Prejudice* – and when two points of view are given, they are usually in different narratives or separated in the book. Clearly, Lawrence does not feel bound by these constraints. In this short extract we dip deep into the minds of Ursula, Gudrun, Hermione, Birkin, the bridegroom, and Gudrun again, in quick succession. Furthermore, we reach a vivid emotional depth during each of these sudden plunges into character.

The narrative viewpoint plunges inside each character abruptly. Lawrence does not write a careful transition; he bluntly tells us that 'Gudrun was impatient of talk', or 'Hermione Roddice was thinking only of Birkin'. In the case of the bridegroom and our second approach to Gudrun there is some pretence of moving from outside to inside: Lawrence tells us that the bridegroom 'looked rather comical, blinking' before we suddenly find ourselves intimately close: 'emotionally he was violated by his exposure'. Our second approach to Gudrun comes through her action: 'Gudrun rose sharply and went away', before we are told that 'She could not bear it'. Nonetheless, the way Lawrence's writing dives into a character is startling, and we can be excused for feeling buffeted by such intensity of emotion, reached so quickly. Even the bridegroom – very much a 'walk-on' character in the novel – is accorded an intense feeling, 'violated' by his 'exposure'.

The relationship between Hermione and Birkin is treated at greater length. They, too, are intense: Hermione 'suffered so bitterly', was 'tormented' and 'in a faint delirium of nervous torture'; while he felt 'acute pity' for her which 'tore his heart'; he was 'tortured' and 'endured' her touch. There are two further features of the way Lawrence portrays this relationship which are worth remarking on. First, the author seems to assign certain words to his characters, and uses them repeatedly. For Hermione, the words 'rapt' and 'demoniacal' are used again and again, and 'gnawed' appears twice; for Birkin, the word 'pity' appears twice. The effect of these repetitions is cumulative. It is as if Lawrence is physically beating us with the same word over and over, so that the emotional pressure of Hermione's 'rapt' and 'demoniacal' personality increases as we read the passage. It is this build-up of pressure that helps us to understand Birkin's agony when he 'endured' her touch, and enables us to empathise with his helplessness when he is 'neutralised, possessed by her as if it were his fate'.

'Demoniacal' raises the second feature for comment. Lawrence

applies a consistent image to Hermione in this passage – that of a
fallen angel. It begins with the comment that her expression is 'spiritual, like the angels' yet associated with 'torture'. The description is
then condensed into the single word 'demoniacal'. The story
Lawrence tells is that before the service Hermione was 'subjected'
and 'tormented' by Birkin's absence. During and after the service,
she first looks at him, then touches him, and finally holds his arm;
and this progressive possession of him leads her to be 'triumphant' at
the end. The image of her as a fallen angel goes through a similar
process, ending with her 'like the fallen angels restored, yet still
subtly demoniacal', and the image story adds to our understanding
of their relationship. Hermione is cast as Satan, which leaves us in
no doubt about her pride, selfishness and hypocritical deceit. The
image story amplifies the continuing undercurrent of possessive selfishness once she is restored to her position: she has gained her point,
but she is still 'subtly demoniacal'. Birkin is cast either as God
(notice that he feels 'pity' for her which causes him acute pain) or as
a human soul possessed by the devil. Again, our sense of Birkin's
pain is enhanced by this image.

The angel/demon image has an additional significance: it connects one particular relationship to universal ideas, and carries
Lawrence's opinion. Hermione's so-called 'love' is a destructive
emotion, deceptively mild in appearance and expression, but
viciously selfish in motive like the blandishments of Satan. Lawrence
implies a hatred of this kind of emotion: the image tells us that it is
evil, dishonest and negative, like Satan. Lawrence may also imply a
criticism of religion, which thrives on and celebrates relationships
which exchange selfish dependence and pity. Additionally, imagery
of the Fall and 'fallen' people connects with a theme of decadence
and impending catastrophe in a 'fallen' world, which is prominent in
Women in Love.

We have made much of an image which is lightly touched in, in
this extract. We make no apology for this, because looking closely at
Lawrence's imagery can be enormously helpful to us. Lawrence's
characters are often in the throes of intense emotion, and feel as if
what they are experiencing is cataclysmic; but they often do not
know what is *really* happening, and the writing comes so much from

inside the character that it is difficult to keep any grip on an objective view. As an example of how useful the imagery can be, read the
following short extract from Chapter III, remembering, all the time
as you read, that Hermione has been compared to Satan:

> 'How do you do, Miss Brangwen,' sang Hermione, in her slow,
> odd, singing fashion, that sounded almost as if she were poking fun.
> 'Do you mind my coming in?'
>
> Her grey, almost sardonic eyes rested all the while on Ursula, as if
> summing her up.
>
> 'Oh no,' said Ursula.
>
> 'Are you *sure?*' repeated Hermione, with complete sang froid, and
> an odd, half-bullying effrontery.
>
> 'Oh no, I like it awfully,' laughed Ursula, a little bit excited and
> bewildered, because Hermione seemed to be compelling her, coming
> very close to her, as if intimate with her; and yet, how could she be
> intimate?
>
> This was the answer Hermione wanted. She turned satisfied to
> Birkin.
>
> (*Women in Love*, p. 37)

In this scene, Hermione is being polite, even considerate, on the
surface; but Lawrence's image remains in the back of the reader's
mind, helping us to see the demoniacal possessiveness in everything
she does and says.

Conclusions

In this chapter we have met Lawrence's style head-on, analysing the
way he writes in considerable and increasing detail. As a result, we
have been able to draw a number of conclusions about the kind of
narrative he provides, and we have noticed several features which
appear consistently in the three extracts tackled so far. In addition,
we have already begun to develop our insight into what Lawrence
writes about – the themes, attitudes and beliefs that inform his
work. The present concluding discussion is therefore divided into

two sections: *Features of Lawrence's style*, and *Themes and subject-matter*.

Features of Lawrence's style

1. Look at **sentences**. Lawrence uses very short sentences, and very long ones: both extremes are worth investigating. We have found that the external narrative is often confined to the shortest sentences; that short sentences are often used for sudden, bald statements of emotion; or that a series of very short sentences struggling to express the same thing may convey the fragmented, staccato nature of a character's thoughts. This happened when Paul Morel sensed industrial bondage: 'Already his heart went down. He was being taken into bondage.' Lawrence's long sentences are often loosely structured, depending on a series of commas, and consisting of a series of phrases each of which strives to explain a particular emotion or thought. Life cannot be expressed in precise words, so each attempted description hits a different aspect of the experience, or they get closer and closer to it without ever arriving.

   Whether in the form of a series of short sentences stabbing at the idea, or one long, loose sentence striving to explain, much of Lawrence's writing shows repetitive features: repeated phrases, repeated words, repeated attempts to communicate. The effect of this style is cumulative – the different elements accumulate to build up the reader's sense of what Lawrence means. It is often called an **accretive** way of writing because each idea accretes or accumulates new aspects and angles which are added to it as we read, or an **incremental** style because we receive the communication in increments.

2. The passages we have looked at in this chapter show **dialogue** used to reveal the failure of spoken communication between characters. In the first two extracts there was virtually no direct speech; and the description of Tom's conversation with the foreigner emphasised its irrelevance. Our passage from *Women in Love* used dialogue in a different way: Gudrun's opinions of Birkin express strong, unresolved emotions in Gudrun – they reveal the speaker to the reader, but do not communicate to anybody else.

The effect of this characteristic treatment of dialogue is to emphasise the level of emotion, thoughts and impulses beneath speech, where the main and real story of Lawrence's characters takes place. Even in these three short passages we have met characters who 'said nothing' at moments of strong feeling (Paul), and who feel compelled to agree, suppressing their own opinion (Ursula). Notice that in our short quotation about Hermione, her polite verbal bullying forces Ursula to say the opposite of what she feels. We already have a strong conviction that people cannot communicate their real thoughts or feelings in speech.

3. In Lawrence's novels we have to be extremely alert to changes in the **point of view**. This means more than just attitude or distance: we have to think precisely in order to work out exactly where the writing is coming from. Lawrence is an omniscient author – his narrative goes where it likes, jumping into and out of characters at will; but we have noticed that he does this in different ways. Sometimes he speaks *from* inside a character, at other times he speaks *about* the inside of a character. So, when Tom Brangwen comments on his afternoon with the girl that it was 'something like!', it is as if he is talking to himself in his own colloquial language. On the other hand, when Tom wonders, after meeting the foreigner, 'What was there outside his knowledge, how much? What was this that he had touched?' these seem to be Tom's thoughts, but using Lawrence's language rather than his own. Finally, when Lawrence describes the 'gnawing at her heart' in Hermione, we realise that he is describing something hidden deep inside her – but he is writing *about* her and not *from* her. The level and direction of point of view is constantly changing, then. These changes are sometimes indicated by a single word or short phrase, as when we noticed that Paul Morel was 'supposed to be' a strange and quiet boy – according to the neighbours.

4. Much of the text occurs at an emotional or pre-cognitive level. When we are following a character's thoughts and feelings, we have found that the writing conveys not only what the feelings or thoughts *are*, but also how they *move*. It is very important to notice the **movements of thought and feeling** within the character as well as what they are thinking about: Lawrence writes so

as to communicate the **dynamic energies** that are at work within the character. Remember that the movement of Ursula's thoughts helped us to understand her resistance to Birkin's attraction: a significant insight into her character.

5. **Repetition** is another prominent feature of Lawrence's writing. In particular, we have noticed that he sometimes chooses a descriptive term and uses it repeatedly in connection with the same character, rather like a Homeric epithet. The words 'rapt' and 'demoniacal' were used for Hermione in our extract from *Women in Love*, and we noticed that their repetition increased the tension of the passage. Lawrence uses this technique intensively, applying his repetitive adjectives to places, attitudes and moments of experience as well as to characters. For example, if we look at Chapter XII of *The Rainbow*, we can see how the terms 'red-brick', 'mechanical' and 'mathematical' intensify the description of Wiggiston.

6. Finally, we have already realised the importance of **imagery** in Lawrence's novels. Not only does the image of a fallen angel elucidate our understanding of Hermione in the passage we analysed, it also helps to inform our understanding of her in other passages and different situations. As we continue to study Lawrence and are able to shift our focus towards more general issues of interpretation, we will find that the imagery becomes increasingly significant. Hermione's likeness to a 'fallen angel' will eventually explain a great deal to us about her, the social class she comes from and the society she is part of, and Lawrence's intellectual perspective on England and history (we will return to this discussion in Chapters 4 and 5).

Themes and subject-matter

We are at the beginning of studying Lawrence, but we can already say something about some of his general concerns. The first and strongest impression we have formed is that the real story takes place on a level below social interaction and speech. The significant life in Lawrence's novels is a story of emotions, impulses and half-hidden or hidden thoughts. It is a volatile life full of conflict, struggle and sudden spikes of emotion; and it flows continuously underneath the rather brittle, irrelevant narrative of what people do and say.

Lawrence is therefore a psychological writer: many of his characters' statements and actions are irrational, and their motives are often
hidden from themselves. However, the extracts we have analysed
take us further than this because there are recurrent concerns which
all three novels seem to share.

In all three extracts, we have witnessed individuals struggling to
preserve and develop their own identities. Paul Morel was threatened
and humiliated by economic necessities, which are portrayed as a
threat to his freedom, a kind of enslavement. Tom Brangwen experienced a sudden liberation in which he discovered a far wider and
more exciting range of experience. Afterwards, he 'resented' the
imprisoning limitation of his ordinary life, which is described as a
'mean enclosure' and a 'pound'. In Ursula we met a woman whose
intact identity is threatened by her attraction to Birkin; and we sense
how she fights to defend her individuality. In the same extract we see
Birkin suffering agonies of subjection to the possessive love of
Hermione. Clearly, Lawrence is deeply concerned with the integrity
of the individual.

The people we read about are filled with desires and fears, and are
involved in a continuous struggle to preserve their individual selves
intact. They are threatened and attacked from outside on every level:
the enemies that threaten Ursula and Birkin in our passage from
Women in Love are relationships, the domination of another person;
Paul Morel's enemy, on the other hand, is the economic and social
system itself; and this, in its manifestation of class, manners and the
prison of labour, is at the root of Tom Brangwen's struggle as well.
We should notice, however, that the individual is also threatened
from inside. The attraction Ursula feels for Birkin threatens to make
her vulnerable to and dependent upon him, so her struggle for self-
preservation is also a struggle against herself. Birkin's subjection to
Hermione is a result of the painful pity he feels for her: here again he
must struggle for freedom against himself. The next two chapters
will add to our understanding of these emotional dynamics.

Lawrence depicts society as a threat to freedom, and social class as
a degrading limitation (Tom Brangwen) or corrupting influence
(Hermione). We can already see that his analysis of the social and
economic environment will be radical and subversive. However, we

have come across one character who is described as an 'aristocrat': the foreigner in *The Rainbow*. His outstanding characteristic is that he is separate and independent – he neither fears nor needs other people, and seems to have no insecurity. We can suggest that the idea of an 'aristocrat' represents an achievement of individual freedom, in Lawrence's mind.

The 'aristocrat' has no fears, so he escapes limitations. He has the freedom of infinite potential experience. In the passages we have looked at there are one or two other hints of the infinite. Tom Brangwen is overwhelmed by excitement at the 'unknown' or 'all beyond himself'. Paul Morel has suppressed his artistic desires, yet they continually reassert themselves as an idea or dream which escapes the limitations of ordinary life. It may also be significant that the 'aristocrat' is a foreigner, so that ideas of a wider and fuller life are fixed abroad: he represents something exotically different, something beyond and outside the narrow English round which is imprisoned in the rigidity of its social classes. And, of course, the foreigner's own society, his background and way of life, are unknown.

Methods of Analysis

In this chapter we have used a standard approach to prose analysis. Our attention focused on the following:

1. Narrative of events and actions, and dialogue; narrative of characters' emotions and experiences.
2. Variation in the length of sentences. (Pay particular attention to the extremely short or extremely long.)
3. The structure of sentences. (Look at the phrases which make up a sentence, and describe how they are linked together. Find ways of describing the structure, and the effect it produces. Compare this with the progress of ideas in the sentence, including the movement of thought in a character.)
4. Other noticeable effects of diction such as repetition, or frequent use of conjunctions.

5. Imagery, both of actual objects which are part of the narrative, and in figurative references which commentate on a character or event.

This amounts to observing *the way in which the passage is written* very closely, and involves an open-minded, detailed scrutiny. Whatever you *notice* about the writing is of interest, because it must be *noticeable*, i.e. a feature of the style. Describe the feature and its effect as accurately as you can.

You will find that close analysis of this kind reveals an overwhelming richness and subtlety in the text; and you will notice different features from those I might single out, or pass over others because something different catches your attention. For example, we have not included in our lists the feature of sentences beginning with conjunctions, which we noticed in the extract from *Sons and Lovers*. At the time, we commented that this device conveys the seesaw effect of Paul's inner conflict. We did not notice this device at all when it appeared again in *Women in Love*. Lawrence uses it in the same way – to present an inner struggle, when Ursula is attempting to define her feelings about Birkin: 'But there had been no time for the understanding to develop. And something kept her from him . . .' The point is that you bring yourself to your reading: the text is subtly different for each reader. Perhaps this is what we mean when we say that literature is 'alive'.

Suggested Work

At this stage, you can gain insight from almost any analysis you undertake along the lines that have been demonstrated in this chapter. Remember that you begin by looking closely at the *way in which the text is written*; then think about the purpose of the features you notice. However, you already have a rough agenda based on the tentative conclusions we have reached, and you should use this to help you focus your thoughts when you approach a new passage. Turning our conclusions into questions will give you a direct lead into thinking about the passage you choose to study. Ask yourself:

- Does this passage show an individual struggling for self-preservation?
- What are the threatening forces which attack individuality in this passage?
- Does speech or irrational action reveal a character's unconscious emotions?
- Do the themes of social class or economic/industrial bondage figure in the passage?

The following are three suggestions of passages which would be rewarding to study, one from each of the three novels.

In *Sons and Lovers*, study the passage on pp. 180–3, beginning at the paragraph starting 'Miriam came later' and continuing to the paragraph ending ' . . . the medium through which she came distinctly at her beloved objects'. This passage describes scenes from the early stages of Paul's friendship with Miriam.

In *The Rainbow*, study the passage which describes Will's arrival at the Marsh Farm, beginning 'He appeared at the Marsh one Sunday morning' on p. 100, and analyse as far as '. . . She could not help it: she laughed outright, a figure of shame' on p. 105. In this extract, the combination of disparate effects produced on Anna by her cousin's presence makes a rewarding study.

In *Women in Love*, look at the episode when Gudrun and Winifred release Bismarck the rabbit, and focus on the level of communication that exists between Gudrun and Gerald during this incident. What does their mutual recognition signify? Begin studying on p. 239, at the paragraph beginning 'Gerald watched them go, looking all the while at the soft, full, still body of Gudrun . . .' and go on as far as p. 242 where the paragraph ends 'He was unconfident, he had qualms of fear'.

2

Impulse and Emotion in D. H. Lawrence

In Chapter 1 we identified a level of characterisation underneath the surface level of conscious thoughts and speech. We commented that the 'real' story of D. H. Lawrence's novels takes place on this level; and we noticed how Paul Morel, Tom Brangwen and four of the characters from our *Women in Love* extract are all portrayed as struggling with inner conflicts and unconscious or half-suppressed urges.

There are still further questions to ask about this. In particular, we fudged the issue of consciousness: does the character 'know' their emotions at the time? How much are they aware of, how much is hidden from their conscious knowledge of themselves? If they 'sense' or 'know' their sudden feelings, in what way are they aware of them, and do they understand what is *causing* the way they feel? These questions can only be answered on a case-by-case basis: in such a variety of characterisation as Lawrence provides us with, the only thing we can be sure of is that we must proceed with extreme caution.

Was Lawrence familiar with psychoanalysis? It is not certain how much he knew of Freud's theories while writing *Sons and Lovers*, although Frieda Lawrence was well informed about Freud and some neo-Freudian theories, and the novel was finished during the six months after their elopement. However, by the time he wrote *The Rainbow* and *Women in Love*, Lawrence was well acquainted with Freud's work, was fascinated by psychoanalysis, and certainly sought to represent unconscious forces in his characterisation. During 1914 Lawrence became friends with Dr David Eder and Barbara Low, and discussed Freudian theory with them at length. He even suggested his own amendment of the theory, and urged Dr Eder and his friend Ernest Jones to present his ideas to Freud himself, at a psychoanalytical conference.

Another difficulty faces us in two of the three novels we are studying. Both Paul Morel in *Sons and Lovers* and Rupert Birkin in *Women in Love* are regarded as self-portraits, and argument rages among critics about whether Lawrence really understood his own nature. Many hold the view that Paul and Birkin are failed characterisations because the author could not penetrate his own unconscious. These critics go on to psychoanalyse the author instead of his creations. We will therefore have to start very carefully, tying our observations firmly to what the text reveals.

We begin with an extract from Chapter VII of *Sons and Lovers*, which describes an early stage in the friendship between Paul and Miriam:

> Then sometimes he hated her. Her youngest brother was only five. He was a frail lad, with immense brown eyes in his quaint, fragile face; one of Reynolds' 'Choir of Angels,' with a touch of elf. Often Miriam knelt to the child, and drew him to her.
>
> 'Eh my Hubert!' she sang, in a voice heavy and surcharged with love. 'Eh my Hubert!'
>
> And folding him in her arms, she swayed slightly from side to side with love, her face half lifted, her eyes half closed, her voice drenched with love.
>
> 'Don't!' said the child, uneasy. 'Don't Miriam.'
>
> 'Yes you love me, don't you!' she murmured deep in her throat, almost as if she were in a trance, and swaying also as if she were swooned in an ecstasy of love.
>
> 'Don't!' repeated the child, a frown on his clear brow.
>
> 'You love me, don't you?' she murmured.
>
> 'What do you make such a *fuss* for!' cried Paul, all in suffering because of her extreme emotion. 'Why can't you be ordinary with him?'
>
> She let the child go, and rose, and said nothing. Her intensity, which would leave no emotion on a normal plane, irritated the youth

into a frenzy. And this fearful naked contact of her soul on small occasions, shocked him. He was used to his mother's reserve. And on such occasions, he was thankful in his heart and soul, that he had his mother, so sane and wholesome.

All the life of Miriam's body was in her eyes, which were usually dark as a dark church, but could flame with light like a conflagration. Her face scarcely ever altered from its look of brooding. She might have been one of the women who went with Mary when Jesus was dead. Her body was not flexible and living. She walked with a swing, rather heavily, her head bowed forward, pondering. She was not clumsy, and yet none of her movements seemed quite *the* movement. Often, when wiping the dishes, she would stand in bewilderment and chagrin, because she had pulled in two halves a cup or a tumbler. It was as if, in her fear and self mistrust, she put too much strength into the effort. There was no looseness or abandon about her. Everything was gripped stiff with intensity, and her effort, overcharged, closed in on itself.

She rarely varied from her swinging, forward, intense walk. Occasionally she ran with Paul down the fields. Then her eyes blazed naked in a kind of ecstasy, that frightened him. But she was physically afraid. If she were getting over a stile, she gripped his hands in a little hard anguish, and began to lose her presence of mind. And he could not persuade her to jump from even a small height. Her eyes dilated, became exposed and palpitating.

'No!' she cried half laughing in terror, 'No!'

'You shall!' he cried once, and, jerking her forward, he brought her falling from the fence. But her wild 'Ah!' of pain, as if she were losing consciousness, cut him. She landed on her feet safely, and afterwards, had courage in this respect.

(*Sons and Lovers*, pp. 183–5)

Paul has only recently begun to know Miriam, so we may be shocked by the strong bald statement with which this extract begins: 'Then sometimes he hated her.' The sentence is like a jolt, it makes us sit up and ask why? Paul is her brother's friend, and she seemed so 'humble' that he 'condescended' to her.[1] Why does he hate her?

---

[1] Diane S. Bonds (see Chapter 9 below) sees this bald statement as the narrator's way to escape from the unsatisfactory conversation on pp. 182–3, in which Paul has tried to impose his false idea of Miriam's personality, but is frightened of the arousal this has produced in her.

Why should he feel this strongly about her at all? An answer must be contained in what comes next, which describes her behaviour and his reaction to it as if to explain his hatred.

What do we find out about Miriam? On one level it is very simple: she hugs her younger brother too tightly, demanding love and irritating the child; she walks in a steady, brooding way; she is a little clumsy and over-strong; and she is a physical coward. These facts about Miriam are given to us one after another, punctuated by quick, intense dips into Paul's reaction. Clearly, Paul reacts violently against her open shows of emotion. We can tell this partly from the way her emotion is described as 'surcharged', 'drenched', 'swooned in an ecstasy' and 'intensity', and partly because the author explicitly tells us so: 'Her intensity . . . irritated the youth into a frenzy'. Even her fear is so extreme that it causes Paul pain – her cry when he jumps her from a stile is 'as if she were losing consciousness', and it 'cut him'. It is Miriam's intense emotion, then, that causes Paul to 'hate her'. Lawrence also tells us explicitly why Paul should hate such displays of feeling: it 'shocked him' because 'he was used to his mother's reserve'.

On the next level of understanding, we can look at certain features of Lawrence's style that we have already met to add overtones to this picture. There are characteristic examples of repetition – either of words or ideas – in this extract. So, Miriam's voice is 'heavy' with love for her brother, and she is said to walk 'heavily'; while one word used for her thoughtfulness is 'pondering' which calls 'ponderous' to mind. Next, we find that Miriam is repeatedly represented as enclosed or enclosing: she was 'folding' her brother, and her attitude was one of 'brooding' with 'her head bowed forward'; she seems to hold so intensely that her effort 'closed in on itself'. An equally insistent motif in the extract, however, is nakedness. Paul is irritated by the 'naked contact' of her soul, and 'frightened' by her eyes which 'blazed naked' when she ran and 'dilated' when 'exposed' in fear. 'Blazed' forms part of another motif in the description of her eyes which 'could flame with light like a conflagration'. Finally, there is an insistence on Miriam fainting or becoming overwhelmed due to emotion: she is 'surcharged' and 'drenched', 'in a trance . . . as if she were swooned'. In fear she 'began to lose her presence of mind' and when she is falling she is 'losing consciousness'.

Some of these motifs lead us into patterns of imagery. For example, 'blazed' and 'conflagration' associate Miriam with fire; while 'drenched' has her flooded with emotion. There are other elements which do not quite amount to imagery: they are rather metaphorical ways of describing character, like the idea of a 'naked' soul or 'palpitating' eyes. The most concrete metaphor among these is of Paul 'cut' by Miriam's cry. There are also two references in this extract, the first to Reynolds' 'Choir of Angels', and the second to the New Testament. We should take notice when we find such references, as we did in the last chapter with the 'fallen angel' idea for Hermione. Sir Joshua Reynolds was an eighteenth-century English painter. Lawrence clearly refers to the angelic sweetness of the children's faces in his paintings: they tend to have charming curls and cheeks that look as if they have been dabbed with a little rouge. The 'women who went with Mary' (Luke: 24,1–10) found an empty sepulchre because Christ had risen. Lawrence is referring to the women casting their eyes down to the ground because they were unable to look at the two angels 'in shining garments' who told them that Christ had risen. This reference is odd. It purports to describe Miriam's usually veiled look, but it is Paul who cannot bear the brightness ('blaze' and 'conflagration') of Miriam's look, so the reference has an ambiguous effect.

By this time, we may feel that we are receiving a conflicting impression of Miriam. Her extreme emotion is confusingly likened to fire and water at the same time; and she is both intensely held in, enclosing, and simultaneously exposed or naked. On the other hand, all the little details in this passage ring true. We understand the girl who smothers her little brother with love – and we appreciate his discomfort. We also understand the vague, unconfident, slightly motherly girl who is usually shy and brooding but always very emotional. So, in spite of the inconsistent elements in this passage, Lawrence has conveyed a vivid impression of Miriam.

This is not the point of the writing, however. If we now turn our attention to Paul, we quickly realise that Miriam is only there as a series of impressions to which Paul reacts: it is his experience, and his hopeless struggle with that experience, which is the continuing story in this extract, as elsewhere in the novel. This is indicated by the ambiguity of the biblical reference, which applies to Paul more obviously than it does to Miriam. It is confirmed by Paul's illogical behaviour. We know that Paul suffers moments of intense feeling in the company of Miriam. He sometimes 'hated' her, she drives him to 'frenzy', she sometimes 'frightened' him, and her cry 'cut' him. Now we can ask the obvious questions about Paul. Why does he feel these things, do the feelings have anything in common, and what does he do about them?

We do not need to spend a long time on the first two questions. Lawrence is explicit about the cause of Paul's sudden reactions: Miriam's 'intensity' shocks and frightens him, and he responds with anger and irritation. All his reactions in the extract have this in common, except the pain he feels when she is frightened. Lawrence has even added that Mrs Morel's 'reserve' is responsible for Paul's fear – and he is conscious of this, being thankful that he has his 'sane and wholesome' mother. So, Paul's relationship with his mother has made him frightened of open displays of emotion. Up to this point, Paul's character and Lawrence's characterisation are both explicit and unarguable.

Our third question is, what does Paul do about his feelings? In this extract, Paul does two contradictory things. First, he objects to Miriam's emotion, saying 'What do you make such a *fuss* for!', and this achieves the desired result of stopping her, pushing her back into her silent and suppressed mood: 'She let the child go, and rose, and said nothing'. Secondly, Paul insists on her jumping from the fence, shouting 'You shall!' and 'jerking her forward', and he has led up to this by persuading her to run down the fields with him, which excites her in a way he finds frightening. Put simply, Paul's behaviour is illogical: if he wants her to stop displaying her emotions, why does he provoke her? What does he get out of this behaviour? When he reprimands her, she is subdued; and we can imagine her with bowed head, in a 'brooding' state. When he provokes her by persuading her to run with him, or by jumping her from the fence, Paul becomes 'frightened' and feels a sudden sharp pain – he is 'cut'. Obviously, his reaction to this girl is much more complicated than he comprehends.

When a character does the opposite of what he consciously

intends, or wilfully seeks experiences we expect him to avoid – as Paul does here – our analysis must broaden itself to include the fact of an unconscious. We are no longer studying the mechanics of motive, decision, perception and action: we have to take into account that something *unknown* is at work in the character, underneath the conscious 'mechanics' of existence. This something confuses and complicates his life for reasons he does not understand.

At this point, many critics veer away from the text of the novel, and, equating Paul and his author, explain the action in terms of Lawrence's own problems. Much later in his life, Lawrence apparently said '. . . that he had not done justice to his father in *Sons and Lovers*, and felt like rewriting it. . . . as Lawrence had grown older he had come to see him in a different light; to see his unquenchable fire and relish for living. Now he blamed his mother for her self-righteousness, her invulnerable Christian virtue in which she was entrenched'.[2] Critics argue that Lawrence was still averse to his father's emotional nature, and clung to his mother's 'reserve', when writing *Sons and Lovers*, so the characterisation of Paul is a flawed self-portrait.

Psychoanalysing Lawrence, however, is a digression: it may be enlightening as biography, but it only distracts us from what the novel presents. In this extract, Paul is consciously devoted to his mother, and 'thankful in his heart and soul' for her 'reserve'. Yet Lawrence shows him behaving irrationally – seeking the very emotion he tells himself he hates, even when doing so frightens and hurts him. Clearly, Lawrence undermines the validity of Paul's pro-mother thoughts, and shows us a boy who compulsively seeks emotional contact, despite what he says to himself.

Furthermore, Lawrence expresses the emotional moments Paul experiences in a powerful way: the metaphorical descriptions we have already mentioned make moments of feeling very concrete (the intense heat of 'blazed', for example, or the sudden sting of 'cut' – short words giving strong impact); while the motif of 'naked' and 'exposed', and the sensational intensity of 'dilated . . . palpitating'

---

[2] E. and A. Brewster, *D. H. Lawrence: Reminiscence and Correspondence* (London, 1934), p. 254, quoted in R. E. Pritchard, *D. H. Lawrence: Body of Darkness* (London, 1971), p. 35.

imbue these moments of contact with a kind of breathless, sensual excitement. In sharp contrast, the words for his mother – 'reserve', 'sane' and 'wholesome' – are very drab.

We can draw two clear conclusions from this extract, then. First, that a choice between restraint and emotion is a problematic issue for Paul, and these problems are related to his mother's influence. The attitudes he has learned from his mother are also value-judgements – expressed by the words 'ordinary' and 'normal' which represent the behaviour he prefers, implying that Miriam's emotions are 'abnormal' – and are based on a concept of proportion which she offends, because the 'naked contact of her soul' occurs on 'small occasions'. Here we can recognise a common problem, which is a legacy of English culture: the long tradition of a battle between 'reason' and 'emotion' which has been related to a struggle between 'reason' and 'romanticism' or 'moderation' and 'excess' in our culture for hundreds of years. Paul's difficulty with Miriam, then, touches on universal cultural themes, and his characterisation highlights the painful confusion in which his particular background, and his cultural heritage, have left him.

Secondly, Paul's relationship with Miriam arouses a crucial conflict *within Paul*. His actions when he provokes Miriam into states of extreme emotion are compulsive. Paul does not consciously *wish* to expose himself to the nakedness of Miriam's soul, yet he repeatedly does so; therefore, we know there is an unconscious desire in Paul which pushes him towards emotional contact. At the same time, he consciously fears contact with her, feels hurt by it, and tells himself that he prefers to avoid it. Clearly, Paul is struggling in a conflict between opposed desires: fear and defensiveness, on the one hand; and the powerful unconscious desire for contact, on the other.

Having studied Paul's character in this extract, it is worth confirming the insights reached by looking at passages from elsewhere in the text. We cannot proceed far down this road in the present chapter, but we can briefly expand on what we have learned to show the benefits of this method of study.

At the beginning of Chapter IV, 'The young Life of Paul', Lawrence describes an incident when Paul accidentally breaks his sister's doll. At first, as long as Annie wept, he 'sat helpless with misery'; but once he is forgiven, Paul suggests that they burn the broken doll. Lawrence tells us that 'He watched with wicked satisfaction the drops of wax melt off the broken forehead of Arabella [the doll], and drop like sweat into the flame. So long as the stupid big doll burned, he rejoiced in silence.' The explanation of this disturbing event is that 'He seemed to hate the doll so intensely, because he had broken it' (the incident is described on pp. 82–3). Clearly, this early anecdote expands on the more irrational side of Paul's behaviour with Miriam: his ambivalent approach to her is similar to his treatment of the doll. He is driven to frighten and hurt her, then hates her because he has hurt her. Another coincidence which may strike us in comparing the two incidents is that Paul broke the doll because he 'must practise jumping off the sofa arm'. Again, it is his boyish boisterousness which breaks the female symbol – the doll – and later Miriam. This brief reference to Paul's earlier life, then, helps us to understand his complex of feelings about women: his inhibitions, his irrational risk-taking behaviour, and his fear and hatred of the whole business, are prefigured here.

We have met similar opposed impulses within character already. In Chapter 1, we found that Ursula feels a simultaneous repulsion and attraction towards Birkin, in our extract from *Women in Love*. We can now think of this as a paradigm, common in Lawrence's novels: a repeated feature of the love-relationships he writes about. The lover feels a simultaneous attraction and repulsion, or desire and fear; and there is a struggle between these forces which pulls the individual in opposite directions.

Our extract from *Sons and Lovers* has, therefore, led us beyond the vivid characterisation we find on the surface: an unconfident, emotional girl, with a shy boy who is under his mother's influence. Lawrence's characters imply much broader themes and truths, about an unnatural cultural inheritance, and a fundamental conflict between desire and fear which may affect all sexual relationships.

*   *   *

We now turn to an extract from *The Rainbow*. Skrebensky is going away to South Africa to fight in the Boer War. He pays a short visit to the Brangwens, then Ursula and her uncle Tom see him onto his train:

> The train was rushing up. Ursula's heart heaved, but the ice was frozen too strong upon it.
>
> 'Good-bye,' she said, lifting her hand, her face laughing with her peculiar blind, almost dazzling laugh. She wondered what he was doing, when he stooped and kissed her. He should be shaking hands and going.
>
> 'Good-bye,' she said again.
>
> He picked up his little bag and turned his back on her. There was a hurry along the train. Ah, here was his carriage. He took his seat. Tom Brangwen shut the door, and the two men shook hands as the whistle went.
>
> 'Good-bye – and good luck,' said Brangwen.
>
> 'Thank you – goodbye.'
>
> The train moved off. Skrebensky stood at the carriage window, waving, but not really looking to the two figures, the girl and the warm-coloured, almost effeminately-dressed man. Ursula waved her handkerchief. The train gathered speed, it grew smaller and smaller. Still it ran in a straight line. The speck of white vanished. The rear of the train was small in the distance. Still she stood on the platform, feeling a great emptiness about her. In spite of herself her mouth was quivering: she did not want to cry: her heart was dead cold.
>
> Her uncle Tom had gone to an automatic machine, and was getting matches.
>
> 'Would you like some sweets,' he said, turning round.
>
> Her face was covered with tears, she made curious, downward grimaces with her mouth, to get control. Yet her heart was not crying – it was cold and earthy.
>
> 'What kind would you like – any?' persisted her uncle.
>
> 'I should love some peppermint drops,' she said, in a strange, normal voice, from her distorted face. But in a few moments she had gained control of herself, and was still, detached.
>
> 'Let us go into the town,' he said, and he rushed her into a train moving to the town station. They went to a café to drink coffee, she sat looking at the people in the street, and a great wound was in her breast, a cold imperturbability in her soul.
>
> This cold imperturbability of spirit continued in her now. It was as if some disillusion had frozen upon her, a hard disbelief. Part of her

had gone cold, apathetic. She was too young, too baffled to understand, or even to know that she suffered much. And she was too
deeply hurt to submit.

She had her blind agonies, when she wanted him, she wanted him.
But from the moment of his departure, he had become a visionary
thing of her own. All her roused torment and passion and yearning
she turned to him.

She kept a diary, in which she wrote impulsive thoughts. Seeing the
moon in the sky, her own heart surcharged, she went and wrote:

'If I were the moon, I know where I would fall down.'

It meant so much to her, that sentence – she put into it all the
anguish of her youth and her young passion and yearning. She called
to him from her heart wherever she went, her limbs vibrated with
anguish towards him wherever she was, the radiating force of her soul
seemed to travel to him, endlessly, endlessly, and in her soul's own
creation, find him.

But who was he, and where did he exist? In her own desire only.

She received a post-card from him, and she put it in her bosom. It
did not mean much to her, really. The second day, she lost it, and
never even remembered she had had it, till some days afterwards.

The long weeks went by. There came the constant bad news of the
war. And she felt as if all, outside there in the world, were a hurt, a
hurt, a hurt against her. And something in her soul remained cold,
apathetic, unchanging.

(*The Rainbow*, pp. 307–9)

This extract vividly portrays a confusing emotional moment. Ursula
and Skrebensky have been lovers, he is going away to war, and this is
their farewell. The departure of the train is described effectively in
short sentences as it diminishes in the distance. Ursula weeps on the
platform, and she apparently misses Skrebensky after his departure.
The emotions are those of Ursula, and we easily recognise the
sudden intensities that are characteristic of Lawrence's writing: we
read about 'All her roused torment and passion and yearning', her
limbs which 'vibrated with anguish'; and we read 'endlessly, endlessly' and 'a hurt, a hurt, a hurt'. All this seems appropriate to the
parting of lovers, but the passage as a whole is still confusing because
Ursula's feelings are more complicated than mere grief at parting. We
have to look more closely to find out just what they are.

Ursula does feel the plain distress at parting we have already noticed, but there is also a counter-current of feeling in her. First, she is in an unexpected relation to her own emotions. When Skrebensky does what she must expect him to do (he stoops to kiss her goodbye), we are told that 'She wondered what he was doing'; and when she cries, she begins weeping 'in spite of herself', and 'she did not want to cry'. At the end of the passage her contradictory feelings show again: she puts Anton's post-card 'in her bosom', then promptly loses it because 'it did not mean much to her, really'.

Lawrence seems to play with conventional expectations here. On the surface, Ursula behaves in the expected manner – she is a young girl whose fiancé is off to war, so she accedes to his farewell kiss, watches the train out of sight, cries on the platform, fixes her emotions upon him in his absence, and, in the most conventional gesture of all, treasures his post-card in her bosom. The word 'bosom' stands out: it is a vague and rather prurient word, specially chosen to indicate romantic cliché; and it is unexpected from a writer like Lawrence. How does a girl put a post-card 'in her bosom'? Does it slot in between her breasts, or does she pop a corner of it inside her bra? Either way, it sounds very uncomfortable, and the vagueness of the phrase 'in her bosom' (Victorian euphemism for chest, breasts, heart) suggests impracticality. However, the difficulty of placing a scratchy piece of cardboard 'in her bosom' is nothing compared to the difficulty of losing it once it is there: how did she manage to do that? Other elements of this scene which ease us towards laughing at Ursula, as a lovestruck adolescent, are the mannered description of the departing train, with its short sentences and inversion ('The speck of white vanished. The rear of the train was small in the distance. Still she stood . . .'), and the gushing sentence she writes in her diary about the moon.

We are beginning now to think of this scene as a parody: it is a satire on teenage romantic posturing. Yet Lawrence also undercuts this reading, because he tells us that her behaviour, although predictable, is involuntary: she 'did not want to cry', yet she cried. There is no irony when the author tells us of Ursula 'feeling a great emptiness about her', and her absurd sentence about the moon really 'meant so much to her' because she 'put into it all the anguish of her youth and her young passion and yearning'. No, this is not simply a parody, although there are satiric elements. Ursula really does feel this way: there is a powerful, involuntary force within the character which compels her to behave like a teenager with a crush. Her will is distinct from, and even in conflict with, the gush of teenage romance; yet she cannot help herself and breaks down when Skrebensky's train departs.

We began with the conventional surface of Ursula's behaviour, so we have not yet mentioned one of the most noticeable features of this passage. The repeated motif of coldness adds a further element to her character in this extract. Although Ursula's heart 'heaved', we are told that at first 'the ice was frozen too strong upon it'; when she starts to cry, 'her heart was dead cold', and while she cries it is 'cold and earthy'. She has a 'cold imperturbability' (twice) in her soul because disillusion had 'frozen' on her, making her 'cold, apathetic', and even after she has created an illusion of Skrebensky 'In her own desire only', Lawrence tells us that 'something in her soul remained cold, apathetic, unchanging'.

A summary is a useful way to highlight illogical elements in a character's behaviour. Here are three statements summarising our study of Ursula in this scene:

1. She does not want to behave like a romantic teenager.
2. She behaves like a romantic teenager.
3. She has a detached, cold heart throughout.

The combination of conflicting elements in Ursula's emotions and behaviour presents us with a puzzle, then; just as Paul Morel's behaviour seemed irrational when put next to his feelings and thoughts. As in our extract from *Sons and Lovers*, this complexity opens the text to psychoanalytical questions. Why does Ursula cry, when she is simultaneously 'cold' and 'detached'? Why does she make her 'soul's own creation' of Skrebensky despite being 'imperturbable'; and why does she forget to act out her romantic intention, and lose the postcard? Clearly, we are reading about a character who is dealing with unconscious energies by creating a fantasy, and attempting to keep up a façade of romance, while unconsciously forgetting and losing the invested object. This implies that Ursula does not want to know that she is *not* in love with Skrebensky. On the other hand, she does not want to show that she *is* emotional about his departure, when she tries not to cry. There is nothing inconsistent about these two statements, if we think about them carefully. The romantic parody has been a smokescreen all along, in fact. All we have to realise is that Ursula's tears are genuine, but they are not a sign of love. She cries because she no longer loves him: it is her own cold heart, which no longer feels any passion for Anton, that makes her cry. It is her lack of love for him, the lonely isolation of her cold self, which makes her feel 'a great emptiness', and prompts her to weep. Thus, Ursula is emotional about Anton leaving, but her emotion is aroused by her loss of romantic illusion, not loss of the man.

This is as far as we can go, using the extract we are studying. The natural question to ask is: why does she so dislike her own detachment that she represses it, constructing a romantic illusion to help bury the knowledge of it and hide it from herself? There is no answer to this question in the current extract, but following the same procedure as with *Sons and Lovers*, we keep it in mind and look for a related passage elsewhere in the text.

Only a few pages before Anton's departure, Lawrence describes the couple's love-making among the corn-stacks (see pp. 298–300). Ursula emerges from this experience 'triumphant'; she has been 'corrosive' and was 'destroying' Skrebensky, while he is described as 'the victim, consumed, annihilated'. As Ursula regains her everyday awareness after making love, her feelings are clearly described:

> What horrible thing had possessed her? She was filled with overpowering fear of herself, overpowering desire that it should not be, that other burning, corrosive self. She was seized with a frenzied desire that what had been should never be remembered, never be thought of, never be for one moment allowed possible. She denied it with all her might. With all her might she turned away from it. She was good, she was loving.
>
> (*The Rainbow*, p. 299)

There is no question that this moment is the root of Ursula's repression – Lawrence tells us that Ursula cannot accept herself and 'denied it with all her might'. If we reread the intervening pages, it is

clear that Ursula succeeds in burying her frightening, 'corrosive' self
and continues to act the affectionate girlfriend on the surface: she
gives him her photograph, for example, and sends him snowdrops.
However, the experience in the stackyard has 'annihilated' him, and
this leads to a development of his opinions:

> . . . his self, the soul that aspired and had true hope of self-effectuation
> lay as dead, still-born, a dead weight in his womb . . . What did a man
> matter, personally? He was just a brick in the whole great social fabric,
> the nation, the modern humanity.
>
> (*The Rainbow*, p. 304)

Skrebensky's submission to the army machine, to his 'duty', shows
that his individuality has been destroyed; so he becomes a 'nullity'.
Ursula resists this insight because she has repressed all consciousness
of how she destroyed him. As it becomes more and more obvious
that Skrebensky is a 'nullity', however, she is 'more and more terri-
fied' and feels 'a great sense of disaster impending' (all from p. 305).
The 'disaster' she fears, clearly, is a confrontation with the fact that
she is not 'good . . . loving', but is a 'burning, corrosive self'. In
other words, in the classic Freudian manner, she fears that her
unconscious will burst out and she will have to confront it.

Our brief excursion through these events has completed the psychoanalytical picture of Ursula at this stage of her development; and
it has confirmed the effectiveness of our method. Detailed study of
an extract highlights illogical elements in character so that the question, 'why is the character illogical?' is answered either within the
extract itself or by a related passage elsewhere in the text. Lawrence
does not hide his character's unconscious from us – indeed, he is
remarkably explicit about it. However, he does expect us to question
inconsistencies in characters, and he does expect us to notice, and
string together, separate explanations and incidents, connecting the
clear analytical 'story' of character for ourselves.

We have two literary points to remark before moving on to look
at *Women in Love*. First, notice the subtlety with which novelistic
convention is not quite parodied in the farewell scene at the station.
Lawrence has included elements of the conventional romantic

parting, and has highlighted these in the most gentle manner (we noticed his diction in the 'atmospheric' description of the departing train, and his choice of the word 'bosom', for example). At the same time, he both undercuts these elements of naïve romance by including a counter-current of conflicting emotion (Ursula's 'cold imperturbability' and so on) and he restores the relevance of romantic convention, showing it to be a real part of her psychology, an element of her environment and her self-expectation, with which she must struggle to come to terms. This scene is both parody and not-parody, at the same time.

Secondly, analysing Ursula's personal experiences is not the end of it. There is a fundamental opposition between her and Skrebensky's new opinions about society and the individual. So, Ursula's emotional struggles are related to a much larger, more intellectual theme, of how we relate to our society and species, and how we conceive of our existence. In this chapter, we are focusing on characters in a close study, considering them as lifelike – treating them almost as if they were real people. This enables us to appreciate the analytical subtlety of Lawrence's imagination. Characters are not real, however, they are parts of an artificial whole, and exist in the context of a novel which has wider concerns. Skrebensky's false doctrine of 'duty', and Ursula's simplified romance-fantasy, contribute to the wider themes of the novel.

*   *   *

In Chapter XI of *Women in Love*, Birkin and Ursula row to an island in a pond, and while there they argue about the future of humanity, nature and love. Then Birkin begins to play with flowers:

> Again they looked at each other. She suddenly sprang up, turned her back to him, and walked away. He too rose slowly and went to the water's edge, where, crouching he began to amuse himself unconsciously. Picking a daisy he dropped it on the pond, so that the stem was a keel, the flower floated like a little water lily, staring with its open face up to the sky. It turned slowly round, in a slow, slow dervish dance, as it veered away.
>
> He watched it, then dropped another daisy into the water, and after

that another, and sat watching them with bright, absolved eyes, crouching near on the bank. Ursula turned to look. A strange feeling possessed her, as if something were taking place. But it was all intangible. And some sort of control was being put on her. She could not know. She could only watch the brilliant little discs of the daisies veering slowly in travel on the dark, lustrous water. The little flotilla was drifting into the light, a company of white specks in the distance.

'Do let us go to the shore, to follow them,' she said, afraid of being any longer imprisoned on the island. And they pushed off in the punt.

She was glad to be on the free land again. She went along the bank towards the sluice. The daisies were scattered broadcast on the pond, tiny radiant things, like an exaltation, points of exaltation here and there. Why did they move her so strongly and mystically?

'Look,' he said, 'your boat of purple paper is escorting them, and they are a convoy of rafts.'

Some of the daisies came slowly towards her, hesitating, making a shy bright little cotillon on the dark clear water. Their gay bright candour moved her so much as they came near, that she was almost in tears.

'Why are they so lovely?' she cried. 'Why do I think them so lovely?'

'They are nice flowers,' he said, her emotional tones putting a constraint on him.

'You know that a daisy is a company of florets, a concourse, become individual. Don't the botanists put it highest in the line of development? I believe they do.'

'The compositae, yes, I think so,' said Ursula, who was never very sure of anything. Things she knew perfectly well, at one moment, seemed to become doubtful the next.

'Explain it so, then,' he said. 'The daisy is a perfect little democracy, so it's the highest of flowers, hence its charm.'

'No,' she cried, 'no – never. It isn't democratic.'

'No,' he admitted. 'It's the golden mob of the proletariat, surrounded by a showy white fence of the idle rich.'

'How hateful – your hateful social orders!' she cried.

'Quite! It's a daisy – we'll leave it alone.'

'Do. Let it be a dark horse for once,' she said: 'if anything can be a dark horse to you,' she added satirically.

They stood aside, forgetful. As if a little stunned, they both were motionless, barely conscious. The little conflict into which they had fallen had torn their consciousness and left them like two impersonal forces, there in contact.

(Women in Love, pp. 130–1)

This passage is rich with suggestion. The daisies Birkin drops onto the water, and the chocolate-paper boat Ursula previously set afloat on the pond, are part of a symbolic pattern in the novel. They float on the 'dark, lustrous' water, the 'dark clear' water as it is described with typically cumulative repetition; and there are parallels with other symbolic descriptions in *Women in Love*, particularly the discussion of '*Fleurs du Mal*' between Birkin and Ursula, which is followed by a description of the dark Willey Water with many bright lanterns upon it, on the evening of 'Water-Party' (see pp. 173–4 and Chapter 5 below). There are many interpretations of these symbols, and it is not our job in this chapter to pursue them. However, the flowers are generally associated with human beings – whether 'humanity' as a whole, or aspects of Birkin's and Ursula's spirits emblematically floating; and the 'dark' water is certainly identified with primal forces, akin to nature, and the underlying, unconscious flow of life and death. 'Dark' and 'darkness' are important words wherever they occur in *Women in Love*, and they always seem to indicate pre-conscious forces which are primitive. Our present interest is in characterisation, so we are most interested in what the daisies represent to the two characters involved, and how Lawrence uses the scene as a means of conveying two people and their relationship.

The extract opens and closes with an emphasis on the loss of consciousness. Birkin begins to 'amuse himself unconsciously' by setting the daisies adrift, and at the end of the passage they are both 'forgetful', 'stunned', 'barely conscious'. What comes in between, then, is on a more intimate level than the intellectual arguments about the end of humanity and the validity of love that they have pursued in the earlier part of the chapter. Their arguments have led to discord and physical separation. His final utterance was 'baffled, withdrawing', and hers has the by-line 'she mocked', before she 'turned her back to him, and walked away'. The beginning of Birkin's absorption in 'unconscious' amusement, then, changes the couple's mood. What happens to them?

Birkin watches the flowers with 'bright, absolved' eyes. 'Bright' is positive, suggesting that he is pleased with the daisy-boats; and in the language-pattern of the novel, 'bright' relates to assertive, independent maleness. 'Absolved' implies more. It suggests that he feels both forgiven, as if he has confessed and received absolution for his sins, in the religious sense, and that he is 'absolved' in the sense that he has been relieved of responsibility. Both of these implications are perhaps present: Birkin forgives himself for his anger and rudeness when they were arguing, and he no longer feels the need to pursue the argument, or no longer feels the need to pursue his growing relationship with Ursula. For once, Birkin is not trying to define the kind of 'love' he offers Ursula, or the kind of 'love' he wants from her in return. 'Bright, absolved', then, introduces a kind of gaiety, and freedom from ties and guilt, to Birkin's mood.

Ursula reacts differently to the flowers, and her response is described with an emphasis on uncertainty. She has a 'strange' feeling, and although she is aware of an event, it is only a 'something' which is 'intangible'. However, she feels Birkin's power as 'some sort of control' but 'could not know'. Ursula continues in this unknowing, hesitant frame of mind for the remainder of the scene. She asks questions, both in her mind and aloud: 'Why did they move her so strongly and mystically?' and 'Why are they so lovely?'; and her professional knowledge of botany is glossed by Lawrence explaining that 'Things she knew perfectly well, at one moment, seemed to become doubtful the next.'

Just as Ursula is uncertain, we are not sure how the scene affects her; and although we have attempted to define the implications of 'bright, absolved', we do not have a clear grasp of Birkin in this scene either. Typically, the characters' conversation seems detached from their impulses and what they mean to each other. Conversation fails them in three ways. First, they do not say what they feel. For example, Ursula uses the daisies as an excuse to escape from the island, asking if they can 'go to the shore, to follow them', when her motive is really that she is 'afraid of being any longer imprisoned on the island'. Birkin says 'They are nice flowers', a bland, conventional remark, while in fact he feels 'her emotional tones putting a constraint on him'. His reaction here is similar to Paul's response to Miriam, in *Sons and Lovers*.

Secondly, they talk irrelevantly, Birkin in particular introducing an element of pure whimsy into the conversation. He comments on daisies and their position in a botanist's hierarchy, then asks Ursula to confirm his comment from her teacherly knowledge, which she does. Birkin then puts forward two neat interpretations of daisies, which are obviously intellectual exercises, not to be taken seriously. He calls the daisy 'a perfect little democracy'; then, when she objects to this, he comes up with a satire of Marxist interpretation: 'It's the golden mob of the proletariat, surrounded by a showy white fence of the idle rich'. The absurd phrase 'golden mob' highlights Birkin's mischievous humour here – we cannot mistake his tone for seriousness.

Finally, conversation runs out. The only thing the characters do say to each other, which is a real communication between them, is that they cannot put the meaning of the daisies into words at all. Birkin acknowledges this when he says 'Quite! It's a daisy – we'll leave it alone'. The word is merely a label for the thing, but does not explain the mystery of the thing. Ursula agrees, deliberately ridiculing language by mixing metaphors: the daisy is a 'dark horse'. They cannot say anything about the daisies in words, then; and by implication they cannot answer Ursula's earlier question – 'Why are they so lovely?' – either. Scientific description and symbolic interpretation have ludicrously failed, the noun itself is a mere signifier, and they are left with nothing to say.

On the other hand, they have not said nothing in this exchange – to conclude this would be to miss Lawrence's point completely. There has been conflict between them, and it has raged around two particular bones of contention. First, Birkin is full of theories about society, and about humanity as a whole. When he tries to argue his theories (for example, that the word 'love' has been vulgarised, and cannot be used any more), Ursula hates him because she senses that he is suppressing his individuality. She thinks of it as 'mean effacement into a Salvator Mundi and a Sunday-school teacher, a prig of the stiffest type' (p. 130). Secondly, and related to this, Ursula objects to Birkin's intellectualising habit. She senses that life exists with potential infinity; and she objects when his intellectual analysis makes life appear to behave like a machine. When they argue whether love still exists, or not, and Birkin puts forward his theory that the word has been vulgarised, Ursula's reply is 'But still it is love' (p. 130). Her assertion here uses the word 'love' as a signifier, consciously avoiding any attempt to anatomise or explain the thing, but merely allowing it to exist and be named, in the same way as Birkin's 'It's a daisy'.

The dialogue in our extract reconciles their argument. Essentially, Birkin admits that his theorising is absurd by satirising himself. His 'perfect little democracy' and 'golden mob of the proletariat' are conscious satires on his own social theorising – and an implicit apology to Ursula. His 'It's a daisy' is a capitulation in their argument about love. Ursula is still prickly about his intellectualising, so even after he has effected their reconciliation, she ridicules language with the 'dark horse' figure of speech, and tries to goad him by saying 'if anything can be a dark horse to you'. We notice that he does not rise to this. So the conversation between them, in its oblique way, has both brought them closer together, and made it less possible for them to communicate in words. Lawrence's touch is subtle, as he conveys reconciliation by means of these indirect references back to the argument. Notice that they do not refer to the actual contentious issues between them, but use parallel substitutes – the daisy for love, Marxist nostrums for the final dissolution of humanity, and so on.

We can now turn our attention to the daisies themselves, and the way they are described. Are we any closer to understanding what they represent? Lawrence provides us with a variety of perceptions of the daisies. Birkin sees them as 'like a little water lily, staring with its open face up to the sky'; then, to Ursula, they are 'brilliant little discs' and a 'little flotilla', a 'company of white specks in the distance'. When she sees them from the bank near the sluice, she describes them as 'tiny radiant things, like an exaltation, points of exaltation here and there'. Birkin then calls her paper boat an escort, 'and they are a convoy of rafts'.

These descriptions differ from each other, but share the quality of brightness. Lawrence – as usual – bombards us with alternative images which have certain qualities in common; so despite the apparent abundance of similes and metaphors, we can pick out two underlying factors. First, both Ursula and Birkin imagine the daisies either facing or yearning upwards. Birkin imagines them 'staring . . . up to the sky', and Ursula's word 'exaltation' contains upward movement, the idea of rising to something above. Secondly, both characters see them as vessels on a voyage – Ursula mentioning the word 'flotilla' and Birkin saying 'convoy of rafts'.

We have already mentioned the primitive associations of the 'dark' water, and the human associations of the flowers. So, the various pictures of these floating flowers become emblematic of life: people, humanity as a whole or individuals, are somehow afloat on a dark primitive stream, going towards the sluice where they will be destroyed. Their attention and their hopes are fixed upon the sky, not the dark stream which is their true element. Life is this kind of a voyage.

Our interpretation may be too simple, and too definite to contain Lawrence's suggestive creation. Nonetheless it seems to fit and to help us. We can relate this emblem both to Birkin's ideas about the 'dark river of dissolution' and modern people as the 'white phosphorescent flowers of sensuous perfection' which are the '*Fleurs du Mal*' borne on that stream (see p. 172), and further forward to Ursula's sense of 'the beauty of fate, fate which one asks for, which one accepts in full' when the car 'lurched and swayed' in 'darkness' which 'held them both and contained them' on their drive towards sexual consummation (see p. 318). So the daisies are related to both the helpless fate of all humanity, and, on another level, the fated inevitability of their relationship.

Finally, there are two images for the way the daisies move. Both Birkin and Ursula imagine the flowers' movement as dancing. Birkin sees 'a slow, slow dervish dance'; Ursula imagines a 'shy bright little cotillon'. Lawrence picks these images in order to define, simultaneously, the identity of their essential vision because they both think of dances; and the distinction between them because Ursula imagines a formal eighteenth-century dance, while Birkin sees a wild and primitive one. This distinction is further developed and explored when Birkin dances to provoke and tease Ursula by the lake-side in 'Water-Party' (see pp. 168–9).

The brief interlude we have studied, then, is created as a kind of 'plateau' for the two characters: they have argued, and afterwards find this way of being reconciled. Lawrence uses a variety of means – inferential dialogue, imagery, emblematic symbolism – all the features we have explored in our analysis, to describe and define the 'plateau' they have reached. This plateau shows differences between them, and some continuing constraints and conflicts, but at the same time reveals something in their perceptions and feelings that they share. At the end of our extract, Lawrence explains this to us clearly: 'The little conflict into which they had fallen had torn their consciousness and left them like two impersonal forces, there in contact'. So, this extract reveals Ursula and Birkin at a deeper, less conscious level, with their surface brittleness and hostility torn away.

Our analysis of one small interlude has led us a little way into the symbolic and linguistic patterns of *Women in Love*. We will find it to be a characteristic of this novel that everything is tightly, yet inferentially and indirectly, related to everything else. The beauty of the patterns we have briefly allowed ourselves to explore, is the way in which ideas, words, images and even the underlying properties of things (I mean momentary attitudes, or directions of movement) flow, change and repeat themselves throughout the book. Lawrence does not seem to fix his emblems and symbols at all firmly: they grow and change with the characters and the story. For example, in our passage the word 'daisy' stands for 'love', momentarily, between Birkin and Ursula, because of the pattern their dialogue makes with the preceding argument; and the insistent brilliance of the daisies in this passage links them to the 'phosphorescence' on Birkin's 'dark river of dissolution', which is in turn linked to the 'solitary, frail flames of lanterns' on dark Willey Water later that evening (see p. 174).

Conclusions

Psychology and analysing characters

Our analyses in this chapter have been like a process of digging: we have deliberately sought to pass down through the vivid, volatile and confusing surface of behaviour and spikes of emotion that Lawrence gives us, to reach a level beneath speech and conscious thought: the level of impulse, and often contradictory urges, where the 'real story' of Lawrence's characters takes place. In doing so, we have confirmed that Lawrence is a 'psychoanalytical' writer: the tools of analysis we apply to these characters can justifiably be taken from Freud's work-room.

It is not enough merely to say this, however: psychoanalysis can be a good servant of literary criticism, but it is a dangerous master. We have noted that many critics analyse Lawrence rather than the figures he created – and we deliberately shied away from this activity. It is important to keep our primary purpose in mind: our job is to elucidate the text, to scrutinise the imaginative work itself, not to add to biographical knowledge of its author. Another warning comes with the use of psychoanalytical ideas: never go beyond what the text indicates. This rule is easy to obey if you remember, at all times, that the characters are not real people. They are not alive outside the text, so we cannot justify guessing about them. All our conclusions are indicated somewhere among the words the author has written.

When studying Lawrence's characters, then, you have to be ready to say to yourself: 'This is as far as I can go. My understanding may not be clear or final, but it is as far as the text allows me to go'. Notice that we reached this point in discussing the significance of the daisies from *Women in Love*. Birkin looked at them with 'absolved' eyes, and we are still not quite sure what this tells us about him. Also, we only have a hunch, but no clear answer, to Ursula's question: 'Why did they move her so strongly . . . ?'

Studying the psychology of these characters is not all pitfalls, however. We could not ask for a clearer account of repression than Lawrence gives on page 299 of *The Rainbow*, which clarifies Ursula's inner conflicts about Skrebensky; and we cannot ask for a more explicit statement about consciousness than that at the end of our

extract from *Women in Love* when the couple are 'like two impersonal forces, there in contact'. Lawrence himself tells us what is happening whenever possible. In this forest of analysis, we are led by a
helpful author who wants to explain it to us.

Underlying patterns in Lawrence's characters
Our studies of Miriam and Paul, Ursula in *The Rainbow*, and Ursula
and Birkin, have turned up numerous insights into these individuals.
Miriam has a heavy, swaying walk, for example; and Birkin has an
entertaining faculty for self-satire. So, we have come away with a
vivid impression of them as distinct people. However, we have also
begun to notice some underlying similarities in the way Lawrence's
people feel, think and live. These similarities lead us into the author's
own understanding of humanity, his own principles and beliefs. The
following points are only indications at this stage, but they can begin
to serve as axioms, governing the varieties of human behaviour we
find in the novels, as you carry out further work on characters.

1. *The romantic/sexual relationship.* All of the characters we have
studied are more concerned about finding and forming a relationship with somebody of the opposite sex than about anything else.
The other major themes of traditional fiction are secondary to this
search for a male–female relationship. Skrebensky, for example (*The
Rainbow*), goes off to war, but he is a 'nullity' before he leaves, and
Ursula feels contempt for his concept of 'duty'. Lawrence does not
follow the soldier, he stays with the girl and her struggle to find her
equal in a love-relationship. Work appears in these novels as a degradation, something hostile to be fought through (Ursula's teaching in
The Rainbow); an irrelevant activity which pays thirty-five shillings a
week (Paul's job in *Sons and Lovers*); something to be escaped from
into the perfect relationship (Ursula and Birkin in *Women in Love*)
or a demonic obsession (Gerald in *Women in Love*) or a tyrant
machine, enslaving and destroying its servants (Tom Brangwen,
Ursula's uncle, in *The Rainbow*).

It would be easy to find a number of statements of this principle –
the primacy of the sexual/romantic relationship – from the novels
we are studying. However, it is succinctly expressed in Lawrence's
novella *The Captain's Doll*:

'We must all be *able* to be alone, otherwise we are just victims. But when we *are* able to be alone, then we realize that the only thing to do is to start a new relationship with another – or even the same – human being. That people should all be stuck up apart, like so many telegraph-poles,' is nonsense.'[3]

This making of a relationship with another is what the characters in Lawrence's novels do; and it is the most fascinating, problematic and important thing they do in their lives: it takes priority over war, work, learning or religious faith.[4]

Passages describing sexual experience are often rhapsodic, metaphorical and written in Lawrence's most urgent, breathless style. It can be helpful for the student of Lawrence to have an overview at the outset, to know that hardly any of the characters succeed in the quest for a love-relationship. Most of the characters, in most of his fiction, fail in this all-important life quest. Birkin and Ursula in *Women in Love* succeed to a great extent, but not absolutely, in finding fulfilment in each other; and it can be argued that Connie and Mellors, in *Lady Chatterley's Lover*, succeed. Yet, the vast bulk of Lawrence's writing is an unremitting chronicle of failed relationships: partial failures, small measures of success, escapes and possessions, and some cruel distortions of love.

2. Fear and desire. We have noted that several of the characters struggle between conflicting compulsions when they approach a sexual relationship. We have discussed this conflict in terms of 'attraction and repulsion', but we have found more than once (Ursula in *Women in Love*, Paul Morel) that the 'repulsion' or their tendency to criticise and reject the other, is really only the rationalised symptom: the cause is self-defensive fear.

Lawrence portrays sexual desire as a challenge to the individual. In order to fulfil the relationship, it is necessary to abandon your

---

[3] From 'The Captain's Doll' in D. H. Lawrence, *Three Novellas*, London (Penguin Books), 1960, p. 207.

[4] Many critics have objected to this feature of Lawrence's novels, suggesting that the individual's quest for sexual/romantic fulfilment is a delusion. They either castigate Lawrence for ignoring society and history, as a bourgeois-romantic revisionist; or they suggest that he unconsciously transmuted the social struggles of his time into personal and sexual ones.

defences, to 'give' yourself to the other. In love, you are dependent on the other also – your emotions are subject to them as they can cause you either misery and pain, or bliss. In love and sex, then, the individual is open, raw and terribly vulnerable. This fact presents the individual with a terrifying prospect: how can he or she protect themselves? Can they survive the self-abandonment, the terrible openness and intimacy?

Lawrence portrays his characters as subject to a primitive, selfish survival instinct. They are driven by an absolute need to protect and defend themselves, and this may show itself in a variety of different forms. What it always involves is a violent battle within the character, a struggle which often seems to tear them apart. The battle is between the absolute instinct of physical desire and attraction, on the one hand, and the absolute instinct of self-preservation, which fears and hates and seeks to destroy desire, on the other hand.

This struggle within the individual is axiomatic in Lawrence's fiction. When we study his characters we find violent swings of mood, combinations of hatred and desire, and sudden, volatile spikes of intense emotion. Often, their behaviour and words are vicious, destructive of each other, despite the attraction between them. So particular scenes, and particular relationships, can appear confusing on the surface of the narrative. This axiom – that what you see is the manifestation of an inner battle to the death, between desire and fear – helps us to grasp the courtships of Lawrence's characters with firmer understanding; and it can often make the process of deeper analysis much quicker, providing a clear answer to some of the puzzles along the way.

The two basic drives we have identified can be called the **struggle into existence**, on the one hand, and the **struggle towards unity with another** on the other hand. Lawrence thinks of both of these as primal forces in the individual. In other words, they are forces inside the character, which fight and shove and force whether the character likes it or not. For this reason, they often act on an unconscious level – as we found when analysing Paul in *Sons and Lovers* and Ursula in *The Rainbow*.

The **struggle into existence** is the drive to become a separate and complete individual. It resists all attempts to overwhelm it, to make it subservient to any external agency, whether its enemy appears in the form of another person, or social pressure of service or belonging. Sometimes, our practical common sense is perplexed by this, as the offer of 'belonging' appears, on the surface, to be such a benefit that we do not understand why the character resists it. For example, Ursula offers 'love' to Birkin several times in *Women in Love*; and we know that he – in the common phrase – 'loves' her. So, why does he not just get on with it, accept her words and marry her? Why does he argue and cavil over the terms of their relationship, fighting her tooth and nail with what appear, on the surface, to be silly theoretical arguments? We will examine the 'battling' process in their relationship in the next chapter; for the moment all we need to understand is that Birkin's individuality is fighting for its life. It is fighting to survive, not because he does not *love* Ursula, and not for logical reasons, but because that is its nature.

3. *The intact individual.* We have focused on the struggle for individual survival between attracted pairs of lovers. The same dynamic forces are at work between individuals and their environment. The **struggle into existence** therefore also fights for survival when social pressures, work, industry, profit, country, church or any other 'higher ideal' threatens to encroach on the individual's separateness and force it to submit. The point is that the individual essence will not willingly serve *any other*: that is its nature.

In these battles there are winners and losers, of course. Some characters are not strong enough to survive the onslaught of another powerful personality, or the temptation of an external service. The example we have met in this chapter is Skrebensky, in *The Rainbow*. Ursula's sexuality is 'fierce', and he is not able to match her destructive passion. The battle of wills between these two ends with 'She had triumphed: he was not any more' (p. 299). Subsequently, as we have seen, Skrebensky loses all sense of separate individuality. He submits to his 'duty' and becomes merely part of a machine – the army – serving his country. In this case, then, the individual essence has been defeated. Ursula now senses that he is 'nothing' and a 'nullity'. Lawrence is equally forthright in his opinion: people who have been beaten, who have lost their all-important separateness, are 'nothing'. They are merely parts of one machine or another, and therefore slaves.

It is therefore of supreme importance for the individual to continue fighting, to carry on with the **struggle into existence** against all temptations and blandishments. Much of the power of Lawrence's writing comes from his success in presenting this as a fearful and confusing battle. He portrays the enormous temptation to give up the struggle; while at the same time his characters fight blindly, often unreasoningly, for their survival.

4. *The aristocrat.* In Chapter 1, we noticed that Lawrence used the word 'aristocrat' to describe the 'foreign gentleman' who has such a powerful effect on Tom Brangwen. The stranger's quality was specifically that of independence, an absence of need for other people and their approval: he looked around 'calmly' and 'unconcerned', 'without referring to' other people and looking at Brangwen 'without considering it necessary to know him at all'. We can now connect this idea with the **struggle into existence.** In Lawrentian terms, an 'aristocrat' is someone who has achieved freedom and independence in their personality – the foreign gentleman is an individual, intact, no longer troubled by battles against class, education, religion or sexuality.

5. *Equality in sex and love.* What happens when love succeeds, then? The will fights for its survival, desire for the other fights both with and against it – there seems no way that love can succeed without destroying both individuals. We have already found that the defeat of Skrebensky's will leaves him as 'nothing', a 'nullity'. Yet Lawrence continually suggests that successful love is possible, and is the goal of his characters' existence – however far short of it they fall in their various attempts at relationships. How can separateness be preserved in love? How can destruction of one or the other be avoided?

Lawrence provides a paradoxical answer to this question, which we examine in more detail in our next chapter. The axiom we can deduce at this stage is that a man and woman in a love relationship must in some sense be equals. If one of them is weaker, we know from the example of Skrebensky, they will be destroyed by the experience. So, they must both carry the battle as far as it can go: they must both have a strong will, a strong drive towards separate, individual identity; and they must both resist to the end of their strength.

Methods of Analysis

1. We have made use of the various approaches to prose analysis demonstrated in Chapter 1, using them as and when they seemed appropriate. The characteristic features of Lawrence's style – such as repetition, incremental descriptions in successive clauses or sentences, the effects of different dictions, imagery and references· – often throw light on puzzling aspects of character, or draw attention to them.

2. In the analyses in this chapter we have followed a single particular purpose: we were interested in reaching the level of impulse and the unconscious, beneath the behaviour, thoughts and speeches of characters, and we kept this purpose in mind during our analysis. Detailed analysis of a character, followed by a **brief summary** of conclusions, will often highlight illogical aspects of the character and therefore focus your attention on an unconscious element.

3. We have gone further than noticing a dislocation between what the characters say and how they feel or behave, or noticing volatility and conflict in their emotions. In this chapter we have explored the inconsistencies in character, seeking explanations each time. This means that we are constantly asking questions: *why* does Ursula forget the post-card if it is so important to her? *Why* does Paul act so as to provoke the reaction that causes him pain?

4. The answers to these questions are to be found in the text. Remember that you will only find reliable answers by re-reading what Lawrence has written, closely and carefully. Speculating without close attention to the text is dangerous: it can lead you to invent psychoanalytical answers that have nothing to do with what Lawrence intended. However, in this chapter we have sometimes found an answer in the extract itself (for example, Lawrence explains a great deal about Birkin's and Ursula's 'almost unconscious' state in the final paragraph of our extract from *Women in Love*); and at other times we have had to look at other parts of the book, beginning with events leading up to the chosen passage (for example, we found the origin of Ursula's indifference

to Skrebensky, and the motive for her false romanticism about
him, by rereading the description of their love-making in the
stackyard on p. 299, eight pages before our extract).

5. Even when you find answers to your questions within the extract,
   it is always advisable to confirm and expand your understanding
   of the character by looking at parallel or analogous incidents elsewhere in the text. We did this by looking back to Paul's childish
   destruction of his sister's doll, in *Sons and Lovers*.

6. Readers are sometimes carried along by the emotional roller-
   coaster ride of Lawrence's narrative, and fail to notice the author's
   analytical intelligence at work. Never forget to notice what
   Lawrence tells us. He frequently provides us with explanation of
   his character's state of mind. We found a straightforward account
   of both repression and compensation in Ursula, on p. 299 of *The
   Rainbow*, for example; and a clear explanation of Birkin's and
   Ursula's state on p. 131 of *Women in Love*.

Suggested Work

Lawrence is a psychoanalytical novelist. It is therefore not enough to
sympathise or empathise with his characters: we must go further and
understand them better than they can understand themselves. It is a
vital stage in studying Lawrence, to practise this kind of analysis.
Here are suggested passages, one from each of the novels we are
studying, which provide good practice at analysing character in the
way we have done in this chapter.

In *Sons and Lovers*, study the account of part of an evening from
Chapter VIII, beginning on p. 239 at 'Then the three men rose and
went' and going as far as the paragraph ending 'But this was life for
her, and for him' on p. 241. The scene begins as Mrs Morel goes
out, leaving Paul working and watching the bread. Soon after she
leaves, Miriam enters, and she and Paul are alone together. Focus on
Paul's feelings: this passage will lead to insights concerning Paul's
relationship with his mother, and the way this affects both his work
and his feelings about other women – in this case Miriam.

In *The Rainbow*, study the passage that tells of Anna Brangwen becoming a mother, beginning at 'Sometimes she came to him with a strange light in her eyes, . . .' on p. 177, and studying as far as the paragraph ending 'So he was unsure' on p. 180. Analysing this passage, the imagery, and incremental descriptions of Will's and Anna's states of emotion, will reveal insights into the state of their relationship. Try to apply the 'axioms' from our concluding discussion above as a way of measuring their relative successes and failures in the struggle for fulfilling love.

In *Women in Love*, study the incident when Hermione hits Birkin with a paper-weight. During a general discussion, she expressed her opinion that all people are 'equal in the spirit', and Birkin angrily demolished her ideas. Study the aftermath of this argument, beginning at the paragraph which starts 'Hermione was looking at him with leering eyes . . .' on p. 104, and analysing up to the end of the paragraph 'A drugged, almost sinister religious expression became permanent on her face' on p. 106. In this extract, Hermione's unconscious motives and her rationalisations afterwards make a revealing study.

3

The Male/Female Relationship

In the last chapter, we quoted Lawrence's comment from *The Captain's Doll*, that it is necessary for the individual to seek a mate. In the 'Study of Thomas Hardy', Lawrence makes the same point more theoretically, writing of the 'struggle into love and the struggle with love':

> The *via media* to being, for man or woman, is love, and love alone. Having achieved and accomplished love, then the man passes into the unknown. He has become himself, his tale is told. Of anything that is complete there is no more tale to tell. The tale is about becoming complete, or about the failure to become complete.[1]

Each individual, then, seeks another to join with in order to achieve its own further fulfilment as part of a 'Two in One'. In this chapter we examine the experiences of Lawrence's characters as they strive to establish positive sexual relationships, which complete them as individuals and do not destroy them. We can start by remembering the axioms we deduced in the last chapter.

Lawrence's characters are hampered and driven in a number of ways as they try to find a mate. First, they are held back from knowing or expressing their true selves by the many deceptions, limitations and distractions of background, economics and environ-

---

[1] 'Study of Thomas Hardy', in Anthony Beal (ed.), D. H. Lawrence, *Selected Literary Criticism*, London, 1956, p. 167.

ment. They are imprisoned by the influences of family and child-hood, social class, work – or more generally the influence of the great capitalist-industrial 'machine' which may dominate their lives – or they are prisoners of reproductive cycles (see Tom Brangwen at the Marsh Farm, or Anna Brangwen in her cycle of motherhood). Lawrence also depicts numerous other deceptive conventions which entice them into submitting their essential selves to something infe-rior. Among these are courtly/romantic conventions, loyalty, duty, obligation, religion and other forms of individuality-killing 'service'. In short, the characters are constantly waging war to keep themselves intact, in a **struggle into existence**. Secondly, they are driven to pursue conflict *in the relationship*, by a fundamental instinct of com-petition and survival. Their love or desire must fight against this instinct, in a violent **struggle for unity with another**.

Love affairs in D. H. Lawrence's novels, then, are a matter of mul-tiple and violent conflicts, both within each partner, and between them. The wild swings between love and hatred, self-hatred, anger and desire, can be confusing to follow. In addition, Lawrence was acutely aware of gender stereotyping as one of the baleful social influences an individual must resist; yet at the same time, he held his own concept of maleness and femaleness, which differed from con-ventional ideas of 'masculine' and 'feminine'. Lawrence's ideas about male and female 'principles' are part of our investigation in this chapter, and we will understand them best through practical analysis of scenes from the three novels. However, we can gain the begin-nings of an understanding from Lawrence's list of male and female attributes in his 'Study of Thomas Hardy':

> . . . the Male, the Love, the Spirit, the Mind, the Consciousness; . . . the Female, the Law, the Soul, the Senses, the Feelings.[2]

Looking at this list will only provide us with the broadest of con-cepts. Maleness is related to 'Love', femaleness to 'Law'; and these in turn seem to form a rough dichotomy between the mind and con-sciousness (Love) and the body and emotions (Law).

---

[2] Ibid., p. 221.

These two principles throw up connections which may seem peculiar to us at first sight. For example, a 'love' that is of the spirit and consciousness may seem odd to us, conditioned as we are to think of 'love' as a matter of sensuous attraction and emotion. Similarly, emotion and sensuality are not likely to seem natural fellows for 'law'. Clearly, further thought about Lawrence's 'Male' and 'Female' principles will be needed before we can grasp them properly.

One further point needs to be made about 'Male' and 'Female' in Lawrence before we turn our attention to the first extract in this chapter. 'Male' and 'maleness' are not the same as 'man', and 'Female' is not synonymous with 'woman'. Lawrence's view was in line with current psychological theory: he accepted that any person – whether man or woman – has 'Male' and 'Female' elements in their personality:

> For every man comprises male and female in his being, the male always struggling for predominance. A woman likewise consists in male and female, with female predominant.[3]

It seems, then, that male and female elements in the personality provide yet another conflict, yet another struggle, in the individual's fight to exist, survive and mate.

How are all these principles and concepts embodied in the novels? How does Lawrence's text convey what his characters are experiencing and doing? Here is an extract from *Sons and Lovers*, our first passage for analysis in this chapter. Miriam's grandmother is ill, and Miriam looks after her cottage while she is away convalescing. Paul spends the day there:

> They lingered a little while. Then they stood up upon the sweet thyme, and he looked down at her simply.
> 'Will you come?' he asked.
> They went back to the house, hand in hand, in silence. The chickens came scampering down the path to her. He locked the door, and they had the little house to themselves.

---

[3] Ibid., p. 191.

He never forgot seeing her as she lay naked on the bed, when he was unfastening his collar. First he saw only her beauty, and was blind with it. She had the most beautiful hips he had ever imagined. He stood unable to move or speak, looking at her, his face half smiling with wonder. And then he wanted her, and threw off his things. And then, as he went forward to her, her hands lifted in a little pleading movement, and he looked at her face, and stopped. Her big brown eyes were watching him, still and resigned and loving; she lay as if she had given herself up to sacrifice: there was her body for him; but the look at the back of her eyes, like a creature awaiting immolation, arrested him, and all his blood fell back.

'You are sure you want me?' he asked, as if a cold shadow had come over him.

'Yes, quite sure.'

She was very quiet, very calm. She only realised that she was doing something for him. He could hardly bear it. She lay to be sacrificed for him, because she loved him so much. And he had to sacrifice her. For a second, he wished he were sex-less, or dead. Then he shut his eyes again to her, and his blood beat back again.

And afterwards he loved her, loved her to the last fibre of his being. He loved her. But he wanted, somehow, to cry. There was something he could not bear, for her sake. He stayed with her till quite late at night. As he rode home he felt that he was finally initiated. He was a youth no longer. But why had he the dull pain in his soul? Why did the thought of death, the after-life, seem so sweet and consoling?

He spent the week with Miriam, and wore her out with his passion before it was gone. He had always, almost wilfully, to put her out of count, and act from the brute strength of his own feelings. And he could not do it very often, and there remained afterwards always the sense of failure and of death. If he were really with her, he had to put aside himself and his desire. If he would have her, he had to put her aside.

'When I come to you,' he asked her, his eyes dark with pain and shame, 'you don't really want me, do you?'

'Ah yes!' she replied quickly.

He looked at her.

'Nay,' he said.

She began to tremble.

'You see,' she said, taking his face and shutting it out against her shoulder; 'you see – as we are – how can I get used to you? – It would come all right if we were married.'

He lifted his head and looked at her.

'You mean now, it is always too much shock?'

'Yes – and –'

'You are always clenched against me.'

She was trembling with agitation.

'You see,' she said, 'I'm not used to the thought –'

'You are lately,' he said.

'But all my life. – Mother said to me – "there is one thing in marriage that is always dreadful, but you have to bear it." And I believed it.'

'And still believe,' he said.

'No!' she cried, hastily. 'I believe as you do, that loving, even in *that* way, is the high-water mark of living.'

'That doesn't alter the fact that you never *want* it.'

'No,' she said, taking his head in her arms and rocking in despair. 'Don't say so! You don't understand.' She rocked with pain. 'Don't I want your children?'

'But not me.'

(Sons and Lovers, pp. 333 5)

We begin by summarising the story told on the surface: the story of a failed relationship. First, Paul desires Miriam: he finds himself 'blind with' her beauty and 'he wanted her'. However, he wants her to desire him as well, and she cannot do this. As long as he remains aware of her and her feelings, he is aware that she is 'resigned and loving' with a look 'like a creature awaiting immolation'. He can only have her when he has 'shut his eyes again to her'. Miriam loves Paul and will submit to sexual intercourse with him, but 'She only realised that she was doing something for him'. Her mother has taught her that sex is 'dreadful, but you have to bear it'; and although Paul has now taught her that 'loving, even in *that* way, is the high-water mark of living', these precepts do not affect her feelings. As Paul complains, 'That doesn't alter the fact that you never *want* it', and she remains physically tense, unable to welcome his love-making: 'always clenched against me'.

This seems like a clear problem of sexual incompatibility. Their attitudes to physical love-making are different, and Miriam's upbringing has left her with a deep conviction that it is 'dreadful' but must be borne by the woman, while the man takes his pleasure. She does not contradict Paul's more liberal modern ideas, but she has only learned from him theoretically, and cannot make her feelings suit these new beliefs. Paul seeks mutual passion, but cannot provoke a passionate response in Miriam. Their conversation after making love reveals that Miriam denies her feelings. Lawrence tellingly combines the silly euphemism of her upbringing ('loving, even in *that* way') with a phrase we recognise that she has learned from Paul ('the high-water mark of living') to show that her mother's Victorian attitude remains untouched underneath a shallow veneer of parroted agreement with Paul's ideas.

Alongside this clear story of a failed relationship run the more problematic issues of individual identity; Lawrence relates their experience to wider themes by means of imagery and Paul's sense of 'death'. Before we move on to consider these, however, we should pursue the subject Miriam's attitudes have opened up: the influence of gender roles.

Paul and Miriam feel differently about sex, and Paul's attitudes appear more liberal, on the surface. Yet, in this part of the book both of them think about love and their relationship in a way that is confined by convention, by their background and the society around them. So, for example, when Paul arrived, Miriam was 'busy preparing dinner' because she was 'cooking a chicken in his honour'. Paul is clearly delighted by the conventional gender roles they then act out. While she cooks, he 'sat down to watch'; he 'beat the eggs for her' and 'peeled the potatoes', 'carved', and afterwards 'wiped the dishes she had washed'. Lawrence emphasises how much Paul enjoys playing this gender game: he approves of Miriam because she 'looked so perfectly in keeping with the little kitchen, ruddy and busy' and 'gave a feeling of home almost like his mother'. All this is punctuated with phrases from marital convention: the house was 'their cottage' and they 'were man and wife'; then Paul carves 'like a young husband'. The description provides a very detailed and traditional division of activities in the home; and the phrases are filled with gender attitudes. Notice the fine detail of the way attitudes are depicted: Paul beat the eggs 'for her' (presumably because it is 'her' meal – her work, not his, although they will both eat it and it is cooked 'for him' in his 'honour'!).

Their feelings about sex differ, but the description of their divided roles in the meal acts as a template for their behaviour to each other, which is bounded by tradition and convention. Miriam lying naked on the bed, waiting passively, is the sexual counterpart of 'cooking a chicken in his honour'. Paul stands to admire her beauty, before throwing off his things and going 'forward to her'. Lawrence points out the convention in Paul's courtly lust: her hips were 'the most beautiful hips he had ever imagined'. This is a delicate touch: Paul admires and desires her female beauty, but at the same time Lawrence reminds us that Paul has been brought up to contemplate female beauty in his imagination, and he now compares her reality with the ideals he has formed in his shy, woman-worshipping boyhood. After they make love, Paul again responds conventionally. All the social norms of male sexual competition and conquest, of rites of passage and conventional ideas of 'manhood', contribute to Paul's feeling of success: 'he was finally initiated. He was a youth no longer'.

Finally, we should notice that there is nothing unconventional in Paul's love-making. He 'shut his eyes again to her' before 'having' her (Miriam uses this term on p. 327). In Paul's behaviour, then, he only departs from the male stereotype of a man taking his pleasure from a passive female in the brief pause when he asks 'You are sure you want me?' So, both man and woman in this scene exhibit behaviour restricted by the limits of conventional gender roles.

So far, we have highlighted the artificial elements in Paul's and Miriam's encounter: the behaviour and attitudes which do not belong to them as individuals, but which imprison them. We conclude that Lawrence has conveyed these conventions fully, in great detail, showing how the characters are bound by them at every stage of their day together. Now, we need to ask: what of their real, underlying feelings? What are their own, natural feelings and how does Lawrence convey them?

First, remember that Lawrence usually tells us about his characters' emotions: in the last chapter, we came across some unmistakable statements about psychological events – for example, the analysis of Ursula's repressions on p. 299 of *The Rainbow*. In our present analysis, then, we look for a direct, explicit statement of

Paul's and Miriam's underlying emotions. If we cannot find such a thing, we should look for it in the few pages before and after the extract: Lawrence does explain, so the explanation is likely to be there somewhere.

There is a clear account of Paul in our extract: 'If he were really with her, he had to put aside himself and his desire. If he would have her, he had to put her aside.' There is no account of Miriam in the extract, except that 'She only realised that she was doing something for him'; but a little beyond where our extract ends, Lawrence sums up her state. Paul's 'hopelessness . . . grieved her deeply. It had always been a failure between them. Tacitly, she acquiesced in what he felt' (p. 335).

What, then, are their so-called 'real' feelings? Paul is caught between two states, neither of which can satisfy him. When he is aware of Miriam-the-person, he is aware that she submits to him sacrificially, and this cools his desire. He has to see her as an object and not as a person, in order to arouse the sexual, desiring part of himself. So the pronoun 'her', in this passage, denotes Miriam as a person *and* as a sexual object, but not at the same time. The pronoun 'him' or 'himself' is used similarly, to denote both Paul-the-person, who is aware of Miriam and their emotional intimacy, *and* his desire for sexual satisfaction with her, which is confused with his conditioned 'blind' masculine approach of 'brute strength'. The symmetry of this situation is telling. She is passive and sacrificial as she has been conditioned to be; while he is aggressive and selfish, as he has been conditioned to be. Both of them, however, are divided from their fuller selves by sex. Paul shuts himself off in order to indulge his sexuality, and Miriam shuts herself off in order to suffer it.

During their post-coital discussion, Miriam is said to have 'acquiesced' in what Paul felt. This is a carefully chosen word, which continues the idea of her conditioned obedience to the man. Miriam does object ('How can you say so?') when he asserts that she does not want him – but she 'acquiesced' after this, which 'grieved her deeply'. 'Acquiesced' expresses the depth of conditioning which prevents Miriam from opposing Paul's opinion. She regrets, but does not envisage any possible change – there is nothing she can do about it. That it 'grieved her deeply' suggests that she is also divided. She, too, has natural feelings she cannot express because of her gender conditioning (and, of course, her obedience to Paul).

The metaphor of blindness highlights how divided both characters are. This begins when Paul is said to be 'blind with' Miriam's beauty. This is a metaphor – Paul is not literally blind, indeed his physical sight is dominant as he 'saw only' the physical Miriam, gazed at her hips, and stood 'looking at her'. In a metaphorical sense, though, Paul is 'blind' *to* her, and his metaphorical eyes open to her – that is, to her feelings and her as a person – when the 'little pleading movement' of her hands stops him and he looks at her face.

Lawrence introduces a curious effect of reversing our perceptions with the 'blind' metaphor. Miriam's eyes partake of the same division into two kinds of sight. Physically, 'Her big brown eyes were watching him', but Paul notices 'the look at the back of her eyes' which reveals her true feelings about the coming sexual encounter, expressed in another image: 'like a creature awaiting immolation'. Later, Paul 'shut his eyes again to her' and his sexual desire returned. In the continuing sense of the 'blind' metaphor, this must mean that he shut off his *metaphorical* sight, which is his awareness of Miriam-the-person, and we presume that he opened his *physical* sight, but 'saw only her beauty, and was blind with it' again. The metaphor of sight and blindness, then, has allowed Lawrence to create a revealing effect: the external, physical circumstances are relegated to a secondary level, as less real and less central; while the non-physical emotions are metaphorically transported into the form of a concrete narrative: they become the actual, tangible story. The emotions are 'sight', and ordinary 'sight' is blindness.

Miriam's feelings in this extract are represented by her actions. By now, we are becoming used to the hiatus between dialogue and experience in Lawrence, so we easily pick up the falsehood in what Miriam says. She asserts that she wants him ('Ah yes!'), and claims to agree that sex can be 'the high-water mark of living'. She also diverts the conversation to marriage, her mother and children. Her actions, however, express two elements of her response to Paul's challenge. First, there is her increasing distress, which Lawrence mentions in careful stages ('She began to tremble'; 'She was trembling with agitation'; 'rocking in despair'; 'She rocked with pain', and 'she rocked herself in distress'). Secondly, Miriam, like Paul, finds full sight between them intolerable. Just as he must 'put her aside' to make love to her, she puts him aside twice: once 'taking his face and shutting it out against her shoulder', and the second time 'taking his head in her arms'. These actions graphically illustrate the hostile threat Paul poses to her, and her defensive response of 'shutting it out' by hiding his face.

It is a ghastly situation between them, and the symmetry of Lawrence's treatment allows us to consider the full range of 'if onlys', without being able to fix on a single one to blame.[4] We can think '*if only* Paul had approached Miriam more sensitively'; '*if only* Miriam had been more assertive'; '*if only* Paul had not felt a macho compulsion to be "initiated" into manhood'; '*if only* Miriam could have let herself feel sexually aroused'. None of these changes would have solved the problem, however – and the whole point about this couple is that they are not more skilful, or more liberated from their backgrounds, than they are. Lawrence also provokes us to consider a further and wider range of 'if onlys', which extend into every aspect of that society. '*If only* Mrs Leivers had not indoctrinated Miriam with a negative view of sex'; '*if only* Paul had not been brought up conditioned into the angel/whore view of women'; '*if only* Paul had not been pushed towards educational achievement because he was a boy, while Miriam's educational needs were overlooked, which led him to adopt a patronising attitude to her mind, and her to lack confidence in her own opinions'. This wider context reminds us how pervasive and powerful the social and gender 'system' is.

The extract has insistently created an impression of division, fragmentation and shutting away, or putting aside. Clearly, Lawrence implies that the problems and failure here are to do with lack of completeness: both partners have to shut something out, about the other one or about themselves. This truth is embodied in the dominant idea of physical and metaphorical vision being opened and

---

[4] It should be noted that many critics have sided with either Paul (Miriam was 'frigid') or Miriam (Lawrence/Paul was egotistical and insensitive, and 'used' Miriam), and the argument continues to rage to the present day.

closed throughout the account, as they alternately view and hide each other, or parts of each other.

Both Paul and Miriam are unfree: they are divided against themselves by their inability to break free from their gender conditioning. Paul, though, shows signs of struggling to escape from the attitudes to sex he has learned in his boyhood, while Miriam's inner conflict manifests itself as her 'despair' and feeling 'grieved'.

Lawrence tells us that there is a conflict in Paul, between what he feels obliged to do – the selfish, 'blind' pursuit of 'brute' satisfaction, typical of males in his experience – and his yearning for a mutual sexuality. So, 'for a second' he regrets having to act the man, when 'he wished he were sex-less, or dead'; and afterwards he again desires death: 'Why did the thought of death, the after-life, seem so sweet and consoling?'

Paul's feelings represent his failure to break out of the prison his society has built around him. An essential self in him feels degraded, balked and destroyed by his sexual acts, and desires to escape. In this emotional tangle, he identifies the 'dull pain in his soul' and his 'sense of failure and death' with his sexuality. This is why 'death' and 'after-life' – an imagined non-sexual and therefore painless state – becomes 'sweet and consoling'.

This extract, then, has shown us a couple who are unable to attain a satisfying sexual relationship. Lawrence describes their failure as that of individuals who are still buried, who have not **struggled into existence** by throwing off their artificial conditioning. Paul Morel is shown to be struggling to escape: he desires something more or something else. However, he is hardly aware of his struggle as yet, and his pain and dissatisfaction only express themselves negatively – as a desire for sexlessness and death. When he expresses his dissatisfaction, it comes out in an aggressive, masculine form, as an authoritative opinion criticising the woman ('You don't really want me'). Paul's experiment in sexual love with Miriam is therefore a very early chapter in Lawrence's story of love between man and woman.

*   *   *

In *The Rainbow* we meet numerous attempts at love relationships, including some which Lawrence evidently views as distortions of the central quest for a full male–female love, such as the homosexual affair between Ursula and Winifred or the perverted marriage of convenience between Tom Brangwen and Winifred. The central story is of three couples in successive generations: Tom and Lydia, Will and Anna, and Ursula and Anton. Our extract for analysis describes a late stage in the relationship of Will and Anna, after the births of four of their children. Briefly, Anna had established dominance in their marriage by becoming engrossed in childbirth, so that Will no longer competes, and 'In the house, he served his wife and the little matriarchy' (p. 193). However, he makes advances to a young girl while out in Nottingham, and almost embarks on an adulterous affair. The change in their relationship that both Will and Anna sense following this event leads to a period of renewed sensuality between them:

> And she roused him profoundly, violently, even before he touched her. The little creature in Nottingham had but been leading up to this. They abandoned in one motion the moral position, each was seeking gratification pure and simple.
>
> Strange his wife was to him. It was as if he were a perfect stranger, as if she were infinitely and essentially strange to him, the other half of the world, the dark half of the moon. She waited for his touch as if he were a marauder who had come in, infinitely unknown and desirable to her. And he began to discover her. He had an inkling of the vastness of the unknown sensual store of delights she was. With a passion of voluptuousness that made him dwell on each tiny beauty in a kind of frenzy of enjoyment, he lit upon her: her beauty, the beauties, the separate, several beauties of her body.
>
> He was quite ousted from himself, and sensually transported by that which he discovered in her. He was another man revelling over her. There was no tenderness, no love between them any more, only the maddening, sensuous lust for discovery and the insatiable, exorbitant gratification in the sensual beauties of her body. And she was a store, a store of absolute beauties that it drove him mad to contemplate. There was such a feast to enjoy, and he with only one man's capacity.
>
> He lived in a passion of sensual discovery with her for some time –

it was a duel: no love, no words, no kisses even, only the maddening perception of beauty consummate, absolute through touch. He wanted to touch her, to discover her, maddeningly he wanted to know her. Yet he must not hurry, or he missed everything. He must enjoy one beauty at a time. And the multitudinous beauties of her body, the many little rapturous places, sent him mad with delight, and with desire to be able to know more, to have strength to know more. For all was there.

He would say during the daytime:

'Tonight I shall know the little hollow under her ankle, where the blue vein crosses.' And the thought of it, and the desire for it, made a thick darkness of anticipation.

He would go all the day waiting for the night to come, when he could give himself to the enjoyment of some luxurious absolute of beauty in her. The thought of the hidden resources of her, the undiscovered beauties and ecstatic place of delight in her body, waiting, only waiting for him to discover them, sent him slightly insane. He was obsessed. If he did not discover and make known to himself these delights, they might be lost for ever. He wished he had a hundred men's energies, with which to enjoy her. He wished he were a cat, to lick her with a rough, grating, lascivious tongue. He wanted to wallow in her, bury himself in her flesh, cover himself over with her flesh.

And she, separate, with a strange, dangerous, glistening look in her eyes received all his activities upon her as if they were expected by her, and provoked him when he was quiet to more, till sometimes he was ready to perish for sheer inability to be satisfied of her, inability to have had enough of her.

Their children became mere offspring to them, they lived in the darkness and death of their own sensual activities. Sometimes he felt he was going mad with a sense of Absolute Beauty, perceived by him in her through his senses. It was something too much for him. And in everything, was this same, almost sinister, terrifying beauty. But in the revelations of her body through contact with his body, was the ultimate beauty, to know which was almost death in itself, and yet for the knowledge of which he would have undergone endless torture. He would have forfeited anything, anything, rather than forego his right even to the instep of her foot, and the place from which the toes radiated out, the little, miraculous white plain from which ran the little hillocks of the toes and the folded, dimpling hollows between the toes. He felt he would have died rather than forfeit this.

This was what their love had become, a sensuality violent and extreme as death. They had no conscious intimacy, no tenderness of love. It was all the lust and the infinite, maddening intoxication of the senses, a passion of death.

He had always, all his life, had a secret dread of Absolute Beauty. It had always been like a fetish to him, something to fear, really. For it was immoral and against mankind. So he had turned to the Gothic form, which always asserted the broken desire of mankind in its pointed arches, escaping the rolling, absolute beauty of the round arch.

But now he had given way, and with infinite sensual violence gave himself to the realisation of this supreme, immoral, Absolute Beauty, in the body of woman. It seemed to him, that it came to being in the body of woman, under his touch. Under his touch, even under his sight, it was there. But when he neither saw nor touched the perfect place, it was not perfect, it was not there. And he must make it exist.

(*The Rainbow*, pp. 218–20)

This extract is of a different kind from the previous one, which contained narrative of an actual time and an actual dialogue. Here, Lawrence describes the couple's relationship over an extended period of time: only Will's and Anna's inner lives are narrated, and external events, over an unspecified period of months or years, play no part at all. The couple's children are mentioned as 'mere offspring' to them; and Lawrence and the reader join them 'in the darkness and death of their own sensual activities' where they 'lived'.

One characteristic we notice immediately in this kind of writing, is that it is heavily patterned and repetitive. We will begin our analysis by studying these patterns, to see what we can learn from them. Here is a list of repetitions from within our extract:

1. strange, stranger × 4
2. infinite, infinitely × 4
3. dark, darkly, darkness × 3
4. beauty, beauties × 17 including 'absolute beauty' (sometimes capitalised) × 4
5. absolute, absolutely × 7
6. no tenderness × 2
7. (no) love × 4

8. mad, maddening × 7
9. sensual, sensuous, etc. × 8
10. touch × 7
11. enjoy, enjoyment × 5
12. delight × 4
13. unknown, knowledge, know × 9
14. discover, discovery, undiscovered × 8
15. death × 4
16. passion × 3
17. (abandoning the) moral, immoral × 3

This list shows that there is a great deal of repetition, but it still very much understates the repetitive effect of Lawrence's writing. I have only picked out terms which appear again in different parts of the extract, so the list does not mention immediate repetitions such as 'And she was a store, a store of absolute beauties', 'bury himself in her flesh, cover himself over with her flesh', and 'he would have forfeited anything, anything'. Nor does our list include parallelism, where a phrase or construction is repeated, which again occurs many times in the extract. For example, 'as if he were . . . , as if she were . . .' in the second paragraph, or 'Yet he must not hurry, or he missed everything. He must enjoy one beauty at a time' (para. 4), or 'And the thought of it, and the desire for it' (para. 6). Our little list of repetitions also fails to account for the insistent re-expression and re-definition Lawrence uses here, which we have previously called his 'incremental' style because we receive our impressions in increments, understanding through the cumulative effect of a succession of descriptions. In this extract, for example, we find 'her beauty, the beauties, the separate, several beauties of her body' and 'the maddening, sensuous lust for discovery and the insatiable, exorbitant gratification in the sensual beauties of her body', within the first three paragraphs. Notice that the main words in both of these last quotations also belong in the pattern of repetition; and the idea of 'insatiable' connects with the twice-repeated 'inability' at the end of paragraph 8.

We have found these patterning features throughout Lawrence's writing. In this kind of passage the effect is so dense that it conveys a sense of urgency, and at the same time inability to name or pin down the emotion being described: words are not adequate to define experience, so the writer throws several of them at once, trying to hit the elusive experience; then he repeats the main words, as if to double their strength, or as if returning to them because that is the nearest language can get to the experience.

A sense of urgency and excitement is also conveyed by loose sentences with commas introducing each rising phrase: these sentences have a breathless, hurrying rhythm (see, for example, the sentence which is the whole of paragraph 8). Additionally, as we have previously remarked, Lawrence sometimes conveys the movement of his character's mind and emotion in actual time, as we read. For example, Will begins with the generalised term 'her beauty', but seems to realise suddenly that her beauty is plural – many beauties – before becoming increasingly excited as he obsessively focuses on how many 'separate, several' beauties there are in each part of her body. This sentence seems to take us along with Will on his journey of sensual discovery.

In this extract, Lawrence's writing is very densely 'Lawrentian', and it is also characteristically rich in imagery. Here again, it will be useful to make a list:

1. Anna to Will is 'the other half of the world, the dark half of the moon'
2. Will is 'a marauder'
3. Anna contains a vast 'store' of delights
4. Will, as if a bird, 'lit' on her
5. Anna is 'a store' of absolute beauties
6. Anna is 'a feast to enjoy'
7. Their sensuality is 'a duel'
8. Will's contemplation of Anna makes 'a thick darkness'
9. Will wishes he were 'a cat, to lick her with a rough, grating, lascivious tongue'
10. Will wishes to 'wallow' in Anna and 'bury himself' in her flesh
11. Will nearly dies, 'is ready to perish' for his inability to be satisfied

12. Their sensuality is a 'darkness and death' to them
13. Knowing her beauty is 'almost death' for Will
14. He would suffer 'endless torture' for knowledge of her beauty
15. Her instep is a 'white plain' and her toes 'little hillocks'
16. Their sensuality is extreme as 'death'
17. Their sensuality is 'intoxication'
18. Their passion is 'death'
19. Beauty is like a 'fetish' for Will
20. Gothic pointed arches symbolise 'the broken desire of mankind'
21. Round arches symbolise 'absolute beauty'

This is a long list of separate images, but we quickly see that some of them belong in groups. So, the 'other half of the world, the dark half of the moon' join the idea of Will as a 'marauder' and the repeated 'discovery' of 'unknown' and 'undiscovered' beauties, and the combat idea of 'marauder' is continued in 'duel'. Then, a 'store', a 'feast' and 'intoxication' all suggest abundance, and sex as consumption. Anna's body is a landscape in 'plain' and 'hillocks', which connects with Will's wish to 'bury himself' in her and his birdlike 'lit' on her, as well as relating to her as half of 'the world' or 'the moon'.

Next, we notice a series of images related to extremes: 'death' (repeated), then states approaching death ('ready to perish' and 'almost death') and 'endless torture'. The sense is that 'Absolute Beauty' is too much for Will, so it is 'death'. Finally, the sensuality they feel is 'darkness' and his anticipation is 'a thick darkness'.

We have analysed the patterns and images in this extract, then; and this gives us a vivid picture of the relationship Lawrence is describing. It is sensual, insistently associated with death, darkness and images of hostility, and both of them consume each other. There was always something feral, or like a bird of prey, about Will, and this idea is reverted to in his desire to be a cat (we remember Will having hair 'like sleek, thin fur' (p. 100) and being like a 'tom-cat' (p. 107), 'like an eagle' or 'like a gleaming hawk' (p. 109)). This suggests that their relationship is on a primitive animal level, and Lawrence further limits them to sensuality by insistently excluding 'love', 'tenderness', or 'conscious intimacy'. So, the renewed sensuality between Will and Anna is characterised as a kind of sexual feeding and sexual obsession. Sex is compared to a battle between them, and Will is unable to obtain satisfaction because Anna's sexuality is 'something too much' for him – so he wishes to have 'a hundred men's energies' or he will 'perish'.

How does this sensuality fit into the concept of an ultimate male–female relationship? We sense that there is something wrong: it is 'sinister' and 'terrifying' and likened to 'death'. However, it is still difficult to place within the progress of successive couples in the novel as a whole. Does this sensual abandon go further, for example, than Tom Brangwen's assertion that a man and a woman are 'one angel'? In what sense is this a development from Will's and Anna's honeymoon, when they lay together 'at the very centre of all the slow wheeling of space and the rapid agitation of life' (p. 135)? How does it prefigure Ursula's experiences with Winifred Inger, or Anton Skrebensky?

It is very difficult to compare one relationship with another in *The Rainbow*: each couple achieve a measure of success, but none are final. In each case, we can gain some understanding of where these different kinds and levels of relationship fit in to Lawrence's overall ideas, by looking first at the relationship itself: what is included and what is excluded from Will's and Anna's relationship? Then, we should examine this phase in each character's life, asking whether they grow through this sexual experience, as individuals; or is it limiting, enslaving?

Our first inquiry is easily satisfied: Lawrence tells us clearly that everything except a kind of sensual combat is excluded from their relationship. This is far from a full and whole relationship, then.

Where does this new change figure in Will's development? We remember that he felt 'naked' and as if 'in a new world' during their honeymoon; and they had violent quarrels and conflicts in the months after their marriage, which culminated in him giving up the 'master-of-the-house' idea, until finally he burned his carving and, to complete Anna's victory, their first child was born. Anna gradually destroyed his mystic religious passion and his mystic creative passion in his carving. The new sensual activity described in this extract has a liberating effect on Will:

His intimate life was so violently active, that it set another man in him free. And this new man turned with interest to public life, to see what part he could take in it. (p. 220)

Will begins teaching night-classes in woodwork, and this outgoing activity has a positive effect not only on Will himself but also on the rest of the family: 'The house by the yew-trees was in connection with the great human endeavour at last. It gained a new vigour thereby' (p. 221). There is only one element in the extract we have studied that depicts this sensual obsession as a breakthrough for Will: he has always adhered to the 'broken arch' of Gothic form, we are told, and has feared the absolute. Now, in his sexual relationship with his wife, he 'had given way' and 'gave himself' to 'Absolute Beauty'. So now the absolute 'round arch' exists – even if only on a primitive level of sensuality – in Will's and Anna's relationship. The 'round arch' is a potent symbol in *The Rainbow*, an alternative version of the arch of the rainbow itself, which symbolises a gateway to a wider world beyond, and a challenge to each individual to continue travelling forwards in a sort of life-journey. The perfect and absolute rainbow arch also symbolises a complete union, a perfected male–female relationship which is visible and journeyed towards, but – like a real rainbow – is also unreachable. So, in this limited sense, Will comes to life again: he begins to take his place in moving the world forward. His passionate creative feelings are never revived; but he does have influence, ideals and worthwhile work again, as a teacher.

Anna's journey in life appears to have stopped when her children were born. The end of the chapter entitled 'Anna Victrix' explains this clearly:

> If she were not the wayfarer to the unknown, if she were arrived now, settled in her builded house, a rich woman, still her doors opened under the arch of the rainbow, her threshold reflected the passing of the sun and moon, the great travellers, her house was full of the echo of journeying.
>
> She was a door and a threshold, she herself. Through her another soul was coming, to stand upon her as upon the threshold, looking out, shading its eyes for the direction to take. (p. 182)

After the description we have studied, there is little further detail of Anna. We are told of her fear when her step-father Tom is drowned; and the passion between her and Will is underlined again (see p. 234). From this time onwards, however, the narrative focuses on Ursula. Anna appears in the role of a mother, and only her careless-ness about worldly things and respectability is highlighted, which may be related to the intense sensuality she lives with Will. We are told that 'They accepted shame' and engaged in 'natural and unnat-ural acts of sensual voluptuousness' which brought a 'heavy, funda-mental gratification' (all from p. 220). Certainly Anna's personality, 'entirely indifferent to the world' (p. 246) has a powerful influence on Ursula's early desire to escape her unruly family.

The relationship we have studied here, then, is a sinister and limited thing: an absolute, consuming sensuality utterly indulged and likened to death. However, when we view it in perspective, it takes its place in a continuous struggle towards connection with the wider world, and the continuing journey towards the perfected arch of the 'rainbow'.

*   *   *

We now turn to *Women in Love*. We have said that Ursula Brangwen and Rupert Birkin achieve the most complete union found anywhere in the three novels we are studying. The extract we will look at here is the aftermath of a blazing row between them. Birkin means to go to dinner at Shortlands, because Hermione will be there. Ursula goes into a towering rage, denouncing him and his intellectual 'spiritu-ality' as 'obscene and perverse' and 'a foul and false liar'. The end of their row is where our extract begins:

> 'Very good,' he said. 'The only hopeless thing is a fool.'
> 'You are quite right,' she said.
> Still she hesitated. Then an ugly, malevolent look came over her face, she pulled the rings from her fingers, and tossed them at him. One touched his face, the others hit his coat, and they scattered into the mud.
> 'And take your rings,' she said, 'and go and buy yourself a female elsewhere – there are plenty to be had, who will be quite glad to share

your spiritual mess, – or to have your physical mess, and leave your spiritual mess to Hermione.'

With which she walked away, desultorily, up the road. He stood motionless, watching her sullen, rather ugly walk. She was sullenly picking and pulling at the twigs of the hedge as she passed. She grew smaller, she seemed to pass out of his sight. A darkness came over his mind. Only a small, mechanical speck of consciousness hovered near him.

He felt tired and weak. Yet also he was relieved. He gave up his old position. He went and sat on the bank. No doubt Ursula was right. It was true, really, what she said. He knew that his spirituality was con-comitant of a process of depravity, a sort of pleasure in self-destruc-tion. There really *was* a certain stimulant in self-destruction, for him – especially when it was translated spiritually. – But then he knew it – he knew it, and had done. And was not Ursula's way of emotional intimacy, emotional and physical, was it not just as dangerous as Hermione's abstract spiritual intimacy? Fusion, fusion, this horrible fusion of two beings, which every woman, and most men insisted on, was it not nauseous and horrible anyhow, whether it was a fusion of the spirit or of the emotional body? Hermione saw herself as the perfect Idea, to which all men must come: and Ursula was the perfect Womb, the bath of birth, to which all men must come! And both were horrible. Why could they not remain individuals, limited by their own limits? Why this dreadful all-comprehensiveness, this hateful tyranny? Why not leave the other being free, why try to absorb, or melt, or merge? One might abandon oneself utterly to the *moment*, but not to any other being.

He could not bear to see the rings lying in the pale mud of the road. He picked them up, and wiped them unconsciously on his hands. They were the little tokens of the reality of beauty, the reality of happiness in warm creation. – But he had made his hands all dirty and gritty.

There was a darkness over his mind. The terrible knot of conscious-ness that had persisted there like an obsession was broken, gone, his life was dissolved in darkness over his limbs and his body. But there was a point of anxiety in his heart now. He wanted her to come back. He breathed lightly and regularly like an infant, that breathes inno-cently, beyond the touch of responsibility.

She was coming back. He saw her drifting desultorily under the high hedge, advancing towards him slowly. He did not move, he did not look again. He was as if asleep, at peace, slumbering and utterly relaxed.

She came up and stood before him, hanging her head.

'See what a flower I found you,' she said, wistfully, holding a piece of purple-red bell-heather under his face. He saw the clump of coloured bells, and the tree-like, tiny branch: also her hands, with their over-fine, over-sensitive skin.

'Pretty!' he said, looking up at her with a smile, taking the flower. Everything had become simple again, quite simple, the complexity gone into nowhere. But he badly wanted to cry: except that he was weary and bored by emotion.

Then a hot passion of tenderness for her filled his heart. He stood up and looked into her face. It was new and oh, so delicate in its luminous wonder and fear. He put his arms round her, and she hid her face on his shoulder.

It was peace, just simply peace, as he stood folding her quietly there on the open lane. It was peace at last. The old, detestable world of tension had passed away at last, his soul was strong and at ease.

She looked up at him. The wonderful yellow light in her eyes now was soft and yielded, they were at peace with each other. He kissed her, softly, many, many times. A laugh came into her eyes.

'Did I abuse you?' she asked.

(*Women in Love*, pp. 308–10)

We can begin with the dialogue, which falls into two distinct parts, the end of the quarrel and the start of the reconciliation. Much of the dialogue can be dismissed – as usual with Lawrence. The first exchange in this extract is mere 'quarrel-language', and we can pass over it. However, Ursula's parting shot reverts to the subject of their quarrel: his physical and spiritual mess, and his bondage of obligation to Hermione. She also refers to the gift of the rings as an attempt to 'buy yourself a female'. We remember how Paul and Miriam were imprisoned in their gender-role behaviour. Ursula's angry retort here rejects conventional courtship games: she is not a 'female' to be bought with gifts of jewellery; and she distinguishes herself from the 'plenty' who would accept that role. Their argument began with his decision to say goodbye to Hermione, which he called being 'decent' (p. 306), and in her rage Ursula rejects his subservience to the hypocritical code of courtesy and 'decency'. She accuses him of belonging to Hermione and her 'dead show', so her fury is a challenge to him to break free from sham courtesy and the complex, self-degrading rationalisations that have governed Hermione's possession of him.

The advantage of coming to this passage after our studies from *Sons and Lovers* and *The Rainbow* is that we can understand the potency and difficulty of the challenge Ursula issues. Unlike Will and Anna, she is not prepared to settle for 'physical' Birkin only: she demands 'spiritual' Birkin as well, or nothing. So, where Will and Anna excluded all except sensuality from their relationship, Ursula is determined that all will be included in hers. Also, where Paul and Miriam were ruled by the code of conventional male and female roles, Ursula refuses to be bound by any codes foisted on them by their society: both the code of courtship, and that of politeness and what he calls 'decency', are nothing to her, and she demands that they must be nothing to him. Put briefly, she only wants him if he is free; and if he is not free, he is nothing.

There is a further challenge to Birkin in the context of their quarrel. Ursula refers to his physical and spiritual 'mess'. In their quarrel she has objected to his 'word-twisting' (p. 306) and called him a 'purity-monger' saying 'your purity, your candour, your goodness' are like feeding on 'offal' and 'death-eating'. The target of this attack is his rationalising, theorising and his intellectual ideals. She tells him that these are hypocrisy and distorted – he is 'perverse' (all quotations are from p. 307). Clearly, Ursula does not want his physical and spiritual 'mess': she only wants him if he is physically and spiritually not a 'mess'. We could put her challenge in very ordinary words: she is effectively saying to him, 'sort yourself out'. However, Lawrence has provided us with more detail than this, by showing us how many, complicated and powerful are the influences from which he must free himself if he is to attain a true individual identity. Birkin's task goes far beyond anything we have seen in the previous two extracts.

The dialogue at the end of the extract, typically, does not discuss all of this subject-matter. What they say simply marks two actions: she offers and he accepts a flower. Ursula's question 'Did I abuse you?' is clearly a joke, and they both dismiss the subject of their

quarrel with laughter. We have noticed before that Lawrence's characters rarely speak about what is happening to their emotions. On
this occasion, the effect is to treat the quarrel itself as an event that is
over. What they said is no longer important, but that the quarrel
happened is important because it has created a new situation.

We can remember the idea of a struggle into love, to further
explain this effect. We said that lovers are caught in several conflicts:
and that they fight against each other with a fundamental will to
survive intact, in opposition to the attraction they feel, the temptation to give in and submit to the other. Ursula's and Birkin's quarrel
is an example of this principle in action: it is a violent quarrel, and
they must fight to the point where she walks away and he feels 'tired
and weak'. The conflict is not resolved in any logical, conventional
sense: neither of them gives way, or apologises, and they do not
reach a compromise. Instead, they stand up to each other until they
reach breaking-point. It is the struggle itself that is important,
because fighting is the only means to create the openness and
exhaustion needed for them to come together. They have to smash
and break down each other's defences, and destroy each other's old
selves, because only then can they meet as new people. The process
is violent, but conflict is necessary to progress in their relationship.
This point is underlined by a comparison with *Sons and Lovers*.
Miriam submitted to a sexual relationship, not because she wanted it
but because she submitted – even sacrificed herself – to Paul's desire.
Miriam and Paul did not fight and quarrel to the point of exhaustion, there was no cleansing, liberating struggle between them.
Miriam yielded to him, so there was no equal or mutual relationship
and their love was a failure.

Now we can turn to the main, central section of our extract,
which concerns Birkin. We understand the idea of a creative conflict
– a quarrel, out of which a new and finer love is born. This paradox
sounds satisfying, but it is still rather trite. Even if we sense that
there is a clever truth in the idea, we still need an answer to the
logical question: how does it happen? How does a violent quarrel
enhance love? The narrative of our extract follows Birkin through
this process, so we should read it closely.

Birkin's state when Ursula leaves him is described in full. We are

How can a quarrel evoke a new finer
love to be born?

told that 'a darkness came over his mind. Only a small, mechanical speck of consciousness hovered near him'. Nearly all of the long main paragraph is in the form of an indirect internal monologue: Birkin's tone of voice is apparent in 'fusion, fusion, this horrible fusion', 'this hateful tyranny', the argumentative rhetorical questions, and so on. Clearly, we are reading Birkin's thoughts, so this paragraph is what the 'small, mechanical speck of consciousness' left to him thinks. There is a great deal in this paragraph, which can be clarified by a summary.

First, Birkin does give up his subservience to Hermione. He 'gave up his old position' and thought 'It was true, really, what she [Ursula] said'. Birkin recognises that he has taken pleasure in 'self-destruction'. So he acknowledges that her insults are just: he has been 'death-eating' and 'perverse'.

Secondly, Birkin rails against the idea of 'fusion'. He calls it 'horrible' and 'dreadful', a 'hateful tyranny'. He rejects both kinds of female love he has encountered – Hermione's 'abstract spiritual intimacy' and Ursula's 'emotional and physical' intimacy – and is against the whole idea of trying to 'absorb, or melt, or merge'. Birkin looks for a relationship in which each leaves 'the other being free' so both can be 'individuals'.

Thirdly, Birkin makes a distinction between two ways that a person can 'abandon oneself utterly': he accepts self-abandonment to 'the moment', but not 'to any other being'. This is a curious distinction, but seems to be necessary in the context of Ursula's challenge: if he gives himself up *to her*, he would become part of her and owned by her. In that case he would be nothing and she has said that she does not want him as a nothing or as a mess. He must remain *himself*, so that what he gives her is himself, the distinct individual, not a submissive nothing. We have to conclude that, in this case, there will be two distinct selves – him and her – given to the 'moment'. This is as near as we can approach to the meaning of Lawrence's phrase 'Two-in-One'.

The paragraph we have just summarised is Lawrentian in style: there are the usual repetitions ('fusion, fusion, . . . fusion', for example); the two rhetorical questions ('and was not Ursula's way . . . ?' and 'was it not nauseous and horrible anyhow . . . ?') are parallel, building up our sense of Birkin's revulsion from the 'fusion' idea; and Lawrence redefines his concepts in the usual way, creating a sense of Birkin's actual, simultaneous thought: 'this dreadful all-comprehensiveness, this hateful tyranny'. However, summary shows that the principles behind Birkin's thinking are quite clear. First, Ursula is right about him. Then, the idea of 'fusion' in a relationship is repugnant. Finally, Birkin's ideal is a relationship between two individuals who remain individuals.

Clearly, this paragraph represents a considerable move forward, and radically new thinking by Birkin. Despite this, there is still an intellectual problem that is not resolved. Birkin is still trapped in a contradiction, because he persists in thinking that Ursula demands a 'horrible' intimacy, which is a 'hateful tyranny'; and he rejects this. In Birkin's head, then, there is still a gulf between what Ursula offers and what he will accept. Lawrence leaves Birkin's intellectual analysis at this point. In order to understand their reconciliation, therefore, we have to examine other aspects of the scene.

What is the state which has led Birkin to think new thoughts? At the beginning of the paragraph we are told that the quarrel has worn him out: he is 'tired and weak'; at the same time he feels 'relieved', which must mean that he is relieved to be abandoning his defences and his hostility to what Ursula says about him, since the next sentence is 'He gave up his old position'. So, Birkin's self-defensive, self-justifying willpower has been worn away by Ursula's sustained attack. His shell has been broken, and his underlying self is exposed and vulnerable to new ideas.

Before we move on, it is worth noticing the two offers of love Birkin perceives: Hermione offers an 'abstract spiritual' love, and Ursula offers 'emotional and physical' love. At the beginning of this chapter we met Lawrence's lists of male and female attributes. It is interesting to note that Hermione corresponds to 'the Male, the Love, the Spirit, the Mind, the Consciousness', while Ursula is depicted as closer to 'the Female, the Law, the Soul, the Senses, the Feelings'. This may add to our understanding of how 'perverse' Birkin's subservience to Hermione was.

Following the unresolved analytical paragraph, Lawrence narrates a simple action: Birkin cannot bear to see the rings in the mud, so he picks them up. The description stresses paradox, again: the rings are 'little tokens of the reality of beauty' but he cannot have them without dirt: 'he had made his hands all dirty and gritty'. This action resonates with significant overtones, as if it is symbolic: Lawrence calls the rings 'tokens' and relates them to abstract concepts such as 'happiness' and 'creation'. However, like many of Lawrence's symbols, the significance of the rings and this action is shadowy.

We have already referred to the rings as part of a conventional courtship game, and in the whole story of the chapter, this is an important part of their function. Birkin gives them, and Ursula likes them; but she is embarrassed about liking them and eventually interprets them as an attempt to 'buy' her, so she rejects them. The rings, then, represent a gender convention that Birkin and Ursula must surmount. Lawrence's story of the rings makes a fine point: it would be no good for Birkin to avoid ever giving Ursula a present, because that would mean that their freedom to do as they like is limited by a need to avoid conventional gender roles. During the quarrel, Birkin explains this point about freedom: he says that Hermione 'means much more to *you*, if it comes to that, than she does to me. For you can only revolt in pure reaction from her – and to be her opposite is to be her counterpart' (pp. 305–6). So, if they consciously *avoid* gender roles, they will only continue to be imprisoned by them. What is necessary, then, is for Birkin to be able to give and Ursula to be able to receive the gift of the rings, simply because he wants to give them and she wants to have them, *without reference to* the prison of gender stereotypes. After the quarrel they both acknowledge that the rings are valuable. Ursula asks whether he found them, and he admits their importance to him by acknowledging that he picked them up and put them in his pocket. Ursula then admits that she likes and wants them, that she accepts the gift, when she 'put her hand into his pocket and took them out'.

The above commentary chronicles the device of the rings, which Lawrence uses to show how the couple have broken free from their gender-role suspicions. However, we are no nearer to understanding how the rings and mud are related in the short paragraph under discussion. In this situation, it is useful to define the *before and after* very clearly: this will help us to understand the significance of the middle.

Before Birkin picks up the rings he has reached a fine distinction between two sorts of self-abandonment. His 'small, mechanical speck of consciousness' is still whittling down and chopping off different parts of love, rejecting most and obstinately insisting on the only sort of experience he will accept.

After picking up the rings – and getting his hands dirty – Birkin has 'a darkness over his mind' and 'the terrible knot of consciousness that had persisted there like an obsession was broken, gone, his life was dissolved'.

The conclusion is plain: the action of picking up the rings and becoming muddy at the same time coincides with Birkin's loss of the final 'small, mechanical speck' of consciousness. Somehow, beauty and dirt together snuff out his last obstinate analytical effort. Lawrence does not tell us what this means: he leaves the moment of picking up the rings to speak for itself, in between two descriptions of Birkin's mental and emotional state. We can suggest that this moment teaches Birkin a lesson about life – that ultimately, in the last analysis, you have to accept what is offered as it is (i.e. 'tokens of beauty' with mud attached). If he goes on trying to make sure Ursula's love is purified and whittled down to exactly what his mind wants, before he will give himself to it, he will end with nothing. If he wants the experience, he will have to accept what is, and trust in it, and he will have to get his metaphorical hands 'dirty and gritty'.

This interpretation reminds us of the point we mentioned in passing earlier: the distinction Birkin draws between abandonment to 'the moment' and 'any other being' is, of course, rather absurd. If you are going to abandon yourself then you must abandon yourself. If you have to inquire minutely into what will happen afterwards, you are not 'abandoning yourself' at all. Birkin thinks about 'abandoning himself' conditionally and temporarily – which is absurd!

So the rings and the mud act as a kind of lesson; and the action of dirtying his hands in order to retrieve these 'tokens of the reality of beauty' breaks down Birkin's final conscious resistance. He dissolves in a 'darkness' which is over 'his limbs and his body'. Lawrence's use of 'darkness' is often confusing for readers, because our culture tends to associate darkness and evil. Lawrence, on the other hand, uses 'dark' and 'darkness' in a different way. He visualises a personality as containing a full range from 'light', which is consciousness, to 'dark' unconsciousness. Birkin is therefore more natural and open, having had his hard-defended conscious shell removed, in this 'darkness'. However, 'darkness' is not only the natural, true, underlying self – the unconscious is also the seat of primitive and instinctive urges. So Lawrence used 'darkness' repeatedly, but in this slightly different sense, when describing Will's obsessional sensuality. Readers are sometimes confused because Lawrence seems to use 'darkness' rather indiscriminately; but if we use our common sense and look at the two contexts, the difference in meaning is clear. Will, in *The Rainbow*, loses his physical and moral inhibitions and therefore enters a 'darkness'; Birkin loses his intellectual inhibitions, and enters a 'darkness'. The common event is the loss of a restrictive outer shell, the exposing or opening up of the inner person.

We have gone into a great deal of detail about Birkin's changes, between the end of the quarrel and the beginning of reconciliation. The question with which we began this part of our analysis has been answered, because we now understand how a persistent conflict culminating in a violent quarrel can strip away the individual's defences, down to the last 'speck' of conscious resistance, and paradoxically lead to a more intimate connection between lovers. Our analysis has repeatedly emphasised the necessity of this process: Birkin *must* acknowledge that he was wrong; they *must not* submit to each other or 'melt, or merge'; Birkin *must* give up his obsessional intellectual hair-splitting; he *must* accept the dirt with the beauty; they *must* overcome their gender suspicions; Ursula *must* be herself, not a mere reaction against Hermione; and so on. At each stage we are aware that only one way forward exists: if either of them fails to live up to these imperatives, then the relationship will be nothing – it will fail.

Our other two analyses have underlined this point. Paul and Miriam in *Sons and Lovers*, fail to break free from their social and gender conditioning; and Miriam sacrifices herself to Paul, so their relationship is a failure. Will and Anna, in *The Rainbow*, settle for a limited relationship and become only partly free; so they defer the quest for a full relationship – they are only a 'threshold' and it is left to the next generation to go further forward in search of the 'rainbow'.

The remainder of our extract leads into Ursula's and Birkin's reconciliation, and Lawrence emphasises repeated key ideas, in words and imagery, to create the shift in emotion. The key ideas are peace and quiet, newness, simplicity and lack of effort.

'Peace' is repeated five times, and is related to the image of 'asleep . . . slumbering' and the idea of ease as he is 'relaxed' and his soul is 'at ease'. In contrast, 'complexity' has 'gone into nowhere' and 'the old, detestable world of tension' has 'passed away at last'. Newness is contained in the image of Birkin breathing 'like an infant, that breathes innocently' and in the description of Ursula's face as 'new and oh, so delicate'. Life is now 'simple again, quite simple'; and the lack of effort in both of them is emphasised. Birkin 'did not move, he did not look again'; and Ursula moves without purpose, 'drifting' and 'hanging her head'. Lawrence's writing here is so full of these motifs – peace, ease, newness are repeatedly represented in words, ideas and imagery – that it gives the impression that the couple are full of, even overflowing with these qualities.

Conclusions

The quest for a perfect male–female relationship can be called the central subject of Lawrence's fiction. We tentatively established certain 'axioms' at the end of Chapter 2, but the extracts in this chapter have filled in a great deal more detail of Lawrence's thoughts on this subject. This concluding discussion begins by attempting to organise our understanding, building on the simple axioms from Chapter 2. Then we take a wider look at Birkin's theories in *Women in Love*, and in particular his parallel quest for a male love. Finally, we will look more closely at Lawrence's concepts of gender, as he explains them in the 'Study of Thomas Hardy'.

The male/female relationship.

In the conclusion to Chapter 2, we proposed certain axioms which helped us to understand how Lawrence views his characters' attempts at finding sexual love. We identified the following features as common to all the love relationships in the three novels:

- A conflict between **fear and desire** – the two fundamental drives towards union and separateness.
- The idea of an **intact individual**, who keeps himself or herself from submitting to conventions and outside pressures, and refuses to 'serve' any external ideal. We connected this with Lawrence's term, the **aristocrat**, meaning a person who is not dependent or insecure, and who therefore lives and acts in freedom from external constraints.
- The need for **equality in sex and love**, which means that both partners sustain themselves and they fight each other to remain themselves. It does not mean they are the same, but they are equal in the sense that neither one submits to the other.

In this chapter, we have added a great deal of detail to these ideas, mainly by appreciating what they mean to the individuals involved, in practice. For example, we have found that Miriam's submission brings about powerful negative feelings in Paul which lead him to despair, and a desire to be sexless or dead. Their misery is a result of their failure to be **equal in sex and love**; just as Skrebensky's destruction into a 'nullity' is a result of his failure to withstand Ursula's sexual aggression. However, if we put these statements in another way, they relate to another of our 'axioms'. Miriam is a slave to her upbringing, and is imprisoned within a traditional, passive feminine role of self-sacrifice; so she has failed to become an **intact individual**. Paul also feels forced to act the male role and 'sacrifice her', so he fails to act as an **intact individual**, although his feelings revolt against this and he is engaged in a **struggle into existence**. Skrebensky chooses to serve his patriotic duty – an external, abstract ideal; and this marks his failure to be an **intact individual**, also.

The point is that our different 'axioms', when we find them in actual situations in the novels, are really all parts of one idea, a single insight into the nature of sexual love. Lawrence's various thoughts on the love-relationship are convincing because they all lead to, and follow from, each other. This is what gives us the impression of necessity, the idea that there is only one way forward. If the char-

acter avoids or is diverted from the one path of individual development, then that person becomes 'nothing' and any relationship is
doomed to failure.

Lawrence confirms and elaborates the relation between an individual and society in his 'Study of Thomas Hardy'. He sees each
person having a drive towards 'self-preservation' because they are
'people each with a real, vital, potential self' so they 'burst the shell
of manner and convention and commonplace opinion'. They escape
because they desire 'free action' and feel convention as 'comparative
imprisonment'. On the other hand, Lawrence points out that there
is 'a greater idea of self-preservation, which is formulated by the
State, in the whole modelling of the community'. This restricted but
secure form of living endures: 'In the long run, the State, the
Community, the established form of life remained, remained intact
and impregnable'. Lawrence sees a kind of tragedy in these two
imperatives towards 'self-preservation' because they foster 'the division of a man against himself'. He explains:

> . . . first, that he is a member of the community, and must, upon his
> honour, in no way move to disintegrate the community, either in its
> moral or its practical form; second, that the convention of the
> community is a prison to his natural, individual desire, a desire
> that compels him, whether he feel justified or not, to break the
> bounds of the community, lands him outside the pale, there to stand
> alone . . .[5]

The tragedy Lawrence sees in this division applies to many of the
characters in Hardy's novels, about which he is writing, and he comments that they are generally compulsive rather than conscious
rebels against convention. In this, the Hardy characters Lawrence
writes about may be different from his own creations. Paul Morel,
for example, has artistic ideals and develops original thoughts about
convention, rebellion and himself; and Rupert Birkin is a radical
intellectual theorist. However, the dilemma is a very real one, and as

---

[5] 'Study of Thomas Hardy', in Anthony Beal (ed.), *D. H. Lawrence, Selected Literary Criticism*,
London, 1956, p. 168.

we read Lawrence's further description of it we are reminded that the characters in his own novels struggle, and often fail, in this perennial conflict with convention, which is also a conflict within the divided self:

> . . . remain quite within the convention, and you are good, safe, and happy in the long run, though you never have the vivid pang of sympathy on your side: or, on the other hand, be passionate, individual, wilful, you will find the security of the convention a walled prison, you will escape, and you will die, either of your own lack of strength to bear the isolation and the exposure, or by direct revenge from the community, or from both.[6]

Lawrence further clarifies what he means by escaping the prison of convention, by creating the idea of a 'walled city'. The imagery he elaborates in our next extract from the 'Study of Thomas Hardy' conveys the individual's fear and courage when facing the infinite, and the destructive effect of what Lawrence calls the 'code of the walled city':

> Upon the vast, incomprehensible pattern of some primal morality greater than ever the human mind can grasp, is drawn the little, pathetic pattern of man's moral life and struggle, pathetic, almost ridiculous. The little fold of law and order, the little walled city within which man has to defend himself from the waste enormity of nature, becomes always too small, and the pioneers venturing out with the code of the walled city upon them, die in the bonds of that code, free and yet unfree . . .[7]

To venture outside convention, while still subject to the 'code of the walled city', is disastrous, then.

In this chapter, we have witnessed Paul Morel's attempt to find an unconventional love: he believes in sexual love, and impresses this belief on Miriam. Their experiment in physical love is a daring enterprise in the context of respectability that surrounds them. Yet

---

[6] Ibid., p. 168.
[7] Ibid., p. 176.

Paul carries with him, unconsciously, the baggage of gender roles and courtly attitudes he has learned from his background; and at the crucial moment he acts from convention, shutting his eyes to her and acting from the 'brute strength' of his desires rather than acting from his natural feelings. To venture outside the 'walled city' while still subject to its code, brings failure.

In *Women in Love*, Ursula and Birkin have to break free from their mutual fears and suspicions about Birkin's gift of jewellery: they needed to surmount the 'code of the walled city', and show each other that it was powerless over them, that they could give and receive from themselves rather than as slaves to a convention.

In the extract we analysed from *The Rainbow*, Will and Anna reach a compromise with convention. They 'abandoned . . . the moral position' and indulged in 'unlicensed pleasures' and 'unnatural acts', accepting 'shame'. However, they overthrow convention in a strictly limited sphere: their secret, sexual life is private and confined to the night-time. In their public lives, during the day, they remain conventional and unchanged, issuing no challenge to the 'code of the walled city'.

These extracts from the 'Study of Thomas Hardy', and our analyses in this chapter, show how enormous and complex Lawrence believes the individual's struggle to be; and how enormous and frightening the individual's isolation is, in the face of the absolute, if he or she dares to turn away from the 'walled city' and confront it. It is for this reason that Lawrence sees the **struggle into existence** and its necessary partner, the quest for a relationship, as the central and crucial challenges in life.

One final point is worth confirming, before we move on to look at Birkin's idea of a further relationship in *Women in Love*. We picked the word 'aristocrat' from a passage in *The Rainbow* and suggested that Lawrence thus describes a person who has succeeded in the **struggle into existence**: an 'aristocrat' *is* an individual. The 'Study of Thomas Hardy' confirms this:

> By individualist is meant, not a selfish or greedy person, anxious to satisfy appetites, but a man of distinct being, who must act in his own particular way to fulfil his own individual nature. He is a man who,

being beyond the average, chooses to rule his own life to his own completion, and as such is an aristocrat.[8]

Birkin and Gerald, the quest for a male love

Chapter XX of *Women in Love* tells of an occasion when Birkin visits Shortlands just after his first proposal to Ursula. He and Gerald strip and wrestle naked. Their conversation after this intimate encounter circles around the issues of love, friendship and intimacy in which they are involved, with each other, and with the Brangwen sisters. Birkin echoes the words we have read in his thoughts about Ursula, so that the idea of a complete relationship between the two men is brought into the reader's mind: 'We are mentally, spiritually intimate, therefore we should be more or less physically intimate too – it is more whole' (p. 272). They also discuss the significance of wrestling naked together. Birkin asks 'Do you think this pledges anything?' and Gerald answers 'I don't know' before they agree that 'At any rate, one feels freer and more open now'. Later in their conversation, Gerald acknowledges 'I don't believe I've ever felt as much *love* for a woman, as I have for you – not *love*.'

Birkin and Gerald obviously have a very close friendship: they are 'mentally and spiritually' intimate, and the wrestling is a deliberate attempt to become physically intimate as well. The scene contains several parallels with scenes of heterosexual love. Even the opening of the chapter stresses Gerald's alternatives – intoxication, a woman, or Birkin; following the wrestling they clasp each other's hands before 'normal consciousness' returns; and the experience makes them startlingly aware of each other as distinct, different men: 'so different; as far, perhaps, apart as man from woman, yet in another direction'.

A later chapter (Chapter XXV, 'Marriage or Not') provides a clear explanation of Birkin's idea about male love. The two friends are discussing marriage and Birkin tells Gerald that he does believe in a 'permanent union' between man and woman, but this 'isn't the last word'. He explains that conventional marriages are dreadful, likening them to 'hunting in couples'. Conventional marriages are

---

[8] Ibid., p. 183.

full of 'tightness and meanness and insufficiency' because the male–female relationship is made into something 'supreme and exclusive', whereas Birkin believes we should seek something more:

> 'You've got to take down the love-and-marriage ideal from its pedestal. We want something broader. – I believe in the *additional* perfect relationship between man and man – additional to marriage.'
> 'I can never see how they can be the same,' said Gerald.
> 'Not the same – but equally important, equally creative, equally sacred, if you like.'
>
> (p. 352)

Gerald objects that sex provides a stronger basis between man and woman, so the man and man relationship could never be as strong. Birkin contradicts this, and argues his point:

> '. . . You've got to get rid of the *exclusiveness* of married love. And you've got to admit the unadmitted love of man for man. It makes for a greater freedom for everybody, a greater power of individuality both in men and women.'
>
> (p. 352)

Quite how Birkin envisages the love between man and man becoming physical is not clear, although we can detect an implication in the earlier chapter, 'Gladiatorial'. Then, Gerald opined that there are only two cures for ennui, 'work and love are the two. When you're not at work you should be in love'. Birkin then adds a third: 'Work, love, and fighting. You forget the fight'. From this point onwards, their conversation leads into the naked wrestling scene. The implication is that intimate physical contact between men may be obtained through fighting rather than sex.

Birkin's theory of the love between men, and the relationship Lawrence describes between him and Gerald, have been the subject of intense scrutiny and speculation among the critics and the psychoanalysts – most of it directed at analysing Lawrence himself rather than his novel. Our first duty, though, is to see this idea as part of the literary work, *Women in Love*. It is an important idea which resurfaces on the final page, and which Lawrence deliberately leaves unresolved, to resonate beyond the end of the book. Birkin again asserts his need for a further relationship, 'another kind of love', after Gerald's death. Ursula argues against him, and the novel ends on this flat contradiction between, possibly, the happiest, most fully achieved couple in Lawrence's fiction:

> 'You can't have it, because it's false, impossible,' she said.
> 'I don't believe that,' he answered.
>
> (*Women in Love*, p. 481)

The effect of resonance, of unfinishedness, achieved by this ending, is obviously deliberate: it was not written at the compulsion of the author's latent homosexuality, as some critics would have us believe. It represents a deliberate artistic decision, which we as readers should consider.

What can we make of this purposeful but unresolved motif in the novel? We can read more widely through other parts of Lawrence's writings, or read the first chapter of an earlier draft of *Women in Love*, in which Lawrence is less reticent about feelings of physical attraction for men, when he describes the relationship between Birkin and Gerald (see Appendix III of the Penguin edition of *Women in Love*, which prints this early draft; in particular, see p. 515). Certainly, there is no real surprise in the more open expression of homosexual feelings Lawrence included in his early draft: they are implicit in the relationship between Birkin and Gerald as it appears in the final version. However, no material from elsewhere, nor any supposed sexual problems in the author, will help us to answer the challenge of the ending.

The crucial question is, how can we understand this open ending as a deliberate authorial decision? The answer is that it carries an implication, that the individual's struggle into existence will never end. This implication is consistent with the struggles we have witnessed in all three novels, and the 'rainbow' symbol indicates the same idea: that the goal of the individual's journey always glows in the distance, as an ideal towards which people struggle and aspire. And yet we can never actually reach a 'rainbow': however far we travel, the great coloured arc will always remain a vague distance ahead of us. It is only in prophetic vision that Ursula imagines 'the rainbow stood on the earth' (*The Rainbow*, p. 458).

We should therefore not be surprised that Birkin embarks on a new journey. On the final page of *Women in Love*, he says that he has achieved the long sought-after, much struggled-for relationship with a woman: 'You are enough for me, as far as woman is concerned. You are all women to me'. Yet movement, struggle and growth are fundamental to Lawrence's concept of the individual.

For these reasons, the unresolved ending is, as we have said, a deliberate artistic choice on Lawrence's part. We can see this as a rejection of novelistic conventions, as well as true to the spirit of the book's main theme. *Women in Love* clearly evolves, in its main story and central subject-matter, as a double courtship fable. The blissful marriage of Birkin and Ursula, and the melodramatic discovery of Gerald's frozen corpse, provide a climactic denouement. Lawrence, however, does not subscribe to the kind of ending we might expect. In place of the conventional 'ending', he refuses to obey the shapely limits of literature: so, on the final page, a new and deeply disturbing story of further conflict and striving begins.

Lawrence's concepts of maleness and femaleness

So far, we have only looked at Lawrence's raw list of the attributes of the two sexes. There are three difficulties which can make it hard for the reader to grasp how these concepts are worked into the relationships in his novels. First, Lawrence's concepts of gender are abstract, and he describes them in philosophical rather than concrete language, so it is difficult to translate them into the actual life of the characters. Secondly, as we have said, Lawrence believes that each individual is made up of male and female – we all have masculine and feminine sides to our personality – so the individuals in the novels are amalgams of the two principles. This means that we may find female characteristics in a male character, and vice versa. Thirdly, Lawrence's writing is heavily metaphorical; and some of his metaphors have masculine and feminine implications as well, which it can be helpful for us to recognise when they appear.

We cannot 'solve' these three difficulties: they remain a challenge to each reader, and every passage you approach will require thought about these issues. However, we will discuss each of the problems in turn, in order to set them into a usable context.

First, Lawrence's 'male and female' principles are abstract, philosophical ideas. In fact, when he proposes Love, Spirit, Mind and Consciousness for the male, and Law, Soul, Senses and Feelings for the female, Lawrence is attempting much more than a mere description of gender characteristics. The two separate but interactive principles he proposes for the two sexes, Love and the Law, are also two all-pervasive principles in life and history: they are the basis of a whole philosophy, and only related to the two sexes as a subsidiary to their dominance of nature, society and history. Lawrence writes of 'this antinomy between Law and Love, between the Flesh and the Spirit, between the Father and the Son'; then he takes us on a trail leading through Aeschylus and Euripides and classical Greek culture, to Shelley, Swinburne, Spinoza and Tolstoy, explaining his theory that all art is 'a revelation of the two principles of Love and the Law in a state of conflict and yet reconciled: pure motion struggling against and yet reconciled with the Spirit: active force meeting and overcoming and yet not overcoming inertia'. In this disquisition, Lawrence follows his characteristic habit of re-expressing his major ideas in new terms. So 'Love', the male principle, is also rephrased as 'the Spirit', 'the Son', 'pure motion', 'the pure will to motion' and 'aspiration', while 'Law', the female principle, is also rephrased as 'the Flesh', 'the Father', 'inertia', 'the living, positive inertia'. The important idea in these elucidations is the idea of motion associated with the male, and inertia associated with the female. Lawrence eventually puts these two ideas into the plainest terms, rephrasing his 'Love' and 'Law' principles as 'doing' and 'being'. We may now be able to construct a descriptive summary of what Lawrence sees as masculine, and what he sees as feminine.

The male or masculine principle is that which Lawrence calls 'Love'. This means mental and intellectual seeking, hoping and aspiring: the idea is that 'Love' always looks beyond and tries to discover, reach or achieve something further. It is always aspiring and therefore always in motion, 'doing'.

The female or feminine principle is that which Lawrence calls 'Law'. This means physical things as they are, including the body and its sensations, natural laws and their operation, which underpin and endure behind other activity. This principle is always there and enduring, remaining the same, so it is called 'inertia', and exists through 'being', not 'doing'.

Lawrence argues that art which gains 'a reconciliation between the aspiration and the resistant', which reconciles Love and the Law, is the most lasting and satisfying art. He continues, using the metaphor of a couple:

> In this consummation, they are the resistance and response of the Bride in the arms of the Bridegroom. And according as the Bride and Bridegroom come closer together, so is the response and resistance more fine, indistinguishable, so much the more, in this act of consummation, is the movement that of Two-in-One, indistinguishable each from the other, and not the movement of two brought together clumsily.[9]

Lawrence's subject in this quotation is Shelley's poetry, yet the comparison with a love affair aptly illustrates our point: Lawrence saw these gender principles as the two primary forces at work in everything – in people, art, history, society, all endeavour is seen as a struggle between, and an attempt to achieve reconciliation between Love and the Law, motion and inertia, doing and being.

These are all-embracing philosophical principles, then. We can put them into the context of the novels with two brief references. First, it is useful to reread carefully the remainder of 'Excurse', Chapter XXIII of *Women in Love*. This tells of the coming together in perfect equilibrium of masculine and feminine principles in the persons of Birkin and Ursula. We can begin by noticing their gifts. Birkin offers Ursula the rings: manufactured, artistically created beauty. This is a gift expressing aspiration, an ideal of beauty, and 'doing' because the rings were imagined and made by the jeweller. In other words, it is a gift of masculinity. In return, Ursula offers Birkin the 'piece of purple-red bell-heather'. Her gift is of natural beauty,

---

[9] Ibid., p. 187. All of the quotations about Lawrence's gender concepts are drawn from this work, pp. 185–94.

which exists and which she 'found' for him: this is a gift of nature and 'being'. In other words, a gift of femininity.

When they arrive at the inn and as they proceed towards their consummation in the dark forest, Lawrence begins to build up a repetitive incantation of imagery and references around the two of them. Birkin is repeatedly likened to one of 'the Sons of God' and Ursula to one of 'the daughters of men' in a reference to Genesis which begins to relate the man to 'the Son' and the principle of Love, and the woman to a natural existence or 'the Law'. Then, in harmony with the cultural history Lawrence explains in the 'Study of Thomas Hardy', the descriptions of Birkin contain references to the Egyptian and Greek ancient cultures:

> His arms and his breast and his head were rounded and living like those of the Greek, he had not the unawakened straight arms of the Egyptian, nor the sealed, slumbering head. A lambent intelligence played secondarily above his pure Egyptian concentration in darkness.
>
> (*Women in Love*, p. 318)

Birkin, then, is a combination of Greek and Egyptian characteristics. Broadly, Lawrence ascribed the spiritual and intellectual aspiration, 'Love', the masculine, to the Greeks; while the 'unawakened' and 'slumbering' Egypt was aligned with unconscious nature and the sources of life, in other words closely related to the female principle of 'the Law'. So, this passage represents Birkin as a completed individual comprising both male and female energies, but with the masculine 'Greek' characteristic of 'lambent intelligence' set 'above' his 'Egyptian' darkness. In other words, in Birkin the masculine principle is dominant in a whole, male-and-female personality. In imagery, Birkin's masculinity is associated with fire in the word 'lambent', and repeatedly associated with fire and electricity in these pages (see, for example, 'It was a dark fire of electricity that rushed from him to her' (p. 314)).

The imagery for Ursula is appropriate to the female principle of nature and 'the Law': she is repeatedly likened to a flower. For example, her face was 'upturned exactly like a flower, a fresh, luminous flower, glinting faintly golden with the dew of the first light', and 'she was beautiful as a new marvellous flower opened at his knees, a paradisal flower she was' (both from p. 313).

Lawrence's concepts of masculine and feminine principles are thus worked into the love relationships in the novel in detail. At the same time, the repeated motif of a return to the beginning of the world ('in the beginning', 'paradisal', and so on) beautifully conveys the sense of rebirth and newness, as well as the primal, archetypal force, in the couple's consummating experience.

Lawrence's references are worth some further thought here. We have noticed the phrases Lawrence borrows from Genesis 6, 'the Sons of God' and 'daughters of men'. Another image used repetitively in this passage is of a 'flood', to describe the flow of passion between them. Lawrence allows these two ideas to exist side-by-side, but we can notice that Genesis 6 introduces Noah, his ark, and the Flood of the Old Testament. The suggestion exists that this 'flood', like the biblical one, washes away a corrupted world and leaves only the pure who 'walked with God' (Genesis 6:9). In this chapter, we have looked in some detail at the lovers' need to break free from all corrupting external fears and influences, in order to purify their individuality. Lawrence's reference to the biblical flood seems to be another metaphor for this process.

In *The Rainbow*, Ursula has a homosexual affair with her schoolmistress, Winifred Inger. Lawrence clearly regards the girl's desire for a woman as a temporary and unnatural phase, and further study would show that this phase in Ursula's development is a reaction against her initial experiences with Skrebensky, a stage in her struggle into being, before, on the final pages of the novel, she recognises her need to wait for 'a man created by God' who should 'come from the Infinite and she should hail him' (*The Rainbow*, p. 457). The wrongness of Ursula's temporary infatuation with Winifred is conveyed by means of terms and imagery which directly relate to the male and female principles we have been discussing:

> But a sort of nausea was coming over her. She loved her mistress. But a heavy, clogged sense of deadness began to gather upon her, from the other woman's contact. And sometimes she thought Winifred was ugly, clayey. Her female hips seemed big and earthy, her ankles and

her arms were too thick. She wanted some fine intensity, instead of
this heavy cleaving of moist clay, that cleaves because it has no life of
its own.

(The Rainbow, p. 319)

Winifred is described in terms of the earth and nature: she is 'clayey',
'moist clay' and 'earthy', and the characteristics of 'heavy', 'thick' and
'clogged' are added to this. Even the sounds of these words convey
Ursula's nausea, conjuring sticky dullness with guttural and indefinite consonants. In contrast, Ursula comes to realise that she desires
'fine intensity', a masculine 'other'. Again, the sounds of these words
enhance the concept, with clear consonants and a ringing sound.
Clearly, Lawrence uses this passage to describe much more than the
death of Ursula's attraction towards Winifred: the imagery and terms
set this event in the context of male and female gender characteristics, and imply Lawrence's judgement that the attraction was always
something perverse and unnatural.

The second problem we mentioned at the start of this section –
that characters are made up of both male and female characteristics
– has already been partly discussed. We noted that Birkin consists of
both male and female elements in 'Greek' and 'Egyptian' references,
with the masculine 'lambent intelligence' above, or dominant; and
we noted that the feminine characteristics of Winifred Inger eventually lead Ursula to feel a revulsion from her. Winifred is not only
feminine, however: when Lawrence describes the beginnings of
Ursula's attraction to her, the emphasis is on conspicuously masculine qualities in the mistress; she is 'clear, decided' and with 'a look
of nobility'. She appears to have 'a fine, clear spirit' and her voice is
'ringing and clear'. These descriptions associate with Lawrence's concepts of Spirit, Mind and Love – the masculine characteristics. He
makes clear that Winifred is an amalgam of masculine and feminine
elements: 'She was proud and free as a man, yet exquisite as a
woman' (all quotations are from *The Rainbow*, p. 312).

We have also touched on our third subject – the pattern of
imagery that is related to the concepts of gender. We have referred to
fire, particularly 'dark fire', which is an image of masculinity; and
flowers, earth, clay, and a countryside or landscape – which are

usually used as images of femininity. Some further detail will be added to this understanding in Chapter 5. We do not have the space to engage in any more thorough study of this large subject, however: as you focus on further close analyses of particular passages, you will not only find the images we have mentioned, which are repeatedly used in a gender-related way, you will also discover modulations and developments of them. For example, fire and flames are a basic and repeated masculine metaphor; but we additionally found 'electricity' as a related development of this masculine metaphor, used as one of the repeated motifs in Chapter XXIII of *Women in Love*.

It is worth noting that the natural imagery for the feminine principle sometimes grows into a larger symbol, as a complete cycle of natural regeneration and reproduction. This happens, for example, in the opening pages of *The Rainbow*. See particularly the fifth paragraph (pp. 9–10) and the idea of 'the drowse of blood-intimacy' (p. 10) and 'the teeming life of creation' (p. 11) as Lawrence opens the novel with a general description of the Marsh Farm and the cycle of an agricultural year. A similar effect occurs later in *The Rainbow*, but this time it is the 'matriarchy' established when Anna Brangwen has her five children, which takes over the cottage so that a cycle of human reproduction dominates all domestic life: 'She seemed to be in the fecund storm of life, every moment was full and busy with productiveness to her. She felt like the earth, the mother of everything' (p. 193). It is characteristic of these depictions of the 'feminine' principle and its natural operations, that they are accompanied by a strong impression of completeness, enclosure: an all-embracing and self-repeating containment. It may be helpful, when conceptualising Lawrence's ideas about gender, to remember another sentence from the 'Study of Thomas Hardy': 'The male lives in the satisfaction of some purpose achieved, the female in the satisfaction of some purpose contained'.[10]

Any reader of this discussion will be left feeling frustrated, because issues remain unresolved, or cause problems of interpretation when we think about the novels. For example, the ending of *Women in*

---

[10] Ibid., p. 191.

Love declares a continuing quest towards love between men; but the Winifred Inger episode of *The Rainbow* seems to reach a negative conclusion about love between women, and no reason is given for this difference in treatment. Also, the masculine quest towards the 'beyond' and a wider world seems to be allotted to the female – Ursula – in *The Rainbow*; and Mrs Morel is more intellectual-masculine than her 'female' earthy husband, in Lawrentian terms, in *Sons and Lovers*. This inverted pattern appears to be repeated in the opening pages of *The Rainbow*, where the men live 'dazed' with female 'being', while the women look out to the 'beyond'.

These issues remain unresolved. The novels leave us with a number of contradictions and inconsistencies, and perhaps these only enhance the powerful impression of a struggle into existence, and towards a complete relationship, which they create.

Methods of Analysis

1. In this chapter we have made use of many of the tools already demonstrated for close analysis of prose narrative, calling on them when and where the features of the passage suggest they are appropriate. As you become more practised at the detailed approach, your study will develop in this way, and you will come to recognise which kind of analysis is likely to yield the most enlightening results from the particular passage you are focusing on.

2. We brought two **advantages from earlier study**, also, and made use of them. First, we came to this chapter with a good knowledge of the characteristic features of Lawrence's style, and some idea of the effects he gains as well as of his purpose in writing in his own particular way. Secondly, we brought with us certain 'axioms' regarding individual character, and the workings of male–female relationships. These provided us with a basis on which to build a fuller understanding of the central theme – individuality and the quest for a full relationship – from our analyses.

3. Much of the analytical work we have carried out in this chapter, however, has been based on one particular method: **noticing and**

classifying repeated words, ideas and images in the passages we studied. This process is most fully demonstrated in our analysis of Will and Anna, from *The Rainbow*; but we have used the same method again and again throughout the chapter. For example, this helped us to follow Birkin's thoughts in the crucial paragraph between quarrel and reconciliation; and helped us to appreciate how Lawrence fills his narrative with peace and newness as the reconciliation begins. The same technique was again invaluable when we looked at the actual consummation of Birkin's and Ursula's love, in the remainder of Chapter XXIII of *Women in Love*. It is in the nature of the rhapsodic, incantatory way Lawrence writes about sexual and love experiences, that focusing on repetitions and recurring motifs will help us to understand the actual content of his writing, while we respond to the build of its emotional power.

4. In this chapter, we have referred to Lawrence's expository writings – in particular the 'Study of Thomas Hardy'. Lawrence wrote a great deal of theoretical prose, as well as his fiction, and there is no reason to avoid reading it when it can give a more explicit 'handle' on his philosophical ideas. However, this is a luxury which should be used with caution. First, you should obey the principle that Lawrence's general opinions are only relevant, in literary study, when they correspond to what is demonstrably present in the fictional text as well. Thus, there is no doubt, from the text of these novels alone, that the writer has specific ideas about masculinity and femininity; but what these ideas are can remain confusing and require a lengthy and complex study to clarify. In these circumstances, the 'Study of Thomas Hardy' can increase understanding and act as a short cut, so it enhances our reading of the fiction. Secondly, be cautious in applying Lawrence's expository writings to his fiction: his philosophy and opinions changed considerably during his life and it is important to relate his ideas to fictional work from roughly the same period.

Suggested Work

Follow up the three analyses in this chapter by practising your analysis on other love relationships from the novels. Each couple reaches a different kind of failure, partial success, distortion or compromise; you should become confident in your grasp of positive and negative elements in these love affairs.

In *Sons and Lovers* we happen to have looked at two episodes involving Paul and Miriam. For further work, I suggest studying the very different relationship between Paul and Clara Dawes. A revealing passage is one beginning on p. 403, at the paragraph starting 'She stood and looked at him' and continuing to the end of the paragraph on p. 405 ending 'Each wanted a mate to go side by side with'. In this passage Lawrence struggles to express both what is present and what is missing in the relationship; and it is helpful to consider this in relation to what we know of Paul and Miriam, working out how Paul's two sexual relationships are complementary, as well as how far his mother-love interferes with both.

In *The Rainbow*, look at the fulfilment of love between the first Tom Brangwen and his wife Lydia after two years of marriage. Begin your detailed analysis on p. 87, when Lydia asks 'Why do you go?', and continue as far as p. 91 and the paragraph ending 'her response came at once, or at length'. Again, it will be important to define what is not achieved, and to look carefully at the terms and imagery Lawrence employs to convey what is achieved between them. In studying this extract, you should also consider the longer-term character development of Tom, as one of a succession of Brangwens stretching from original farming unconsciousness to the hyper-awareness of Ursula: how far has he travelled on the road towards a 'wider world' where men move 'dominant and creative' (*The Rainbow*, p. 11)?

In *Women in Love*, we have twice found ourselves looking at stages in the relationship of Birkin and Ursula; it would therefore be appropriate to complement these studies, by studying the relationship between Gudrun and Gerald. A fascinating passage to study will be that beginning on p. 443, with Gudrun's request 'Try to love me a little more, and to want me a little less', and continuing after their argument over the mountain-top sunset, to Gudrun's line 'I am not afraid of your threats!', on p. 447. In this passage, the **struggle into being** and each individual's struggle against annihilation by the other make a complex of vicious conflicts between them: the 'battle of the sexes' is seen at its most destructive. At the same time, it will be important to recognise and define each partner's failure to achieve individual completeness.

4

Class and Society

In our conclusions to Chapter 3, we pointed out that Lawrence's ideas about gender, and the quest for reconciliation between male and female principles, are part of an all-embracing theory which he explains in terms of cultural and social history. We have also found several situations where the characters are subjected to external – social and environmental – pressures to conform. The individual must fight, or reach an accommodation with society, in order to survive. For example, we have seen Paul Morel struggle with the male gender role of a 'young husband'; Tom Brangwen becoming aware of an infinite world beyond his dull round of day-to-day work as a farmer; and Anton Skrebensky dedicating himself to the service of 'duty' and 'country', sacrificing his individuality in the process.

Lawrence's story of the individual, then, is only a part of his insight into society. The pressures and codes of social existence – what Lawrence calls the 'walled city', the 'little fold of law and order'[1] – impinge upon the characters' lives and generate conflicts within and between them. Additionally, Lawrence's novels discuss the state of society and in *Women in Love* a recurrent topic of conversation between the characters is the decline and disintegration of society, and how it can be redeemed.

In this chapter, we will analyse extracts with this specific inquiry in mind: we look at Lawrence's individuals in relation to their social

---

[1] 'Study of Thomas Hardy', in Anthony Beal (ed.), D. H. Lawrence, *Selected Literary Criticism*, London, 1956, p. 176.

context. We will begin with two short extracts from *Sons and Lovers*, the first being a description of Walter and Gertrude Morel's courtship, from the first chapter of the novel:

> When she was twenty three years old she met, at a christmas party, a young man from the Erewash Valley. Morel was then twenty-seven years old. He was well-set-up, erect and very smart. He had wavy, black hair that shone again, and a vigorous black beard that had never been shaved. His cheeks were ruddy, and his red, moist mouth was noticeable because he laughed so often and so heartily. He had that rare thing, a rich, ringing laugh. Gertrude Coppard had watched him fascinated. He was so full of colour and animation, his voice ran so easily into comic grotesque, he was so ready and so pleasant with everybody. Her own father had a rich fund of humour, but it was satiric. This man's was different: soft, non-intellectual, warm, a kind of gambolling.
>
> She herself was opposite. She had a curious, receptive mind, which found much pleasure and amusement in listening to other folk. She was clever in leading folk on to talk. She loved ideas, and was considered very intellectual. What she liked most of all was an argument on religion or philosophy or politics, with some educated man. This she did not often enjoy. So she always had people tell her about themselves, finding her pleasure so . . .
>
> Walter Morel seemed melted away before her. She was to the miner that thing of mystery and fascination, a lady. When she spoke to him, it was with a southern pronunciation and a purity of English which thrilled him to hear. She watched him. He danced well, as if it were natural and joyous in him to dance. His grandfather was a French refugee who had married an English barmaid – if it had been a marriage. Gertrude Coppard watched the young miner as he danced, a certain subtle exultation like glamour in his movement, and his face the flower of his body, ruddy, with tumbled black hair, and laughing alike whatever partner he bowed above. She thought him rather wonderful, never having met anyone like him. Her father was to her the type of all men. And George Coppard, proud in his bearing, handsome, and rather bitter; who preferred theology in reading, and who drew near in sympathy only to one man, the Apostle Paul; who was harsh in government, and in familiarity ironic; who ignored all sensuous pleasure – he was very different from the miner. Gertrude herself was rather contemptuous of dancing: she had not the slightest

inclination towards that accomplishment, and had never learned even a Roger de Coverley. She was a puritan, like her father, high-minded, and really stern. Therefore the dusky, golden softness of this man's sensuous flame of life, that flowed from off his flesh like the flame from a candle, not baffled and gripped into incandescence by thought and spirit as her life was, seemed to her something wonderful, beyond her.

(*Sons and Lovers*, pp. 17–18)

This seems to be a simple description of two people, together with some statements about how they respond to each other. Clearly, each finds the other fascinating because they are of an unfamiliar type. Gertrude thinks Walter 'rather wonderful, never having met anyone like him'; while to him, she is 'that thing of mystery and fascination, a lady'. We are left to infer why she has never met people like Walter, and why he only has an uncomprehending, distant concept of 'a lady' from the background Lawrence gives us. Gertrude is from the 'Coppard' family, a 'good old burgher family' who had fought with 'Colonel Hutchinson', a reference which takes the family's history back to the civil war in the seventeenth century (see *Sons and Lovers* p. 15). Her grandfather was a lace-maker, a well-off tradesman in commercial business, who went bankrupt; her father is an engineer; and she was privately educated. In other words, Gertrude Coppard belongs to the middle class in English society. Walter Morel, on the other hand, has a brief and disreputable family history, works as a miner, and went to work in the pit at the age of ten – having received only an elementary education. In other words, Walter Morel belongs to the working class in English society.

The first point we realise about the class system, then, is the extraordinary division in society between the working and middle classes. Gertrude has 'never met anyone' like Walter, and she is something he has only seen from afar – a 'thing of mystery' to him. These two people have lived in the same society, geographically close to each other, all their lives; and it is evident that there are many other middle-class young ladies in the area, as well as many other young miners. So we are immediately struck by the division between the classes: each of them inhabits a world which is unknown to the other, despite the fact that these worlds exist side by side.

This impression is intensified by their responses to each other, which are essentially an excited response to anything unfamiliar. To Gertrude, he was 'rather wonderful', and his physical presence has 'a certain subtle exultation like glamour'. Lawrence, however, reminds us that Walter is not really 'wonderful': the author adopts a flat, bathetic tone to explain that she had not 'met anyone like him'. The implication is that he is nothing special – any other well-set-up young miner would have created the same impression. This is important, because it defines the attraction and excitement Gertrude feels as a class attraction, not a personal one. Similarly, the author's tone is indulgently contemptuous of Morel, who admires her 'southern pronunciation' and feels a 'thrill' because she speaks well. Clearly, Morel's romantic vision of her as 'a thing of mystery and fascination' is also a feeling which derives from his class attitudes, not a response to her as an individual. The author states what she is to Morel very precisely: she is 'a lady', not herself alone – the indefinite article ranking her with any number of other 'ladies'.

This passage, therefore, describes two groups of people – middle-class and working-class – and shows them responding to each other as to a fascinating, exciting and strange world. Their feelings are determined by their backgrounds; the attraction and delusions exist between social classes, not between these two particular individuals. Even their perceptions of themselves are completely different: to Walter, he seemed to be 'melted away before her'; while to her, he represents 'something wonderful, beyond her'.

Lawrence enhances the contrast between the two classes in the descriptive evocation of Walter, Gertrude and her father George Coppard. The passage builds its effect of contrast in typically Lawrentian fashion: each description consists of repeated and modulated motifs. The summary approach can help to clarify what Lawrence is saying about each social class.

Walter Morel is conveyed in terms of colour and richness. His hair and beard are both strong, an absolute 'black'; his hair is 'wavy' and 'shone', and his beard 'vigorous'; later his hair is active – it 'tumbled'. 'Black' is an absolute, strong colour – mentioned three times in this short passage – and Morel is also 'ruddy' with a 'red' mouth; he is 'so full of colour' and has a 'dusky, golden' softness.

Imagery enhances this strong physical impression, adding references to nature: his voice 'ran' into comic tones, like a stream, and his sensuousness 'flowed off his flesh' – again a streamlike movement. His face is 'the flower of his body'; while the idea of a bouncing lamb is conjured in the meaning and sound of the word 'gambolling'. Further details add an insistence on unrefined physical nature: his mouth is 'moist', and his beard 'had never been shaved'. Finally, the masculine image of a flame is attached to him, but two contrasting kinds of flame are described. His is a 'sensuous flame of life' which, as we have noted, 'flowed from off his flesh like the flame from a candle'. By contrast, Gertrude's life-flame is 'baffled and gripped into incandescence by thought and spirit'.

This contrast with a 'baffled and gripped' life leads us to the contrasting descriptions of Gertrude Coppard and her father. A series of powerful words create our impression of George Coppard: 'satiric', 'ironic', 'proud', 'bitter', 'harsh'; while his daughter Gertrude is 'opposite' to Walter, loved 'ideas' and is 'intellectual'. Heavy, longer words thump down around her: 'religion', 'philosophy', 'politics', 'educated'. She is 'contemptuous' and has no 'inclination' for dancing, which is referred to in typically polysyllabic middle-class euphemism as 'that accomplishment', rather as Jane Austen might describe it; so she is 'high-minded', a 'puritan' and 'stern'. The contrast built up between the middle-class Coppards and working-class Morel is obvious to us as we read, but still not easy to define. Although Morel is conspicuously natural, the Coppards are not exactly unnatural. Two features of the contrast can be clearly identified, however: first, that Morel is seen in terms of easy and natural movement, from 'ran', 'flowed', 'tumbled' and 'gambolling'; while static rigidity is emphasised in the Coppards, in 'harsh', 'proud', 'stern', 'puritan'. The easy natural flow of Morel's personality is also contrasted to a sense of blockage, interruption or artificial diversion of the personality in 'baffled', 'gripped', 'satiric' and 'ironic'. In the middle-class family, nature is somehow interfered with, and expression of the self is limited, constrained ('gripped') and indirect. The image for George Coppard suitably adds to the sense of rigidity, of resistance to natural change: he is compared to the 'Apostle Paul', a man of eighteen centuries ago, and a particularly rigid one at that. The contrast between movement and its absence is extended into the action of the story: quite simply, Walter Morel dances, and Gertrude does not.

Secondly, there is a contrast between mind and spirit, and body. Walter, as we have seen, lives simply in the body – so his 'flame' flows directly off his 'flesh', he is 'gambolling' like a lamb, and his humour is 'non-intellectual'. Gertrude, on the other hand, 'loved ideas' and was 'intellectual'. An 'educated' man is what she enjoys, and academic subjects abound, in their heavy noun-forms: 'religion', 'philosophy', 'politics' and her father's favourite 'theology' as well as his role – 'government'. Gertrude's life, trying to 'flow' from her 'flesh', cannot do so because it is interfered with by 'thought and spirit'. Lawrence places the middle-class attitude to physical living precisely, by saying that George Coppard 'ignored' all sensuous plea- sure. In other places, you can find Lawrence expressing hatred of Victorian middle-class respectability, which never spoke of physical pleasure and – in his view – hypocritically perverted its natural sexu- ality into a pornographic secret, so that he calls the nineteenth century the 'century of the mealy-mouthed lie'.[2] Some of the strength of this antipathy comes out in the damning word 'ignored', and the prepared surprise that George Coppard only sympathised with one man – a dead one – in the passage we are studying.

Gertrude Coppard and Walter Morel are described as representa- tive of their social classes. Lawrence depicts a working-class living without thought, in sensuous physical pleasure; and a contrasting middle-class which has broken the connection between physical exis- tence and life, its life strangled, 'baffled' and perverted by thought, spirit and intellect. In this passage, he highlights the division between these two kinds of people, so that they fail to understand each other, and each is suffused with a glow of mystery or distant glamour to the other.

As we continue to read about the married life of the Morels, we find more and more that the class differences between Gertrude and Walter are a tragic source of conflict between them. So, for example, Gertrude attempts to broaden the intellectual intimacy between

---

[2] 'Pornography and Obscenity', in Anthony Beal (ed.), D. H. Lawrence, *Selected Literary Criticism*, London, 1956, p. 46.

them: 'Sometimes, when she herself wearied of love talk, she tried to open her heart seriously to him. She saw him listen deferentially, but without understanding. This killed her efforts at a finer intimacy' (p. 19).

Our second extract from *Sons and Lovers* is of a different kind. Just as we noticed that Lawrence describes a mixed agricultural and industrial view from the library window during Paul's attempt to find work (see Chapter 1 above), so a background of gradual industrialisation and urbanisation is a constant and often ironical setting in the novel. In the following scene, Paul goes to the pit to fetch his father, with the news that his brother William is dead:

> It was a beautiful day. At Bretty pit the white steam melted slowly in the sunshine of a soft blue sky, the wheels of the headstocks twinkled high up, the screen, shuffling its coal into the trucks, made a busy noise.
>
> 'I want my father – he's got to go to London,' said the boy to the first man he met on the bank.
>
> 'Tha wants Walter Morel? – Go in theer an' tell Joe Ward.'
>
> Paul went into the little top office.
>
> 'I want my father – he's got to go to London.'
>
> 'Thy feyther – is he down – what's his name?'
>
> 'Mr Morel.'
>
> 'What, Walter? Is owt amiss?'
>
> 'He's got to go to London.'
>
> The man went to the telephone and rang up the bottom office.
>
> 'Walter Morel's wanted – Number 42 Hard. Summat's amiss – there's his lad here.'
>
> Then he turned round to Paul.
>
> 'He'll be up in a few minutes,' he said.
>
> Paul wandered out to the pit top. He watched the chair come up, with its wagon of coal. The great iron cage sank back on its rests, a full carfle was hauled off, an empty tram run onto the chair, a bell 'ting-ed' somewhere, the chair heaved, then dropped like a stone.
>
> Paul did not realise William was dead – it was impossible, with such a bustle going on. The puller-off swung the small truck onto the turn-table, another man ran with it along the bank, down the curving lines. 'And William is dead, and my mother's in London, and what will she be doing?' The boy asked himself, as if it were a conundrum.

He watched chair after chair come up, and still no father. At last,
standing beside a wagon, a man's form! The chair sank on its rests,
Morel stepped off. He was slightly lame from an accident.

(*Sons and Lovers*, pp. 166–7)

The effect of this exquisite scene is poignant. First, Paul is clearly in
a state of shock, and has not yet internalised the news he has heard –
that his brother is dead. He knows it, but does not yet believe it:
Paul 'did not realise William was dead'. Paul's limbo-like state is
further conveyed by his reticence. He twice says of his father 'He's
got to go to London', then, when asked if anything is amiss, he
obstinately repeats this phrase. We sense that the boy cannot bring
himself to say that his brother is dead. After the extract and in reply
to his father's question, he speaks the same line for a fourth time,
'You've got to go to London.'

However, perhaps the most subtle and moving effect in the scene
is built up by the relation between Paul's situation and errand, and
the setting. While a personal and family tragedy unfolds, the pit
itself continues to work. So, eventually, William's death becomes
even more unlikely to Paul: 'it was impossible, with such a bustle
going on'. Yet Lawrence does not describe the pit as filthy, violent
and hostile. On the contrary, the happiness of the pit is what he
emphasises. This sense of everything, including heavy industry,
being happy to be alive, begins with the statement that it was a
'beautiful' day. The pit produces 'white' steam which 'melted', the
headstock wheels 'twinkled', and even the screen is described with a
word from playing games – 'shuffling' – and in the language of a
child's picture-book it 'made a busy noise'. When Paul watches for
his father's arrival, all the activity is again smooth and happy. The
great cage has 'rests', the bell 'ting-ed', and the truck is run down the
'curving' lines. It is all a 'bustle', another word reminiscent of a
child's story.

The pit, then, is presented in very positive and cheerful language.
If we compare this apparent style with what actually happens,
however, more sinister elements emerge. The unending business of
production, the great economic machine, does not stop for a second.
Lawrence does not emphasise the dirt, dust and noise, but the happy

indifference of the pit is almost worse. Furthermore, the worker's enslavement to continuous and efficient production is emphasised by the physical details given. Morel does not come up until after several wagons of coal: clearly, he is less important than the product. When he does appear, his humanity is belittled: 'At last, standing beside a wagon, a man's form!' The impression of servant humanity is intensified by the mention that 'He was slightly lame from an accident'. Such small details about the physical effect of his work on Walter Morel recur at odd moments throughout the novel, like a small complaint in the background. For example, when the Morels are chattering about the draught through the scullery door, Lawrence casually interjects a brief description: 'He had still a wonderfully young body, muscular, without any fat. His skin was smooth and clear. It might have been the body of a man of twenty eight, except that there were perhaps too many blue scars, like tattoo marks, where the coal-dust remained under the skin' (p. 235). Through a constant reference to setting, use of background touches, and a shifting, ironic relationship between industrial setting and individual life, Lawrence sets the characters' experiences within a context of the economic 'machine': the necessity of work, and the primacy of the employer's business.

*   *   *

In *The Rainbow*, industrialisation and social mobility are more prominent themes, discussed by author and characters. Our extract comes from Chapter XII, 'Shame', when Ursula takes her teacher and lover Winifred Inger to visit her uncle Tom, deliberately intending to make a match between them. Tom is the manager of the colliery at a town called Wiggiston. Soon after their arrival, Ursula asks her uncle:

> 'But is this place as awful as it looks?' the young girl asked, a strain in her eyes.
> 'It is just what it looks,' he said. 'It hides nothing.'
> 'Why are the men so sad?'
> 'Are they sad?' he replied.

'They seem unutterably, unutterably sad,' said Ursula, out of a passionate throat.

'I don't think they are that. They just take it for granted.'

'What do they take for granted?'

'This – the pits and the place altogether.'

'Why don't they alter it?' she passionately protested.

'They believe they must alter themselves to fit the pits and the place, rather than alter the pits and the place to fit themselves. It is easier,' he said.

'And you agree with them,' burst out his niece, unable to bear it. 'You think like they do – that living human beings must be taken and adapted to all kinds of horrors. We could easily do without the pits.'

He smiled, uncomfortably, cynically. Ursula felt again the revolt of hatred from him.

'I suppose their lives are not really so bad,' said Winifred Inger, superior to the Zolaesque tragedy.

He turned with his polite, distant attention.

'Yes, they are pretty bad. The pits are very deep, and hot, and in some places wet. The men die of consumption fairly often. But they earn good wages.'

'How gruesome!' said Winifred Inger.

'Yes,' he replied, gravely. It was his grave, solid, self-contained manner which made him so much respected as a colliery-manager.

The servant came in to ask where they would have tea.

'Put it in the summer house, Mrs Smith,' he said.

The fair-haired, good-looking young woman went out.

'Is she married and in service?' asked Ursula.

'She is a widow. Her husband died of consumption a little while ago.' Brangwen gave a sinister little laugh. 'He lay there in the house-place at her mother's, and five or six other people in the house, and died very gradually. I asked her if his death wasn't a great trouble to her. "Well," she said, "he was very fretful towards the last, never satisfied, never easy, always fret-fretting, an' never knowing what would satisfy him. So in one way it was a relief when it was over – for him and for everybody." – They had only been married two years, and she has one boy. I asked her if she hadn't been very happy. "Oh, yes Sir, we was very comfortable at first, till he took bad – oh, we was very comfortable – oh yes – ! But you see – you get used to it. I've had my father an' two brothers go off just the same. You get used to it."'

'It's a horrible thing to get used to,' said Winifred Inger, with a shudder.

'Yes,' he said, still smiling. 'But that's how they are. She'll be getting married again directly. One man or another – it doesn't matter very much. They're all colliers.'

'What do you mean?' asked Ursula, ' – "they're all colliers"?'

'It is with the women as with us,' he replied. 'Her husband was John Smith, loader. We reckoned him as a loader, he reckoned himself as a loader, and so she knew he represented his job. Marriage and home is a little side-show. The women know it right enough, and take it for what it's worth. One man or another, it doesn't matter all the world. The pit matters. Round the pit there will always be the side-shows, plenty of 'em.' – He looked round at the red chaos, the rigid, amorphous confusion of Wiggiston. – 'Every man his own little side-show, his home, but the pit owns every man. The women have what is left. What's left of this man, or what is left of that – it doesn't matter altogether. The pit takes all that really matters.'

'It is the same everywhere,' burst out Winifred. 'It is the office, or the shop or the business that gets the man, the woman gets the bit the shop can't digest. What is he, at home, a man? He is a meaningless lump – a standing machine, a machine out of work.'

'They know they are sold,' said Tom Brangwen. 'That's where it is. They know they are sold to their job. If a woman talks her throat out, what difference can it make? The man is sold to his job. So the women don't bother. They take what they can catch – and *vogue la galère*.'

'Aren't they very strict here?' asked Miss Inger.

'Oh no. Mrs Smith has two sisters who have changed husbands. They're not very particular – neither are they very interested. They go dragging along what is left from the pits. They're not interested enough to be very immoral – it all amounts to the same thing, moral or immoral – just a question of pit-wages. The most moral duke in England makes two hundred thousand a year out of these pits. He keeps the morality end up.'

Ursula sat black-souled and very bitter, hearing the two of them talk. There seemed something ghoulish even in their very deploring of the state of things. They seemed to take a ghoulish satisfaction in it. The pit was the great mistress. Ursula looked out the window and saw the proud, demon-like colliery with her wheels twinkling in the heavens, the formless, squalid mass of the town lying aside. It was the squalid heap of side-shows. The pit was the main show, the *raison d'être* of all.

How terrible it was! There *was* a horrible fascination in it – human bodies and lives subjected in slavery to that symmetric monster of the colliery. There was a swooning, perverse satisfaction in it. For a moment she was dizzy.

Then she recovered, felt herself in a great loneliness, wherein she was sad but free. She had departed. No more would she subscribe to the great colliery, to the great machine which has taken us all captives. In her soul, she was against it, she disowned even its power. It had only to be forsaken to be inane, meaningless. And she knew it was meaningless. But it needed a great, passionate effort of will on her part, seeing the colliery, still to maintain her knowledge that it was meaningless.

(The Rainbow, pp. 322–4)

The subject-matter of this extract is quite clear: the characters express different feelings about what is happening in the society of Wiggiston, but they do not disagree about the facts or how to understand them, so Lawrence's exposition of a modern industrial and commercial society proceeds without contradiction or interruption. This is despite the fact that it is cast into dramatic form, with three characters and differing reactions. Our first task is to understand exactly what Lawrence's analysis of industrial society is, and relate that to other knowledge we already have.

The genesis of conversation is Ursula's reaction to seeing Wiggiston and the men hanging about in streets 'like visions of pure ugliness' (p. 320); then her reaction to uncle Tom when he calls his servant '*Mrs* Smith'. The conversation reaches certain clear conclusions, and we can pick these out to focus on each one in turn:

1. 'They believe they must alter themselves to fit the pits and the place, rather than alter the pits and the place to fit themselves.'
2. 'You get used to it', meaning that wives get used to the miners being expendable and replaceable.
3. 'Marriage and home is a little side-show.'
4. '. . . the pit owns every man. The women have what is left.'
5. 'It is the same everywhere [i.e. in office, shop or business] . . . [a man at home is] a machine out of work.'

6. 'The man is sold to his job.'
7. 'The most moral duke in England makes two hundred thou-
    sand a year out of these pits. He keeps the morality end up.'

These all have the tone of definitive statements. Some are in the
form of definitions ('Marriage and home is a little side-show'),
others have symmetrical constructions ('alter themselves . . . alter the
pits and the place') and the final comment has an irony so heavy to
point out the owner's hypocrisy, that it conveys a feeling of symmetry: the literal and implied meanings are diametrically opposed.
Imagery used in these statements is also simple: we have no difficulty
understanding the emphatic weight of 'side-show', 'machine out of
work', and 'sold'. These images are like the figures of speech found
in proverbs or common sayings – they are even similar to political
slogans. In fact, there is a neatly turned, brutal harshness in this
style, which underlines what Ursula thinks of the speakers: 'They
seemed to take a ghoulish satisfaction in it'.

The seven statements we have picked out serve as a complete
analysis of society. This begins with individuals who choose to adapt
to the pit, then focuses on how they become used to being expendable units. The next stage is to broaden the analysis to include all
economic activity – all work – in the same analysis. Finally, they
assert that all relationships are economic – the worker is 'sold' to his
job – and the owner is making enormous, unthinkable profit with
staggering hypocrisy.

The analysis is straightforward socialism: the capitalist boss, owner
of 'the means of production', exploits workers without compunction
in order to maximise his profit. However, Lawrence's angle differs
from that of a political movement. Politics always looks to action by
governments or by groups. So, trade unions are groups who unite in
order to have more power than an individual can have, and they use
that power to fight for the redistribution of wealth, or to gain a
quality of life closer to that enjoyed by the owner (shorter hours,
better leisure facilities or educational opportunities, and so on),
seeking greater fairness. Socialist political parties try to assemble
massed votes: again the emphasis is on groups and numbers of people
uniting in order to use their massed power to force a change for the
better. Revolutionary groups follow the same route – recruiting, con-

verting masses of people to fight with them, until, united, they have enough support to attempt taking over the government.

A socialist would say that Lawrence's nerve fails him before he reaches these obvious decisions about how to change society. However, we could say that Lawrence's thinking is more fundamental than political aims can ever be. Lawrence focuses on the individual. First, each person makes a choice – to adapt to the machine, because that is easier. From that moment of subjection onwards, a process of dehumanisation takes place. A man dies, and 'You get used to it'. They are all the same because 'They are all colliers'. The men are 'sold', and are nothing apart from their job.

At the end of our extract, Lawrence returns to the crucial moment – the moment when the individual has a choice, to submit to the system or not. This time, the choice occurs in Ursula: 'No more would she subscribe to the great colliery, to the great machine which has taken us all captives. In her soul, she was against it, she disowned even its power. It had only to be forsaken to be inane, meaningless'. The direction in which Lawrence points is towards the individual, not any group serving a common interest. We should remember one of our conclusions from the last chapter: that whenever an individual serves any external duty or extrinsic purpose, that individual has died, has ceased to amount to anything. So, for Lawrence, the route of political change is as arid as continuing within the ghastly capitalist system. What would be changed if the workers rose up, and became owners of the 'means of production'? From Lawrence's point of view nothing would have changed, because production itself, and money, would still subject and dehumanise individuals. Even in a perfect communism, with ownership communally shared, individuals would still have to make the same choice – to adapt themselves to fit some external system. Then the dehumanising process would continue, just as Tom and Winifred describe it.

This extract implies, then, that the only escape lies with the individual, and there is some optimism in the narrative because Ursula makes her choice: she removes herself from being influenced by the 'great machine which has taken us all captives'. In doing so, she realises the futility of the entire system of work and money. It is all 'inane, meaningless'.

Ursula succeeds at this point in the novel: she keeps her soul intact and rejects the creeping power of 'that symmetric monster'. This process occurs within Ursula at several points during *The Rainbow*, so that we should recognise it as a recurrent pattern in the development of her character. For example, she almost succumbs to the drudgery and violence of her school-teaching job, but eventually manages to rise above it; she almost succumbs to the temptation of marriage to Skrebensky and joining his pre-planned, systematic career in service in India, but her individualism fights back and rejects this, even though the battle is painful. In a larger and more metaphorical sense, the final two pages of the novel chronicle another, similar event as she recovers from breakdown and miscarriage. At first she is overwhelmed by despair, seeing 'a dry, brittle, terrible corruption spreading over the face of the land', so that 'she perished as she sat'. Then, her despair is gradually replaced by an optimistic vision of 'the old, brittle corruption of houses and factories swept away, the world built up in a living fabric of Truth'.[3] Ursula's constant swings between despair and optimism make a significant contribution to the sense of continual struggle by individualism, fighting to preserve itself against the 'symmetric monster' in the novel.

Before leaving this extract, we should notice the power with which Lawrence invests the system. First, it is uniformly victorious: the thousands of inhabitants of Wiggiston, and its servant uncle Tom, are firmly under its sway. They are thoroughly dehumanised. Secondly, Lawrence shows that understanding alone is not enough to set people free. Tom and Winifred understand – the whole ghastly analysis is their explanation to Ursula – yet they are 'ghoulish' and Ursula feels the strength of the temptation they have succumbed to. Talking cynically to each other, they obtain a 'perverse' satisfaction and indulge a 'horrible fascination'. These phrases, and the flat brutality we have already noticed in their manner of speech, imply that they take a twisted pleasure in their own cynicism. In the present extract Ursula's weakness, her despair, is conveyed by her dizziness when she recognises these temptations: 'There was a swooning, per-

---

[3] We will return to these final pages of *The Rainbow* in more detail in Chapter 5, when discussing the 'rainbow' symbol and other imagery from the novel.

verse satisfaction in it'. Finally, Ursula's emotions are described in full in the final paragraph. She is 'against' the monstrous system, 'disowned even its power'; and it seems 'inane, meaningless' to her. On the other hand, her individualist choice is far from easy. It leaves her in 'a great loneliness' and 'sad'; and it needed 'a great, passionate effort of will on her part, seeing the colliery, still to maintain her knowledge'. In short, conformity and convention offer security and a measure of happiness; while the path of the individual is lonely and leads to constant pain and strife.

This extract, then, conveys a complete analysis of the hostile, dehumanising 'system'; and it depicts Ursula making her 'individualist' choice. We know that Lawrence regards this moment of choice as crucial, and we understand why. However, many readers and critics regard this as only half the story. Once Ursula has chosen, what will she do next? How can she live separate from the 'system', and still within the society it rules? As we have seen, Lawrence is unequivocal about what she chooses to reject; but the questions remain about what she chooses to embrace. Many critics castigate Lawrence on this matter, saying that his individuals unnaturally cut themselves off in an impossible isolation and withdrawal; and they see his social vision as a step backwards because he advocates – in their terms – an outdated bourgeois-romantic solution.

*   *   *

Turning to *Women in Love* we will analyse an extract from the conversation at Hermione's country-house, Breadalby, in Chapter VIII:

> The great social idea, said Sir Joshua, was the *social* equality of man. No, said Gerald, the idea was, that every man was fit for his own little bit of a task – let him do that, and then please himself. The unifying principle was the work in hand. Only work, the business of production, held men together. It was mechanical, but then society *was* a mechanism. Apart from work they were isolated, free to do as they liked.
>
> 'Oh!' cried Gudrun. 'Then we shan't have names any more – we shall be like the Germans, nothing but Herr Obermeister and Herr Untermeister. I can imagine it – "I am Mrs Colliery-Manager Crich –

I am Mrs Member-of-Parliament Roddice, I am Miss Art-Teacher Brangwen." Very pretty that.'

'Things would work very much better, Miss Art-Teacher Brangwen,' said Gerald.

'What things, Mr Colliery-Manager Crich? The relation between you and me, *par exemple?*'

'Yes, for example,' cried the Italian. 'That which is between men and women –!'

'That is non-social,' said Birkin, sarcastically.

'Exactly,' said Gerald. 'Between me and a woman, the social question does not enter. It is my own affair.'

'A ten-pound note on it,' said Birkin.

'You don't admit that a woman is a social being?' asked Ursula of Gerald.

'She is both,' said Gerald. 'She is a social being, as far as society is concerned. But for her own private self, she is a free agent, it is her own affair, what she does.'

'But won't it be rather difficult to arrange the two halves?' asked Ursula.

'Oh no,' replied Gerald. 'They arrange themselves naturally – we see it now, everywhere.'

'Don't you laugh so pleasantly till you're out of the wood,' said Birkin.

Gerald knitted his brows in momentary irritation.

'Was I laughing?' he said.

'*If*,' said Hermione at last, 'we could only realise, that in the *spirit* we are all one, all equal in the spirit, all brothers there – the rest wouldn't matter, there would be no more of this carping and envy and this struggle for power, which destroys, only destroys.'

This speech was received in silence, and almost immediately the party rose from table. But when the others had gone, Birkin turned round in bitter declamation, saying:

'It is just the opposite, just the contrary, Hermione. We are all different and unequal in spirit – it is only the *social* differences that are based on accidental material conditions. We are all abstractly or mathematically equal, if you like. Every man has hunger and thirst, two eyes, one nose and two legs. We're all the same in point of number. But spiritually, there is pure difference and neither equality nor inequality counts. It is upon these two bits of knowledge that you must found a state. Your democracy is an absolute lie – your brother-

hood of man is a pure falsity, if you apply it further than the mathematical abstraction. We all drank milk first, we all eat bread and meat,
we all want to ride in motor-cars – therein lies the beginning and the
end of the brotherhood of man. But no equality.

   'But I, myself, who am myself, what have I to do with equality – with
any other man or woman? In the spirit, I am as separate as one star is
from another, as different in quality and quantity. Establish a state on
that. One man isn't any better than another, not because they are equal,
but because they are intrinsically *other*, that there is no term of comparison. The minute you begin to compare, one man is seen to be far better
than another, all the inequality you can imagine, is there by nature.

   'I want every man to have his share of the world's goods, so that I
am rid of his importunity, so that I can tell him: "Now you've got
what you want – you've got your fair share of the world's gear. Now,
you one-mouthed fool, mind yourself and don't obstruct me."'

(Women in Love, pp. 102–4)

We can think about Lawrence's approach to society as divisible into
two broad subject areas. First, there is the critical analysis of society
he presents in the novels, or his insight into the way things are.
Secondly, there is another and different subject, which is the whole
question of what we should do about it. Society is bad and corrupt:
that is one subject. What can we do about it? That is another. Our
extract from *The Rainbow* focused predominantly on the first of
these subjects: uncle Tom and Winifred Inger presented an accurate
and perceptive analysis of the economic and social system. As we
remarked at the time, none of the characters contradicts this view,
and neither does the author – so there is no reason to distinguish
between their insights into the deplorable influence of the 'great
machine', and Lawrence's own views. However, when we turn to the
second subject – what can be done about it – we find that Lawrence
parts company with Tom Brangwen and Winifred Inger. They
accept the status quo and enjoy their cynicism, and Lawrence
implies that this is 'ghoulish'. In our extract from *The Rainbow*, the
second subject is only implicitly presented, in the form of Ursula's
reactions when she refuses to accept pessimism and struggles free
from capitalism's 'monstrous' power. We know, then, that the way
forward is associated with an intact individual consciousness.

The present extract from *Women in Love* centres its attention on the second subject. Sir Joshua sets the theme by stating his theory and each character involved in the discussion makes a contribution by stating or implying what they think a better society should be like. The best way for us to approach this is to attempt a summary of each of the views put forward by the different characters.

Sir Joshua proposes the '*social* equality of man'. It is far from clear what he means by this – although we can guess that he wishes to abolish class differences and hierarchies, or social 'rank'. Lawrence's opinion of this is not given, except in the speed with which he dismisses the idea and moves on to Gerald's view. Clearly, Lawrence has no interest at all in 'social equality', whatever that means. He only uses the secondary character's opinion as a device to set the discussion in motion.

Gerald proposes that the unifying element in society is 'the work in hand'. Society is 'a mechanism' and the mechanism of 'work, the business of production' holds people together in a 'society'. Gerald takes a deliberately limited view, however: he does not look for anything more than the 'mechanism' of work from society, so he is not concerned about happiness, individual freedoms and fulfilment, or any social ideals such as justice or equality. In his opinion, all other issues are not social, because when they are not taking part in 'the business of production' people are 'isolated, free to do as they liked'. In other words, Gerald says that people are not part of society in their private lives.

Gerald's opinion is subjected to satirical opposition from Gudrun, Birkin and Ursula: it is obvious that all three of these characters disagree with him. Gudrun begins the attack by building a satire on names, ironically suggesting that people should be called by the name of their job instead of an individual name. She proposes absurd-sounding titles such as 'Mrs Colliery-Manager Crich' and 'Miss Art-Teacher Brangwen', likening these to the portmanteau titles used in Germany, 'Obermeister' and 'Untermeister'. When Gerald insists that his solution has practical advantages ('Things would work much better'), Gudrun changes the focus of her attack, pointing out that Gerald's solution will only help production: personal relationships will not work any better than they do at present.

The Italian, Birkin and Ursula all ridicule Gerald's idea. Gerald insists on his division of people into 'social being' when they are at work, and 'private self', when 'the social question does not enter'. Birkin finds this division so absurd that he can only say sarcastically what Gerald says in earnest – that love and sex are 'non-social'; Ursula points out how individuals would be split when she says 'But won't it be rather difficult to arrange the two halves?'.

Where is Lawrence in all this? Referring back to our extract from *The Rainbow*, we know that Gerald's idea is monstrous. 'Work, the business of production' is the same as the 'great machine' Ursula rejected in Wiggiston. People are dehumanised, turned into expendable units. In that passage it became clear that the 'machine' kills individuality in the workers ('They are all colliers'), the manager (uncle Tom is a 'ghoulish' and 'perverse' servant of the system), and the hypocritical owner. All – both winners and losers – are locked into a destructive, dehumanising system. Lawrence does not believe that people can live two separate lives, because the pit takes 'all that really matters' and leaves only 'the bit that's left' for a 'side-show' private life.

Lawrence has also shown us his agreement with Gudrun's point about labels and types. We remember that Gertrude Coppard and Walter Morel were deceived by confusing individuality with class 'type': to him, she was 'a thing' and 'a lady' – the indefinite article revealing that he thinks of her as one of a social batch. To her, he was new because she had not met 'anyone like him'. The class-based attraction between them leads to individual misery for both of them when they marry. A further version of this personal tragedy is replayed in uncle Tom's remarks about marriage in Wiggiston: men are a type, 'colliers', not individuals: 'What's left of this man, or what is left of that – it doesn't matter altogether'.

We have referred to *The Rainbow* to underline the flaws in Gerald's proposition. We can easily confirm this from within *Women in Love*. Gerald's idea is that his work as a colliery-owner is social, and otherwise he is free; and that his work is of primary importance. The fact is that his idea does not work for himself, as we learn in Chapter XVII, 'The Industrial Magnate'. Gerald has created a 'system . . . so perfect that Gerald was hardly necessary any more'.

This brings him moments of 'terror, not knowing what he was'. We understand that Gerald has not developed his own individuality – in Lawrentian terms he is still a 'nullity' outside his work. Gerald's fear when he senses his own emptiness is conveyed in gruesome images which may remind us of unnatural aliens or monsters from horror-films: 'His eyes were blue and keen as ever, and as firm in their sockets. Yet he was not sure that they were not blue false bubbles that would burst in a moment and leave clear annihilation', and 'He was afraid that one day he would break down and be a purely mean-ingless babble lapping round a darkness' (all quotations are from *Women in Love*, p. 232). Lawrence clearly reminds us here that work is limited: it is not enough for a complete human being, and an incomplete human being is a nothingness.

Gudrun, Ursula and Birkin all stand for an individualistic view: that people cannot be divided into different functions, they must be whole people. They also imply that all participation in life is 'social': society is made up of personal relationships and work. However, their opinions are expressed indirectly in their satire of Gerald, not put forward as a solution of their own.

The next positive contribution to the debate comes from Hermione. She believes that all society's problems would be solved if people could 'realise, that in the *spirit* we are all one, all equal in the spirit'. She identifies society's ills as its destructive 'carping and envy' and 'struggle for power'. The passage only tells us that 'This speech was received in silence', but before treating Hermione's opinion with the contempt it deserves, we should set it within the context of Lawrence's discussion, where it is part of a deliberate, symmetrical progress. Gerald proposes that society is all materialism – all 'work' and 'a mechanism', and he excludes everything else. Hermione puts the opposite view: she wishes to ignore all material things, so that society can become all 'spirit' where she dreams that we are all equal and 'all one'. Hermione's opinion is nonsense, as Birkin will quickly tell us. However, the presentation of Hermione implies more tren-chant criticisms, because of who she is.

Hermione is part of the establishment, she belongs in the 'owning' class and they are enjoying a privileged country-house weekend. Hermione can ignore material things because, frankly, she has them. She can ignore work because she does not have to do it. The irony lies in her hypocritical attempt to be modern, her pretence of being 'concerned'. The language Hermione uses betrays the origin of her ideas. She passes through 'all one', to 'all equal', and finally suggests 'all brothers'. These phrases together with her repetition of 'spirit' recall religion. Lawrence was well aware of the socialist analysis of Christianity: Marx's famous view, that religion is the 'opiate' of the people, sees the Church as part of an exploiting establishment lying to the masses, persuading them to accept flagrant injustice and suffering in this world by promising them a false vision of bliss in the afterlife. This analysis of religion's oppressive social role – or modulations and developments of this view – was commonly held by Lawrence's progressive atheist friends. In the present extract Lawrence puts a parody of the great religious lie into the mouth of a so-called 'progressive' upper-class woman. This is bitter satire. It reveals that Hermione is, inescapably, a prisoner of her leisured, privileged class; because whatever she *thinks* she is saying, and however different she *thinks* she is, Hermione is only able to recycle the old religious lie in a new form. She, like Victorian Protestantism, urges the workers to ignore their dreadful lives and poverty and fix their minds on some mystical, insubstantial dream. The only difference is that a Victorian clergyman would call it 'heaven' and Hermione calls it 'in the spirit'.

Finally, we come to Birkin. He does not respond to Hermione's view immediately, but waits until some of the other people have left. Then he turns on her, and demolishes her opinion with fury. Birkin is angry and contemptuous, and Lawrence allows his invective to express this: 'Your democracy is an absolute lie', he says, and 'your brotherhood of man is a pure falsity'. Birkin's anger is not directed only at Hermione, however. He wants to be 'rid of' everybody's 'importunity' and snaps at all other people 'mind yourself and don't obstruct me'. This part of Birkin's irritation is directed against all materialists – all those who are concerned about material conditions and material inequality. Birkin scathingly calls such a person a 'one-mouthed fool'. Part of his solution to society's ills is the same as a mainstream socialist's: Birkin wants 'every man to have his share in the world's goods'. However, his fury betrays his motive for putting forward this solution: he wants everybody to have material equality because he finds the whole business of materialism so grindingly boring. If they all have the same amount, then they can all shut up about it.

A brief reference back to *The Rainbow* is appropriate here. Ursula struggled against the power of the 'great machine' until she realised that it is 'inane, meaningless'. The contempt behind Lawrence's word 'inane' is clarified by Birkin's anger: he regards materialism as too stupid to think about. We can identify Lawrence with Birkin's feelings here. He expressed the same kind of impatience with the whole social reform subject in letters to Bertrand Russell. For example, Lawrence proposed immediate nationalisation of every-thing and commented dismissively 'which practically solves the whole economic question'.[4]

Birkin's contribution, then, demolishes everything that has gone before. He places '*social* differences' with 'material conditions' and says – with Sir Joshua – make them equal. However, he insists that all the 'social' programmes are no use at all as an answer to the crucial question, which is, how can we improve our lives? So 'democracy' and 'brotherhood' as well as 'social equality' or any other real 'equality' are lies.

Birkin's positive contribution is his assertion of individualism. Between different individuals, he says, 'there is pure difference', so people are 'intrinsically *other*' from each other (if we can put it in this way'), and cannot be compared. In fact 'all the inequality you can imagine, is there by nature'. He asserts his belief in individuality forcefully. 'I am as separate as one star is from another, as different in quality and quantity', and his challenge to the argument is: 'Establish a state on *that*'.

Very well, but how can a 'state' be established on 'inequality' and 'difference'? Birkin has impatiently given part of an answer: that people need to be set free from needing material goods, and this can

---

[4] From a letter to Bertrand Russell dated 12 February 1915, quoted in *The Priest of Love: A Life of D. H. Lawrence*, by Harry T. Moore, London 1974, p. 278. The 'Sir Joshua' of *Women in Love* is generally thought to be a portrait of Bertrand Russell, a friend of Lady Ottoline Morrell, who in turn was the original for the character of Hermione.

be done by giving everyone an equal share. However, his further point goes beyond this: people need to be set free from *thinking about* material goods as well.

Birkin does not provide a practical or political answer to the question of society, then. Just as in *The Rainbow*, we find that the answer is said to lie in each individual, where freedom of thought, a revolution in ideas and emotions, needs to take place. In our extract from *The Rainbow*, we found part of this revolution, this liberation in the individual, taking place within Ursula. In the extract from *Women in Love*, Birkin seems impatient to get on with his own internal revolution; and he feels that the whole question of society, politics, reform, material equality and all the rest of it, is merely getting in his way – it impedes him, can 'obstruct' him.

If we are used to political arguments, we can quickly spot the weakness in Birkin's position, and hear the counter-accusation: 'this is pure escapism. You are avoiding the whole question, you have no practical answer, and all you want is to stick your head in the sand like an ostrich, and escape the whole business of real life!' The truth in this is apparent from Birkin's and Ursula's behaviour when they consummate their love. As soon as they come together in the chapter called 'Excurse', Birkin says 'We'd better get out of our responsibilities as quick as we can' and 'There's nothing for it but to get out, quick'. Ursula poses the practical question, doubting whether they can find anywhere to live free, saying 'we've got to take the world that's given – because there isn't any other'. Birkin's answer to this is in two parts: first he tries an impractical paradox ('to wander away from the world's somewheres, into our own nowhere'); then he asserts that there *are* places where you can live freely, and even that there *are* a few people 'who have gone through enough, who can take things for granted' with whom you can live. The people Birkin imagines can be likened to his ideal of an 'aristocrat' – they would not impinge on his freedom because they are independent in themselves, neither domineering nor demanding. However, Ursula finds the 'few other people' depressing, so there is not complete unanimity between the couple – the question of escape from the world, and a free form of living, is not resolved. We also remember that the end of *Women in Love* leaves the question of further and more complex relationships unresolved. It is fair to conclude that this question, the *social* question of how individuals can more positively interact in larger populations than a single couple, resonates unresolved in Lawrence's work. The shadowy dissatisfactions in the scene from 'Excurse' we have just referred to, and the ending of *Women in Love*, show that the author is aware of and creates this unanswered challenge as an integral part of his fiction.

A final ambivalence in Birkin's position is the fact that he is vulnerable to the same criticism as Hermione. Birkin, conveniently, has some money of his own – independent means. This enables him to indulge in the grand gesture of resigning from his job and urging Ursula to do likewise: he is privileged because he does not need to work. We can contrast this with Paul's situation, facing the economic necessity of work, in *Sons and Lovers*.

There is a single, clear conclusion to be drawn from our analyses, however. Throughout these novels there is a consistent drive towards liberation of the individual, struggling to gain freedom from all external powers. At the same time, Lawrence expresses a consistent hatred of all typing, grouping and labelling – from the mistaken class attitudes of Gertrude Coppard and Walter Morel, to the job labels we have found in *The Rainbow* and *Women in Love* as well as the 'equality' label Sir Joshua and Hermione, in their different ways, make use of. Lawrence rejects membership of any group, rejects any idea of a person as 'a something', from 'a working-class man' right through to the final erroneous label 'a human being'. All are totally different, he insists.

Finally, then, Lawrence's answer merely contradicts the question: it is a sociological question, and he refuses to think in sociological terms. Instead, Lawrence's answer – his vision of a better future for mankind – comes in an artistic and mystical form. We have touched on this vision in our reference to the final pages of *The Rainbow*, but a closer examination of its significance belongs properly in the next chapter, because it is inextricably bound up in the metaphoric and symbolic texture of the novels.

Conclusions

The subject 'class and society' in D. H. Lawrence is huge and various. In this chapter we have centred our attention on only four brief extracts, so our analysis can only be a 'sample' of the way these themes are integrated into the three novels we are studying. Our conclusions come in the form of some insights into the way Lawrence creates and discusses 'class and society', but each of these conclusions should only be seen as a starting-point for further study. The method to follow is to think outwards from an extract you have studied in detail. Look for scenes and passages which are analogous to or which contrast with the presentation of society you have found; and look for confirmation or development of the ideas you have found. In this chapter, for example, we noticed Gerald's opinion that 'work' is the basis of society. We briefly referred to Chapter XVII of *Women in Love*, 'The Industrial Magnate', where the flaws in Gerald's ideas, which do not even work for him, are revealed. In the same way, we picked up Birkin's impatience, and the implied escapism in his feelings. This led us to remember the escapist plans he makes with Ursula in Chapter XXIII, 'Excurse'. In each case, following up our deductions in a different part of the text added to our understanding, and developed our sense of the way Lawrence builds the theme of 'society' into his narrative. Each of the following conclusions can be pursued through other parts of the text, in the same way.

1. Lawrence creates a constant background in these three novels, by means of descriptions of the setting. The setting is an ambiguous mixture of agricultural, natural and industrial landscapes (except in the London and continental episodes of *Women in Love*), and analysis of imagery shows that Lawrence uses his descriptions in an emblematic way. In particular, we found that the relation between the personal story and its setting is often complicated and ironic, producing an effect which highlights elements of society and industry, and their impact on the characters' lives.

2. Particularly in *The Rainbow* and *Women in Love*, social and economic problems are increasingly discussed, both by author and characters. These discussions can be thought of as addressing two

subjects: first, analysing society as it is and defining how it works; secondly, exploring the question of what should be done to reform or revolutionise society.   – *what theories do 'is' & ' is not'*

3. Lawrence's analysis of society is broadly in line with socialist ideas, which see the exploitation of the masses by a capitalist elite, owners of the means of production. Lawrence also exposes and satirises religious and establishment hypocrisy, and other forms of social pretentiousness (see, for example, Hermione Roddice's spiritual idealism in our extract from *Women in Love*). Lawrence does advocate a socialist solution to material inequalities: he agrees with nationalisation and the equal distribution of wealth. However, he does not think this is an interesting issue, and accepts this solution as a way of dismissing the economic question quickly. Lawrence does not think this will increase happiness, but he does want people to be free from want, so they do not have to think about material things.

4. Lawrence does not put forward a political or practical solution to society's ills. Instead, he urges a revolution within each individual, to liberate the mind from its materialist chains. This 'liberation' or 'spiritual revolution' is presented in rhapsodic, often metaphorical or symbolic terms in the novels, and will be considered in more detail in the next chapter.

5. The lack of a 'social' answer to the 'social' question is something the author is aware of, and leaves as a continuing but unresolved theme in these novels. For example, continuing uncertainty governs relations between Ursula and Birkin, on the one hand, and other people, as we found in the 'Excurse' chapter; and Ursula struggles with a continuing temptation to despair and submit to the 'great machine' throughout *The Rainbow*.

6. The theme of **individualism** which we discussed in Chapter 3 in relation to love and sexual relationships is pursued consistently throughout Lawrence's evocation of society and class as well. Lawrence is insistent that people must become individuals, independent of each other and able to live free from all external influences, including social and economic constraints; and he insists on the difference of each person from every other, the 'otherness' of each individual. This also means that any thinking which

treats people by type, class, occupation or as 'part' of any sort of 'group' is anathema to Lawrence. He shows both the tragic misery that can follow from such confused thinking (for example Mr and Mrs Morel's disastrous marriage), and the personal annihilation that results when individual characters identify with their work (see uncle Tom in *The Rainbow*, and 'Mr Colliery-Manager Crich' in *Women in Love*), or their duty (see Anton Skrebensky in *The Rainbow*). The hostility Lawrence feels against all 'group' thinking varies in the quality of emotion and intensity which is expressed (the Morels' marriage is fatally sad; Birkin's hostility is impatient and scathingly angry) but it is unwavering.

In this chapter we have relied on **methods of analysis** already demonstrated during the first three chapters, and summarised at the end of each. It would be redundant to repeat that advice, but remember that each of the above conclusions is an opportunity for further study through researching other parts of the text you are working on.

Suggested Work

Almost every page of each of these three novels will furnish some material relevant to the themes of 'class and society': Lawrence's sympathy for the individual's predicament in society, and his sensitivity to the individual's struggle against encroaching pressures, means that this reality is constant in the narratives. However, it would be helpful to carry out a detailed analysis of a significant passage from each of the novels, or from the novel you are studying. Your analysis should then be used as a basis for wider research in the relevant text, in the manner suggested above. Here are three passages for initial detailed study, one from each of the novels.

In *Sons and Lovers*, it will be worthwhile to make a study of the longish account of Paul's first day at Jordan's. Begin on p. 128 at the paragraph beginning 'Paul followed him round the rectangle of counters', and continue as far as Paul's return home when he ends his speech to his mother 'You must come and see. It's ever so nice. –', on p. 135. This appears to be a longer passage than is normal for close analysis. Remember, however, that you are particularly interested in the world of work, and the effect of work on individuals. In this account of Paul's day, Lawrence includes a number of characteristics in people's work relationships, gender-related behaviour, and so on, which show how these are determined by their allotted place within the 'machine'; and he also touches in the warehouse setting. Paul's emotions during this, his first sensitive day in contact with a 'job', also make a revealing study.

In *The Rainbow*, look at the account of Ursula's experiences as a school-teacher. She begins work full of sensitivity towards the children in her class, but the job turns into a battle for power. Ursula reaches a crisis point when she confronts a particularly naughty boy called Williams and canes him to establish her dominance. After this crisis, Lawrence describes how Ursula feels as she continues teaching. Begin at the paragraph on p. 376 starting 'So the battle went on till her heart was sick', and continue to the paragraph ending 'She would serve them, that she might destroy them' on p. 378. This extract again creates the issues of preserving an intact individuality, and struggling to surmount a challenge, that we have found so prevalent in this chapter and the last. Additionally, the dehumanising effects of work and the question of feminism and a 'man's world' are vividly presented.

In *Women in Love*, study the passage describing Loerke, and Gudrun's fascination with him, from Chapter XXX, 'Snow'. Begin on p. 423 at the paragraph starting 'It was very interesting to Gudrun' and continue as far as the paragraph ending 'He seemed to be the very stuff of the underworld of life. There was no going beyond him', on p. 427. In this extract Loerke's explanation of his artistic theory, shifting art from church-serving to industry-serving, should be compared to what we learned from our extracts in the present chapter. The relation between the surface conversation and Gudrun's hidden feelings will repay analysis also.

5

Imagery, Symbols and Structures

Lawrence's stories do not focus on actions and events. His central interest, and therefore the central subject-matter of his novels, is in emotional sensations, and concepts. Lawrence vitalises this non-concrete material with as much physical reality, energy and life as he can attach to it: his subject-matter naturally generates an enormous amount of imagery. At the same time, it is ideas and states of emotion that Lawrence conveys, so his images are driven by ideas. This dual process, where imagery both physicalises concepts and carries the weight of ideas, produces the interpretative richness of Lawrence's writing. Almost every image grows to a symbolic stature, and much of the description carries interpretable significance as well. The most intense experiences in each novel are expressed by means of metaphors: it is as if Lawrence thinks in metaphors, not in material or literal terms.

In this chapter, we will use some of the images we have already met as starting places for an exploration of recurring and related imagery in the text. In the second half of the chapter, we briefly discuss the structure of Lawrence's novels, with a particular focus on *The Rainbow*, where plot structure and the major symbols are integrated into a 'whole'.

Landscapes in *Sons and Lovers*

In Chapter 1 we noticed the view from the library window, as Paul Morel looks for a job:

> Already he was a prisoner of industrialism. Large sunflowers stared over the old red wall of the garden opposite, looking in their jolly way down on the women who were hurrying with something for dinner. The valley was full of corn, brightening under the sun. Two collieries, among the fields, waved their small white plumes of steam. Far-off on the hills were the woods of Aldersley, dark and fascinating.
>
> (*Sons and Lovers*, p. 114)

In Chapter 4 we met the pretty description of the pit, when Paul has just heard that William is dead:

> At Bretty pit the white steam melted slowly in the sunshine of a soft blue sky, the wheels of the headstocks twinkled high up, the screen, shuffling its coal into the trucks, made a busy noise.
>
> (*Sons and Lovers*, p. 166)

There is a strong similarity between these two pictures: in particular, both of them surprise us by painting a cheerful picture of industry. This is partly done through personification which attributes a friendly (the pits 'waved their small white plumes of steam') or playful (the screen, 'shuffling its coal') character to the pit; and partly through diction, which carries almost metaphoric overtones, reminding us of childlike good humour. In the second short passage, for example, the wheels 'twinkled' and the screen childishly 'made a busy noise', and in Chapter 4 we noticed that the bell 'ting-ed'. Additionally, notice that Lawrence easily adds an effect by choosing an inappropriate word. Here, 'melted' is not what the steam did: it 'evaporated'. Why does Lawrence use 'melted' instead of the appropriate word? We can suggest that 'melted' gives a gentler, more personal and less scientific impression of the landscape: it is often applied to softening emotions, or grief, and combines with 'soft' sky to convey gentleness. In the first passage, the word 'brightening' has a comparably enlivening effect. Lawrence seems to add life and motion by using this in place of the static 'bright'; and a hint of abundance comes from its assonance with 'ripening' which we might expect after 'full of corn'.

So far, we have found that these two short descriptions of land-scape are invested with a great deal of imagery and neo-imagery. Lawrence constantly suggests figurative ideas in this way, by choosing words which attribute life, movement and emotion where none would literally be expected. When we analysed the passages from which these examples are drawn, we looked at both pictures in an interpretative way. In Chapter 1, for example, we commented that 'Here, to our surprise again, the mines are presented as pretty, and "small" underlines their unthreatening appeal. We can speculate that Paul's view out of the window is, in some way, a nostalgic view from his innocent childhood, before industry began to threaten his happiness'; and in Chapter 4 we suggested that the prettiness of the pit is in ironic conflict with the narrative, which shows machinery dehumanising the workers: the picture's cheerfulness carries a chilling message of indifference. In both instances, the particular character with which Lawrence invests landscape, by means of a richly metaphor-suggestive style, prompts the reader to interpret. So we treat the landscape as symbolic.

We can confirm that symbolic significance is present by moving out from these examples and exploring other parts of the text. Do we find collieries in farmland anywhere else? Are there more explicit statements of a correspondence between landscape and underlying meaning?

To answer the second question first, look at the paragraph our first example comes from. The description from the library window is framed between explicit statements about Paul's life situation, and economic imperatives. Before meeting the landscape we read 'Already he was a prisoner of industrialism', and afterwards 'He was being taken into bondage'. This confirms that the apparent harmony of 'corn' and 'collieries' is illusory, and points towards an ironic inter-pretation of the landscape. Certainly, a connection between the theme of industry and this description is clearly established. When we turn to the second example, we find that the landscape continues to be significant. As he hears of his son's death, Morel walks between a 'sunny autumn field' and 'a wall of trucks': symbolically, Lawrence has placed the miner between natural cycles suggesting life and death, and the permanent sameness of industry. In the next phase of grief, Morel 'leaned up against a truck side'. Lawrence places his character within the landscape with care, then. Nature (here represented by the 'sunny autumn field') has dealt the blow, and Morel leans on industry's permanent sameness, 'a truck side', to support him.

The landscape is thus filled with metaphorical life, and it is significant. The answer to our other question is, yes. Look at Paul's conversation with Clara in the following extract:

> They came near to the colliery. It stood quite still and black among the corn-fields, its immense heap of slag seen rising almost from the oats.
>
> 'What a pity there is a coal-pit here where it is so pretty,' said Clara.
>
> 'Do you think so?' he answered. 'You see I am so used to it, I should miss it. – No, and I like the pits here and there. I like the rows of trucks, and the headstocks, and the steam in the daytime and the lights at night. – When I was a boy, I always thought a pillar of cloud by day and a pillar of fire by night was a pit, with its steam, and its lights and the burning bank – and I thought the Lord was always at the pit-top.'
>
> (*Sons and Lovers*, p. 364)

Here, the colliery is not pretty. It is 'still' and 'black' with an 'immense heap' of slag. Lawrence's image this time is of the pit as an incongruous growth which rises 'almost from the oats'; but the force of this image is because the pit is not animate – 'still' 'black' and 'heap' emphasise deadness – so its presence among the corn is incongruous, unnatural. However, the exchange between Clara and Paul complicates matters. Clara takes a conventional view of ugly industry defacing a pretty countryside, but Paul's attitude is much more complicated. In his childhood the pit seemed to him like 'a pillar of cloud by day and a pillar of fire by night'. This is a reference to Exodus, when 'the Lord went before them by day in a pillar of cloud, to lead them the way; and by night in a pillar of fire, to give them light; to go by day and night: he took not away the pillar of the cloud by day, nor the pillar of fire by night, from before the people' (Exodus 13:21–2). In the Bible, Moses is leading the Israelites out of their captivity in Egypt, towards the Red Sea. God is a light leading them through the wilderness as cloud by day and fire by night. Ironically, then, Paul's simile compares the pit to a light which guides his journey from enslavement towards the 'promised land'.

The notes in the Penguin edition provide us with this reference. However, it is always worthwhile to read around biblical references, in order to gain a full understanding of the author's intention. In this case, Chapter 14 of Exodus provides a further interesting point: the Israelites or 'chosen people' find the pillar of cloud and fire is a guide, it 'gave light by night' and helped them. However, it was 'a cloud and a darkness' to the pursuing Egyptians, hindering them.

How does this relate to Paul? He seems to claim that seeing the steam and lights of the pit throughout his childhood has guided him, has helped him to journey towards his desire and freedom. In the image, Paul casts himself with typical individualism and arrogance as one of the 'chosen'; and he knows that if you are not special, like him, you will not see the pit as an illuminating sign. Instead, it will darken and cloud your vision, and prevent you from reaching your goal. Life, we notice, is a journey from captivity to freedom. Success or failure depends on who you are.

This is a surprising comparison, and our next task is to look for corroboration and extension of these ideas, elsewhere in the text. To do this we first need to have a clear idea of what we are looking for, and a summary helps.

Paul is the son of a miner, intimate with pit-work and pit-dominated life. He is born into the 'common people', yet has education and ideas enough to rise socially. Paul's image suggests that he is somehow indebted to the pit, his coal-mining background, for showing him the way; and that he is special, different from others, who can only succumb to the pit's 'pillar of cloud'. The subjects are industry, ugliness, nature and beauty, and social class.

We can look for analogous ideas in the same section of the book. The image of a 'pillar of cloud . . . pillar of fire' occurs in a conversation between Paul and Clara. Looking in the chapter called 'Clara', about forty pages earlier, we find two interesting passages of dialogue. When Paul and Clara climb up to the Castle in Nottingham, he begins conversation by remarking how small people seem from up on the hill. Clara's cynical reply is: '. . . it is not necessary to get far off in order to see us proportionately. The trees are much more significant'. Clara's view seems jaundiced, emphasising the insignificance of people. Paul points out her error – that size is not the same as value – by answering 'Bulk only' (p. 313).

We will pass over the description of the landscape, which would make an interesting study in itself, and continue with their conversation. This turns upon the ugliness of the town, with its urban industrial development, in contrast to the 'natural' countryside. Clara puts this point of view, saying that the town 'is only a *little* sore upon the country yet', and Paul rephrases this as 'A little scab' (p. 313). Here, they are playing with imagery: Paul's more graphic and repulsive metaphor has a satirical intention, suggesting that her town-hatred is really a little melodramatic. He then explains his own feelings:

> 'But the town's all right,' he said. 'It's only temporary. This is the crude, clumsy make-shift we've practised on, till we find out what the idea is. The town will come all right . . .
>
> '. . . I don't hate the town. It's only a clumsy effort. We haven't learned to live together yet.'
>
> (*Sons and Lovers*, p. 314)

This conversation begins with the question of perception: seeing people and nature in proportion. Clearly, Paul understands something more abstract and metaphorical as 'proportion', because he rejects Clara's measure of mere 'bulk'. So the difference between them is that Paul sees something which could be called 'value', something inside people which Clara is too cynical to see. If we relate this back to the Exodus image, Paul is able to see through the ugliness of the town, understanding its direction and potential – in his words it is only a 'make-shift' practice effort, and will 'come all right' in the future. To Clara, on the other hand, the town is a 'pillar of cloud' she cannot see through: it blinds her and makes her hate it. Paul trenchantly identifies where her blinded vision leads when he describes her as hating herself: 'Loathing the very flesh on your bones' (p. 314). To Paul, then, the town's clumsy ugliness is like a light leading him to see the infinite potential of human beings. Paul is cast as an Israelite, Clara as an Egyptian doomed to destruction by God.

This confirms and elaborates what Paul means by comparing the pit he has lived near to all his life to God's 'pillar of cloud, pillar of fire', guiding him through life. We have also found that Paul's difference from others resides in his special ability: his insight which penetrates further than other people's. This may help us understand how he sees himself as 'chosen' in contrast to the common run of people who pursue in helpless blindness, like the Egyptians in Exodus. The mines and industrial towns Paul is surrounded by are growing in significance as we explore their images in the text; and their role is becoming increasingly complex and ambiguous. Ironically, Paul asserts that his understanding of ugly industry is an advantage, it gives him a 'vision' denied to others. What is Paul's attitude to the social class he was born into?

A few pages before the conversation with Clara we have just looked at, Paul announces his class affiliation to his mother: 'I don't want to belong to the well-to-do middle class. I like my common people best. I belong to the common people'. The conversation then analyses this statement, with Mrs Morel critical. Paul claims that he gets 'ideas' from the middle classes and 'life itself, warmth' from the common people; but Mrs Morel rightly points out that Paul does not spend time with ordinary common people – only with 'those that exchange ideas, like the middle classes. The rest don't interest you'. So, Paul's natural friends are people who are losing their identity with their class, people like himself. In the course of the conversation, Paul seems to contradict himself by asserting that he is above class: he considers himself equal to any gentleman 'In myself . . . not in my class or my education or my manners. But in myself, I am' (p. 298). Again, when we find Paul measuring himself against his background, we find him arrogating a special, independent value: he is an individual, ready to take what different social groups have to offer, but not really part of any group himself. Once more, Paul seems to see through his environment, using it as a light to increase his insight, while others remain blinded or imprisoned by it.

In this particular conversation, Paul appears to be struggling to achieve his 'vision' and freedom from social class. Mrs Morel is right, that Paul naturally gravitates towards individualist misfits similar to himself; while Paul appears to contradict himself, saying he 'belongs' to the common people but 'in myself' feels himself equal to any gentleman. This scene dramatises the conflict we have met many times before, between Paul's growing sense of his inviolable individuality and his young man's need for a sense of belonging and companionship. It is only in the final chapter of the novel, after his mother's death, that Paul feels, finally, completely alone.

We began this chapter with two examples of landscape description which were rich in imagery and neo-imagery. We have followed a logical and common-sense method to expand our inquiry outwards from these examples to other parts of the text. We could continue this process: for example, we have ignored the landscape description as Paul and Clara look down on Nottingham, which is again rich in imagery (the houses look like 'black, poisonous herbage', the river glistens in a 'hieroglyph', and on the railway 'smoking toy engines fussed'). A fuller study than we have space for would examine this and other analogous passages, building further understanding of the role of landscape in the novel.

The method we have followed falls into clear stages:

1. Analyse an example, and draw a clear 'summary conclusion' about it (for example, we noticed several images but drew the single conclusion that industry is presented as 'childlike' and 'pretty').
2. Look for comparable examples elsewhere in the text.
3. Repeat the process (i.e. analyse the new example, and this will enable you to draw a more developed, more specific conclusion. We did this with the comparison of the pit to God's 'pillars' in Exodus. Our conclusion set us on the track of Paul's idea that he is different – special or 'chosen').
4. Look for further similar examples, and corroboration of your conclusions, elsewhere in the text.

This process of study can be repeated again and again. We have already, in this limited example, achieved considerable insight into the relation between surprisingly positive representations of industry, and the central theme of Paul's individuality, in *Sons and Lovers*.

Moon symbolism

When we analysed Ursula's parting from Skrebensky (at the end of Chapter XI of *The Rainbow* – see Chapter 2 above) we read:

> She kept a diary, in which she wrote impulsive thoughts. Seeing the moon in the sky, her own heart surcharged, she went and wrote:
> 'If I were the moon, I know where I would fall down.'
>
> (*The Rainbow*, p. 308)

At the time we treated this as a portentous and rather pretentious thing for Ursula to write, as she manufactured a false romanticism around Skrebensky's image. However, our analysis of Ursula's psychology led us back to the scene in the stackyard where her repression began, and in that scene Ursula had 'stood for some moments out in the overwhelming luminosity of the moon. She seemed a beam of gleaming power' (p. 298). It is clear that the moon is a significant symbol in Lawrence. The question we want to pursue here is, how is this symbol created in the text; and what can we understand about its meaning?

The passage in which the moon plays such a large part describes the aftermath of Fred Brangwen's wedding party, the outdoor dance and Ursula's and Skrebensky's love-making later in the stackyard (*The Rainbow*, pp. 294–300). This is an intense episode, much of it written in Lawrence's most rhapsodic, breathless rhythms, and expressed by means of metaphor. We can only pick out certain elements, however, which relate to the way the moon is created and used as a symbol.

First, we want to have some broad idea of what the moon stands for, symbolically. We can do this by noticing and classifying the repetitive motifs in the evocation of the moon's power, using the technique demonstrated in Chapter 3 above. In this case, we find that the moon is insistently associated with hardness, cold, silver and steel metal, and a colourless brightness. So, it awakens a 'fierce, white, cold passion' in Ursula and she compares herself to 'bright metal'. She is a 'steel blade', 'bright', and the light is like 'cold, glimmering, whitish-steely fires'. The moon is also corrosive, like salt, so

Ursula/moon destroys Skrebensky 'cold as the moon and burning as a fierce salt' and 'seething like some cruel, corrosive salt' until she 'crystallised with triumph'.

Obviously, the moon stands for the hardness of self-will which fights to remain separate, and will fight viciously for its own survival. So, the moon represents one force in the struggle we discussed in Chapter 3, the conflict between intact survival and desire.

This is clear enough for the time being. We have a 'broad idea' of the moon's significance. However, notice that this answer is both useful and useless at the same time. As with all symbolism, there is a danger that we will make nonsense of the story if we simply interpret a meaning as if the book were a code. Our other question is: how is the moon symbolism handled? If the moon simply arrives and leaves each time a character's self-will appears and disappears, the book would quickly become an unconvincing nonsense. Also, we still have a number of other questions. For example, we know that Ursula/moon seems to be destructive to Skrebensky, but what is the moon to Ursula? What is her relationship to the moon, and how does she become identified with it?

To answer these questions, we need to re-examine the beginning of the passage: look closely at the situation before the moon's symbolic influence grows, and examine exactly how the moon itself is introduced and developed as the narrative moves on.

Before the moon rises, Ursula already desires escape, wishing to 'be amongst the flashing stars' and 'beyond the confines of this earth. She was mad to be gone'. She is compared to a 'hound' and is both 'the quarry, and she was also the hound'; and she feels compelled to leap 'into the unknown' but is imprisoned 'in bonds'. After the moon has risen, Ursula again desires escape: she 'half started' to 'flee away, away from this dark confusion and chaos of people to the hill and the moon', but the people and Skrebensky are like 'magnetic stones' and a 'loadstone' which 'detained her'.

The moon, then, calls to an urge that already exists in Ursula: an urge to escape from Anton and other people. So there is nothing metaphysical about this experience: Lawrence begins by identifying a powerful emotional drive which is really present in Ursula, and identifying the actual moon, which actually rises. In other words,

Lawrence sets the scene in naturalistic mode. However, as the passage continues, Ursula's urge and the moon gradually draw together and merge until they enlarge Ursula's need with the power of the moon symbol.

The first stage does not identify the moon: it is 'some influence' and 'something'. Its effect on Ursula, on the other hand, is described intimately as 'looking right into her', so the metaphor of her intimacy with the moon begins before we are even aware that it is the moon. As soon as the moon is named and appears ('a great white moon looking at her over the hill') the metaphor of intimacy is rapidly developed, and becomes overtly sexual as 'her body opened wide like a quivering anemone' and she wanted 'consummation'. This is a carefully prepared effect: the emotional state exists before the symbol, and the metaphor for Ursula's relation to the symbol exists before it is named. In other words, the moon takes a prepared place in the order of Ursula's character, not in the natural sky.

It is a curious technique: it is as if the moon enters the narrative at a different level from its actual place as part of the setting. Instead, it comes into the story unrecognised, directly into the level of emotion, impulse and unconsciousness which lies beneath conscious thought and action, within the character. We remarked in Chapter 1 that this is the level where the 'real story' of Lawrence's novels takes place.

How is the total effect created? Again, it is easy to make an interpretative statement: *The moon stands for hard self-will and withdrawal from relationships.* But, a statement like this does not tell us how the moon exists in the text. If we look carefully at Lawrence's writing, we find that the moon's influence and significance are conveyed by means of a typically Lawrentian technique. We have repeatedly noticed his 'incremental' style: lists of successive words or phrases, each one qualifying, modulating or contributing to the sense Lawrence wants to convey; and always highlighting the author's struggle with language, which can never express the complexity of experience itself. Lawrence's words seem to blunder towards the truth: hitting near and around his target, and only conveying the actual emotion by a cumulative effect.

The moon is conveyed in the same way. Nothing can quite define what it means, but Lawrence throws subsidiary metaphors at it, which work together as a cumulative 'batch' of figurative ideas. So, the figurative ideas of a personified entity watching Ursula, hardness, metal, coldness, salt, burning and corrosion are all thrown at the moon repeatedly in this passage. The symbol itself, then, is not a defined and separate thing in the text. On the contrary, there is a rich and multiple level of supporting metaphors which all contribute to the symbol, each one making only a part of the whole living influence which is the moon.

Some of the moon metaphors extend into other parts of Ursula's experience, also, so the symbol is not isolated but part of a larger whole. For example, the moon is associated with 'bright metal' and Ursula's hands are 'steel blades of destruction'. This metaphor of metals extends into the people around, who contrast as 'like magnetic stones', with Skrebensky as a 'loadstone' and 'dark, impure magnetism'. Eventually, Skrebensky is likened to 'warm, soft iron' corroded by the moon's 'salt'. In this way, Lawrence creates the sense of the moon symbol acting as part of a metaphoric whole, and prevents us from reducing it to a sterile, separate and single significance.

One final point from this passage further contributes to the moon idea. This is the biblical reference to Genesis when Ursula is said to be 'cold and unmoved as a pillar of salt' (p. 297). This is a reference to Genesis, Chapter 19, when Lot's wife is turned to a pillar of salt because she turns to witness God's destruction of Sodom and Gomorrah as Lot is escaping to the mountains with his family. Just as we found when considering Paul Morel's reference to Exodus, it is helpful to read around Lawrence's biblical allusion to consider the whole story. In the case of Lot's wife, the story has a clear and immediate relevance to Ursula: when she becomes a 'pillar of salt' she is no longer Lot/Skrebensky's partner in life – she is gone; and this has something to do with her having witnessed a forbidden vision, perhaps in the sense that Ursula desires more than Anton can offer, more than a woman traditionally asks. However, the consequences of Lot's story make an added, bitter reflection on Anton's character: the remainder of Lot's life produces only evil and perversion, as he lies with his two daughters in drunkenness, producing children born out of incest. This suggests a scathing and disgusted comment on the nullified, unproductive future Anton goes into at the end of the novel: his empty dedication to the army, and his makeweight marriage of convenience to the colonel's daughter.

As readers of Lawrence we know, of course, that moon symbolism is a consistent element in his work. In *The Rainbow*, Ursula's moon destruction of Skrebensky is repeated and forms the final crisis of their affair on pp. 443–5. In *Sons and Lovers* the moon figures prominently when Mrs Morel withdraws from her husband after their quarrel (see pp. 33–5), and when Paul decides to break with Miriam (see pp. 337–8). On both of these occasions it is described in terms of white light decolouring the world, and flowers which have a 'brutal' effect on the character. The sensual element we notice in Ursula's 'consummation' is present as Paul feels the 'fleshy throats, and their dark, grasping hands' of the iris (p. 338) and Mrs Morel feels 'dizzy' from the scent of lilies until in the 'mixing-pot' of moonlight she enters 'a kind of swoon' (p. 34). In *Women in Love*, there is a chapter called 'Moony' (pp. 244–65) in which Birkin and Ursula are both unsatisfied in the moonlight and resist its influence. Birkin shatters the moon by throwing stones at its reflection in the millpond. Finally, the moon is agonisingly present as 'a painful, brilliant thing . . . unremitting, from which there was no escape' as Gerald climbs and climbs, forcing himself to his death (see *Women in Love*, p. 473).

As we study Lawrence's symbols, then, we can build further understanding of their significance by connecting elements between the different novels. For example, Gerald's perception of the moon as 'unremitting, from which there was no escape' makes it part of the fatal self-destructive course towards death on which he is bound. This may remind us of Skrebensky's feeling, that kissing Ursula was 'like putting his face into some awful death' (*The Rainbow*, p. 298). So, we can add to the idea of the moon as a hard-willed and selfish withdrawal from relationships: Lawrence implies that this hard, hostile separateness of the selfish will is, effectively, death.

Some Structures and Symbols in *The Rainbow*

In this section we will look at the way Lawrence has structured or 'shaped' *The Rainbow*. We begin to study 'structure' by thinking about the text in a particular way, concentrating on the question of its 'shape', and how it is all fitted together.

Studying structure begins by standing back from the details of the novel and taking an overall view. This can be quite difficult to do when you have just read the novel for the first time. *The Rainbow* is full of characters, relationships and significant experiences; and the story is complicated, crossing three generations and focusing intimately on a succession of individual characters and couples in turn. When you have finished reading it for the first time, and try to think of the 'whole' novel, you are likely to see nothing but a very large number of intense moments all in a long line: the story, experience after experience after experience, from the beginning to the end.

The problem is exacerbated with Lawrence, because his novels do not adopt a conventional plot. The 'real story' in Lawrence is inside the characters, as we have frequently remarked, so it does not depend on external events and action. Additionally, the novels deliberately undercut any idea of finality. In Chapter 3, we noticed that the ending of *Women in Love* is deliberately unfinished: the romantic relationship, which should be the goal of a 'courtship' novel, is emphatically presented as incomplete and unresolved. In the same way, Ursula confronts a challenging, unknown future at the end of *The Rainbow*. Her 'courtship' has failed, so the romantic theme is not resolved. On the other hand, it is not tragic either, as she recovers from her breakdown and miscarriage and turns to face a future, further quest for love.

To perceive the 'structure' of *The Rainbow*, then, we need to stand back from the details, and in order to do this it is helpful to track some simple elements in the external story through the whole novel. We will do this for the physical settings and the characters' occupations.

The novel opens at the **Marsh Farm**, an isolated farmhouse. The farm is in a 'small valley bed' which ends at the nearest settlement, 'a

busy hill and the village spire of Cossethay' (p. 13). Two miles away
the church tower and country town of Ilkeston are visible from the
farm, on a hill-top. Tom Brangwen and his Polish wife Lydia live at
the Marsh Farm; her daughter Anna and their sons Tom and Fred
are brought up there.

Anna marries her cousin Will, and they take a cottage next to the
church in **the village of Cossethay**. He works in the country town of
Ilkeston. From Cossethay, the lives of the Brangwens gradually
branch out and reach into ever-more populated and developed areas.
The five Brangwen children are born and grow nearly into their
teens at Cossethay, but Ursula and Gudrun are then sent to the
Grammar School at Nottingham, a large industrial city. The sense of
progress from a smaller to a larger community, and to a higher level
of sophistication, is underlined in the text: 'So Ursula seated herself
upon the hill of learning, looking down on the smoke and confusion
and the manufacturing, engrossed activity of the town' (p. 250). A
few months after leaving school, Ursula goes to work as a teacher at
Brinkley Street School, at Ilkeston, and she goes to face the challenge
of 'the town, a black, extensive mount' (p. 342), establishing herself
there after a bitter battle.

While Ursula is between her teaching job and going to the
University at Nottingham, the family leaves Yew Tree Cottage in
Cossethay and moves to a bigger house in the middle of a large
industrial conurbation, **Beldover**. This will be convenient for Will's
new job, because his work as Art and Handwork Instructor for the
County of Nottingham requires him to live somewhere more
central, and handy for the Grammar School at Willey Green.

Finally, Ursula goes to University in **the city of Nottingham**, and
spends an Easter vacation of three weeks with Skrebensky in
London. They also have holidays together at a country house in
Oxfordshire, a cottage in Sussex, and again in London, before their
affair ends while they are staying with others at a bungalow on the
Lincolnshire coast. Before the end of the novel, Gudrun has gone as
an Art student to **London**.

The main settings in *The Rainbow*, then, follow a clearly structured progress moving in one direction: from an isolated house,
through village, town, industrial conurbation, to city and finally to

the capital. The original community is a single separate family, and with each successive stage of development the community that surrounds the characters becomes larger, more populous and wider.

The characters' occupations follow a parallel pattern of development. The original Brangwen men are **farmers**: they 'faced inwards to the teeming life of creation' and lived 'their senses full fed, their faces always turned to the heat of the blood' and 'dazed with looking towards the heat of generation'. Lawrence contrasts these farmers and their wholly sensual life with what the Brangwen women sense in the distant town: men 'fighting outwards to knowledge' so that the Brangwen wives were ambitious for their children: 'It was this, this education, this higher form of being, that the mother wished to give to her children' (all quotations are from pp. 11–12). Tom Brangwen, the first main character of the novel, is a **farmer**. He works manually and with primary, living things – livestock and crops.

Will Brangwen, in the next generation, works as a **skilled craftsman**, as a draughtsman in a lace factory. This occupation involves using some education and expertise but is still practical, not yet intellectual, work: the distinction between a 'craft' and a 'profession' was still strong. Also, where the farmer produces a basic commodity – food – Will works in a manufacturing industry producing an embellishment to life, a decorative, luxury item.

Halfway through his career, Will becomes Art and Handicraft Instructor for the County of Nottingham. This is a move forward, as Will has crossed the barrier into **intellectual work** in education, and is now a **professional**. The subject he teaches, however, is still an applied subject, not an academic study: he is a **craft teacher** so he occupies a sort of middle ground between the higher reaches of applied and manual work and pure intellectual work.

Ursula becomes an **academic teacher**. The gruelling work she undergoes in Ilkeston is not very intellectual, but she is working as a **professional** in **academic** subjects – although at a low level. When we meet Ursula in *Women in Love* she has made further progress, since she now teaches Science to secondary level at the Grammar School. By that time, then, she has moved fully into a professional, intellectual level of work.

In the final phase of *The Rainbow*, Ursula goes into **higher education** at Nottingham **university**, although she fails her degree. From Will to Ursula, the intellectual focus has moved from semi-manual craft to pure academic study, and has become more intellectual and more sophisticated. However, the furthest reach of the Brangwens in *The Rainbow* comes with Gudrun, who becomes an **artist**. Lawrence clearly believed that the highest calling is pure, artistic creation. This serves a purified aim and creates beauty, and is the furthest distance travelled from the non-intellectual, sensual and manual occupation of her farmer ancestors.

As we can see, in *The Rainbow*, the characters' occupations move in a straight line of development from manual to semi-skilled to applied academic and professional, to pure academic, to artistic and creative forms of work. Lawrence has therefore structured his novel to show considerable social and intellectual development between the three generations of the Brangwen family. Lawrence's use of the terms 'outwards' to describe the direction from the farm to the town, and 'inwards' to describe the Brangwen men's original direction, facing the 'heat of generation', provides a consistent idea of movement from an original **centre** towards a wider **circumference**; and this in turn gives a physical 'shape' to the development of all related themes in the novel. This 'shaping' language is explicitly used in the two chapters entitled 'The Widening Circle' (Chapters X and XIV).

Notice that the survey we have carried out, of the main settings and occupations in *The Rainbow*, does not call for any detailed research and study: we could write down these lists from memory as soon as we have read the novel. Notice also, that these simple lists show how deliberately Lawrence has imposed a shape on his novel: the steady progress, in clear stages, from isolated farming life at the beginning to a sophisticated, intellectual city life towards the end.

In addition, this structure is an integral part of the novel. We can show this with a brief reference to one part of these developments. We already know that Ursula sensed new and wider opportunities when she went to the Grammar School at the age of twelve, and 'seated herself upon the hill of learning'. Ursula's pursuit of wider and deeper knowledge is fervent, akin to a religion for her: she 'trembled like a postulant when she wrote the Greek alphabet for the first time' (p. 250). When Ursula goes to University, she has similar feelings of awe about 'the wondrous, cloistral origin of education'; the college itself is 'holy ground' and the professors are 'priests of knowledge' (pp. 399–400). However, Ursula's eyes are opened by disappointment in her second year. She realises that the professors are only 'middle-men' and the learning they impart is 'second-hand'. All the academic ideals of pure knowledge are 'spurious' because the aim of it all is only 'a second-hand dealer's shop where one bought an equipment for an examination' in order for students to go on and make more money. Ursula realises that the education system is only a mechanical part of a tainted, commercial world: 'The college itself was a little, slovenly laboratory for the factory' (all quotations are from p. 403). In short, Ursula finds that her increasing understanding brings progressive disillusionment: each stage attained becomes devalued as she grows beyond it and needs a further, new challenge. On p. 405 Lawrence reverts to the idea of a circle in a passage which retrospectively surveys Ursula's journey through life so far. She sees all she has achieved as 'This inner circle of light in which she lived and moved', which is belittled, because she is disillusioned with it, by being compared to 'the area under an arc-lamp'. Other people are like moths and children to whom the light is 'blinding'; but Ursula looks towards 'the glimmer of dark movement just out of range'. There is no question that the idea of a steadily expanding circle of knowledge and experience is thoroughly built into the structure and incidental imagery throughout *The Rainbow*.

This simple study of the 'skeleton' Lawrence has imposed over his novel, of progress through larger communities and higher forms of work and learning, gives us a firm overall grasp of the novel's shape and purpose. However, it does not show us how closely integrated several structural themes are with each other. We can appreciate this point by following up one connection we have already come across: the reference to the 'hill' of learning from Ursula's arrival at Nottingham Grammar School. Hills are significant in *The Rainbow*, and this is signalled in the opening pages of the novel. The topography of the first three significant settings is described then, with the Marsh Farm in a valley, the village of Cossethay on a 'busy hill' and

Ilkeston 'on a hill' two miles away. More detailed study will show that each stage in a character's development involves climbing a hill, reaching a vantage point and looking out from there. So, when Ursula goes to the Grammar School, 'up here, in the Grammar School, she fancied the air was finer, beyond the factory smoke' and she was 'looking down on' the town's industrial activity.

The idea of a hill as a vantage point from which you can view your future journey, or look down upon the small discarded affairs of mankind, is linked to the symbol of the rainbow itself. Anna's achievement as wife and mother sets her upon a 'Pisgah mount' from where she strains her eyes to visualise her future journey through life. 'Pisgah' is the name of the mountain where God took Moses before he died, and from where they surveyed the Promised Land (see Deuteronomy 34:1–4). Like the other biblical references we have met, this one repays some reading around. First, the reference is appropriate to Anna as God tells Moses, 'I have caused thee to see it with thine eyes, but thou shalt not go over thither': Anna does give up her life's struggle at this point and settles into childbirth and a world of 'fecundity'. However, like the Promised Land, what she can see from the 'Pisgah mount' is for her children, who will journey further using her attainment as a 'threshold': this idea is reflected in God's words 'I will give it [the Promised Land] unto thy seed'.

However, what Anna sees from her little 'Pisgah mount' is not the Promised Land but 'a faint, gleaming horizon, a long way off, and a rainbow like an archway, a shadow-door with faintly coloured coping above it' (p. 181). The rainbow is another biblical reference: it is a sign of the covenant between God and all living things:

> This is the token of the covenant which I make between me and you and every living creature that is with you, for perpetual generations: I do set my bow in the cloud, and it shall be for a token of a covenant between me and the earth.
>
> (Genesis 9:12–13)

By this stage, in pursuing the recurrent idea of hill and vantage point, we have realised that Lawrence has integrated the spatial idea of a 'widening circle' with the alternative idea of climbing a hill and looking out from the top. This in turn links with the 'Pisgah mount', one of a series of biblical references which create a further metaphor for the Brangwens' journey from farm to university (there are many biblical references in the novel, particularly to Genesis and Exodus, the books of the emergence of the chosen people, their escape from slavery and journey through the wilderness towards the Promised Land). This in turn is associated with the symbol of the rainbow, an insubstantial but brilliant distant ideal, which – in biblical terms – is like a perpetual promise and hope for mankind, a 'covenant' for 'perpetual generations'. Finally, the rainbow is described using the metaphor of a door or archway, and although we have not yet pursued the idea in this direction, readers of *The Rainbow* know that this links the 'rainbow' idea with a vein of arch symbolism which recurs throughout the novel (we may remember the distinction between Gothic and round arches we noticed in an analysis in Chapter 3; and the surge of idealism Will experiences and Anna mocks in Lincoln Cathedral).

We do not have the space to explore further these complex, interrelated elements in the structure, symbolism and imagery of the novel. However, our short excursion from the physical setting, through the significance of hills, has already made us aware of how densely interwoven all elements in Lawrence's novel are: structural elements work together with symbolism, and the interpretation of imagery, to add a purposeful, shaping energy and meaning to the whole work.

Some Water Imagery in *Women in Love*

In Chapter 2 we analysed a scene between Birkin and Ursula from the chapter 'An Island'. We noticed that Birkin's daisies and Ursula's paper boat upon the mill-pond suggested a larger, shadowy meaning: 'people, humanity as a whole or individuals, are somehow afloat on a dark primitive stream flowing towards the sluice where they will be destroyed. Their attention and their hopes are fixed upon the sky, not the dark stream which is their true element. Life is this kind of a voyage' (see p. 56 above). We did not pursue the role of water further at that time, but a moment's thought about the novel indicates that water figures prominently with swimming, drowning and boating episodes. Now we want to enlarge our understanding of water as a symbol, and we do so by means of our standard method: summarise what we know, identify analogous passages elsewhere in the text, then analyse them.

1. *Summarise what we know*: we know that the water is characterised as 'dark' and it affects Ursula in an unconscious way, moving her 'strongly and mystically'.

2. *Identify analogous passages*: looking in the obvious chapter, 'Water-Party', we find the conjunction of flowers floating on a stream in Birkin's descriptions of two rivers (p. 172). Also, Ursula is strongly moved by water again (p. 185).

The third stage is to analyse the other passages we have found, using these to expand and develop our insight into the water symbol in *Women in Love*. First, then, we can look at Birkin's descriptions of two rivers. This is part of a conversation with Ursula, but Birkin's exposition is more or less continuous, so the following omits Ursula's questions:

> 'It seethes and seethes, a river of darkness,' he said, 'putting forth lilies and snakes, and the ignis fatuus, and rolling all the time onward. That's what we never take into count – that it rolls onwards. . . . The other river, the black river. We always consider the silver river of life, rolling on and quickening all the world to a brightness, on and on to heaven, flowing into a bright eternal sea, a heaven of angels thronging. – But the other is our real reality – . . . the dark river of dissolution. – You see it rolls in us just as the other rolls – the black river of corruption. And our flowers are of this – our sea-born Aphrodite, all our white phosphorescent flowers of sensuous perfection, all our reality, nowadays . . . I mean she [Aphrodite] is the flowering mystery of the death-process, yes . . . When the stream of synthetic creation lapses, we find ourselves part of the inverse process, the flood of destructive creation. Aphrodite is born in the first spasm of universal dissolution – then the snakes and swans and lotus – marsh-flowers – and Gudrun and Gerald – born in the process of destructive creation.'
>
> (*Women in Love*, p. 172)

We met dark water with flowers floating upon it in the first passage. Now Birkin expounds an interpretation of that image. He describes them as 'white phosphorescent flowers of sensuous perfection' and connects them with 'our sea-born Aphrodite'. Aphrodite, the Greek goddess of seductive female beauty, corresponds with Birkin's phrase 'sensuous perfection'. The myth of her birth is somewhat disturbing: Cronus and his mother plotted together, and Cronus castrated his father Uranus. He threw the severed genitals into the sea where they produced a foam which became Aphrodite. In this way, then, she was as Birkin says 'water-born'. However, the background story from Greek mythology adds elements of mutilation, perversion and unnatural reproduction, underlying the 'sensuous perfection' of Birkin's bright flowers.

The flowers are created out of the 'dark' river, and Birkin's diction intensifies our feeling of perversion, wrongness or decadence. The 'black' or dark river is identified with 'corruption', 'snakes', 'dissolution' (twice), 'the death-process' and 'destructive creation' (twice). This 'dark' river, then, is described in terms which are both frightening ('the death-process') and conventionally repulsive ('dissolution' and 'corruption'). We should also notice that there is a paradox in the way Birkin expounds his idea: as far as the sensuous goes, this fearful river does produce 'perfection', Birkin insists that it 'rolls onwards', and his final paradoxical phrase for it is 'destructive creation'. So, the 'dark river' may be rather frightening and disgusting, associated with sides of life we avoid thinking about and so related to the fundamental, primitive truths of the unconscious; but Birkin insists that it is an essential, and ultimately creative, part of our existence.

What does Birkin say about this river? He asserts that it is 'all our reality, nowadays', and although people do not think about it ('We always consider the silver river') it is 'our real reality'. What he seems to mean is that the people and society around him are in a decadent, deathlike phase. Birkin suggests that all the apparent 'flowers' of society (he includes Gerald and Gudrun, and implicitly also the beauty of the lights on Willey Water as 'ignis fatuus', as well as purely sexual relationships) are part of a destruction, a death. His vision is of the 'dissolution' or breaking apart and decay of the whole human spirit.

The other river Birkin describes is 'the silver river of life' and is strongly contrasted with the 'black' one, being described in positive terms as 'quickening', 'brightness', flowing 'to heaven' or into 'a bright eternal sea' with 'a heaven of angels thronging'. These terms suggest idealism and a higher, conscious faith. However, there is something satiric in Birkin's tone. Angels 'thronging', in particular, pokes fun at mannered church vocabulary and implies that people subscribe to a facile and falsely prettified belief.

We may be tempted to think of these rivers as 'delusion' and 'reality' at this point, but this is not what Birkin says. First, he is critical of society's attitudes: he accuses people of pretending that the 'silver river' is everything, and ignoring the dark one. He also accuses people of thinking that the fouler and frightening aspects of existence (such as decay and death) are static, whereas they are in fact part of the whole process, 'rolling all the time onward' and contribute to 'creation'. However, the delusion he criticises is precisely defined. The 'silver river' is just as real and true as the 'dark' one, and the fault is that we ignore one of them. So, Birkin says that the dark river 'rolls in us just as the other rolls'. There are two streams, one of 'synthetic creation' and the other of 'destructive creation'.

Birkin is scathing about the present state of humanity; and he is uncertain about his own potential to escape from the general decadence he sees around him. So, when Ursula asks 'And you and me – ?', he answers 'I don't yet know' (pp. 172–3). Nonetheless, this passage does present two rivers, which symbolise two processes of simultaneous destruction and creation. Birkin's aim in the whole conversation seems to be a call for people to be more honest, to accept and understand life completely, both the dark unconscious processes and the bright, conscious and idealistic flow we think about more readily.

We can relate this principle – that we must accept all aspects of life, in order to become complete – to what we found out about relationships in Chapter 3. There, we noticed that Birkin perceived two offers of love, an 'abstract spiritual intimacy' and 'emotional and physical' love. Both seemed to him equally 'nauseous and horrible' on their own, and the implication is that he will only accept what is complete, a love that includes all of life – not merely one half of it.

Now that we have investigated the two rivers symbol, we understand this principle of completeness in more detail. The point is that the 'dark river', the disgusting, decaying and death-related processes of life, must be included in a 'whole' relationship, otherwise 'love' will be an artificially prettified lie – just as the 'silver river' on its own is a lie. This principle also underlies Birkin's refusal to accept 'love' because the word is romantically falsified, it no longer means the kind of relationship he wants.

Turning back to the scene by the mill-pond, we remember that Ursula was 'strongly and mystically' moved by the flowers on the water, but did not understand her own feelings. We have identified a passage in 'Water-Party' when she is strongly moved by water again. Birkin opens the sluice to drain the lake:

> Then, a real shock to her, there came a loud splashing of water from out of the dark, tree-filled hollow beyond the road, a splashing that deepened rapidly to a harsh roar, and then became a heavy, booming noise of a great body of water falling solidly all the time. It occupied the whole of the night, this great steady booming of water, everything was drowned within it, drowned and lost. Ursula seemed to have to struggle for her life. She put her hands over her ears, and looked at the high, bland moon.
>
> (*Women in Love*, p. 185)

We can begin by appreciating the actual situation, to remind ourselves that Lawrence creates his symbolic effects out of a convincing external reality. Ursula was 'strongly and mystically moved' by a peaceful stream; this time, she meets a much wilder, noisier and more violent manifestation of water – the force and volume of the whole lake. It is strongly depicted, a 'harsh roar' and 'heavy booming noise', and it is natural that Ursula should react by putting 'her hands over her ears'.

However, we now know more about Lawrence's water symbolism. This is clearly a much more violent attack on Ursula's consciousness than she experienced at the mill-pond. Darkness is emphasised by Lawrence confining his description to noise: the scene is described with an absence of vision, and noise 'occupied the whole of the night'. Water is associated with death and destruction, as 'everything was drowned within it, drowned and lost' and she had to 'struggle for her life'.

Ursula, then, seems to be attacked by the enormous force of the dark side of life, and death is literally contained within it (she knows that two drowned bodies are in this flow). It is terrifying, 'a real shock to her', and threatens to overthrow her consciousness, drowning her as well in a destructive, deathlike dark flood. The symbolic role of water in Ursula's character development is clear, then; but interpretation alone does not explain the whole of Lawrence's achievement here. The fact that this enormous flow is an integrated part of the story (draining the lake follows naturally from the drownings), and the vivid description of its power, impresses us both naturalistically and symbolically. So, we understand what a whole lake pounding through a sluice is like – this is naturalism. We also understand, symbolically, how terrifyingly difficult it will be for Ursula to do what Birkin demands: to surrender to this power, and accept the 'dark river' of the destructive side of life. The terrifying nature of the challenge facing the individual, and the violence of the struggle each must engage in, are vividly conveyed through the water symbolism in this passage.

This also makes clear psychological sense. Why are some things hidden in our unconscious? Because we find these things horrible, unacceptable, vile. So, when any person confronts the shock and power of the unconscious, it will be a violent and terrifying experience, and will feel like annihilation.

How does Ursula react? We have already commented that she reacts naturally by trying to shut out the noise. She also 'looked at the high, bland moon'. Here, Lawrence links her confrontation with the symbol of the 'dark river', with another symbol we have already studied: that of the moon. We can therefore interpret Ursula's reaction: when threatened by the 'dark river', her instinctive response is towards hard, separate self-will, symbolised by the moon. Notice, however, that in this passage the moon does not have the 'steely' and 'corrosive' power of Ursula's hostile withdrawal into self that we found in *The Rainbow*. Instead, it is now 'high, bland', and the water is much more powerful. Lawrence is telling us that Ursula's self-will is weakened, almost overthrown by the 'real shock' of the lake roaring through the sluice. His mention of the moon symbol at this moment prepares us for her encounter with Birkin in the chapter called 'Moony', when the moon symbol is shattered.

We now understand a great deal more about the mysterious power that moved Ursula at the mill-pond: that she was unconsciously aware of the other process in life, the 'river of darkness', but could not consciously accept it. 'River of darkness' symbolism returns to develop and complete the story of Ursula's gradual awakening, in the chapter called 'Excurse', when she discovers 'rivers of strange dark fluid richness' flowing from 'the darkest poles of the body' (p. 314) while caressing Birkin.

The method we have employed to explore water symbolism in *Women in Love*, is the same as we used with landscapes in *Sons and Lovers*. As we remarked then, the method can be repeated again and again, each time increasing our awareness of the symbolic texture in Lawrence's narratives. Simply use the more developed understanding we have now reached, and look for further analogous passages to analyse.

Conclusions

1. Much of our work in this chapter has produced interpretative conclusions about Lawrence's characters and themes. We have discovered a great deal about the significance of industrial landscapes, moon symbolism and water symbolism in Lawrence's writing. However, there are a great many other symbols and veins of recurring imagery that we have not studied. We will not reiterate our interpretations here, therefore. Instead, we can make some useful observations about the way Lawrence has constructed his novels into meaningful 'wholes'.

2. First, we found that *The Rainbow* has a clear 'framework', apparent in its settings and the characters' occupations. This gives the novel a strong shape which implies a straight-line development, a purpose in life so that every aspect of the novel journeys towards its goal. Some reflection about *Sons and Lovers* and *Women in Love* tells us that the other two novels we are studying

are similar in this. So, *Sons and Lovers* can be said to begin in a small miner's cottage within a pit-dominated village, and travel steadily outwards until Paul finally turns away from darkness and 'towards the city's gold phosphorescence' on the final page. In *Women in Love*, the sequence of settings is less obvious than in *The Rainbow*, but they are equally carefully arranged. Notice, for example, that the Brangwen sisters penetrate into 'society' in gradual stages, partly through Ursula's professional connection with Birkin, the school inspector. They are invited into the traditional 'society' circle at Breadalby, and the seat of economic power at Shortlands – where Gudrun accepts employment. The scenes in London are also carefully orchestrated, and the novel as a whole continues the movement 'outwards' in a 'widening circle', that is so structurally apparent in *The Rainbow*. In *Women in Love*, the journey eventually goes abroad, and reaches its climax at the furthest point of withdrawal, among snowy peaks at a Tyrol resort. There is, then, **a strong outward and forward movement** which is the main and defining 'shape' in all three novels.

3. We can also consider all three of these novels as making a sequential forward movement between them. *Women in Love* is the sequel to *The Rainbow*, so the relationship between these two, although loose, is clear. However, if we look at *Sons and Lovers* as dealing with the struggles of growing up and establishing the individual's identity separate from his parents, then we can see *The Rainbow* and *Women in Love* beginning to focus on a subsequent struggle: the struggle to establish a sexual relationship in adulthood. All three novels together, then, can be seen as telling one story: the story of the struggle into being and towards a 'complete' relationship.

4. The title of this chapter includes 'imagery', but we have not focused on the smaller effects of individual figurative ideas in Lawrence's text. This is because we quickly found that Lawrence's imagery contributes towards his larger symbols. So, although there are vast and varied riches of simile and metaphor throughout these texts, it all contributes to a continuous symbolic texture and we find ourselves **prompted to interpret the text** all the time. For example, we found that the momentary

prettiness of personification, as the colliery smoke 'waved' at Paul Morel, is part of a larger symbolic metaphor, the 'pillar of cloud', and the two contrasted ways of seeing that are exemplified in Paul and other characters. Thus, much of this chapter has been devoted to symbols.

5. When studying symbolism, we have concentrated **on how the symbol is created**. This means that we focus on the way Lawrence uses his text to build up our impression of the symbolic thing, and how a blend of naturalistic description and metaphor is used when the symbol is introduced. In this way we have increased our appreciation of the effect of the symbol at the same time as interpreting the symbol's meaning.

6. We have found that **minor imagery contributes to a major symbol**, so imagery is used in the same way as Lawrence uses language itself: he continually re-expresses and reiterates, modulating his expression or his idea, and the narrative works by means of a 'cumulative' effect. Lawrence's symbols work in the same way, being built up and enriched by constant addition of accumulated 'sub-symbols' and 'sub-metaphors'. For example, the subsidiary figurative ideas of steel, coldness and salt all contribute to the effect of the moon symbol in *The Rainbow*.

7. **Lawrence's novels are intricately patterned**: their 'wholeness' relies on the complicated integration of background 'structure', various levels of metaphors and symbols which all connect with each other into a whole network, and patterns of repetition of language, with formal and frequent use of key words and phrases. In this chapter we have found numerous links of this kind. For example, one of our investigations began with the journey to larger communities in the structure of *The Rainbow*, and led us through the 'hill' idea to the 'Pisgah mount' reference and on to the 'rainbow' symbol. Another of our investigations turned up interrelations between the water symbol and the moon symbol in *Women in Love*.

8. Our explorations have begun to uncover a number of simultaneous 'stories', and in particular we can look at the **'story' of a symbol**. This occurs with the 'river of darkness' idea in *Women in Love*, which we began looking at as water imagery in Chapter XI.

We followed this to a theoretical discussion in Chapter XIV, and to its reappearance and resolution for Ursula, in Chapter XXIII. We can already guess that the final locale of the story, under snow and ice, continues the 'water' development. The same 'story' can be told about the moon symbol, beginning with its appearances in *Sons and Lovers*, passing through Ursula's experiences in *The Rainbow*, and reaching a kind of resolution in 'Moony', Chapter XIX of *Women in Love*. So, Lawrence's major symbols often tell their own, revealing story; and they can be traced through the stages of their story, both within one novel, and through all three novels.

Methods of Analysis

There is one very useful and noteworthy method for **studying imagery and symbolism**, that has been demonstrated in this chapter.
1. Analyse an example, and draw a clear 'summary conclusion' about it.
2. Look for comparable examples elsewhere in the text.
3. Repeat the process (i.e. analyse the new example, and this will enable you to draw a more developed, more specific conclusion).
4. Look for further similar examples, and corroboration of your conclusions, elsewhere in the text.

This process of study can be repeated again and again: the conclusions you reach will grow in detail and complexity.

When **studying structure**, we need to stand back from the complex details of the text, and think about it as a whole. It is often useful to choose a prominent but straightforward aspect of the story and work out its 'shape' in the whole novel. We did this for the main settings and characters' occupations, in *The Rainbow*.

It is also useful to remember the importance of **biblical and other references**. In each case, it can be extremely helpful to go further than the note in your edition alone. Look up the reference itself, and read around it in the Bible or other original text. Then think about the situation you have found in the reference: how does it relate to the whole situation in Lawrence's text?

Suggested Work

The imagery and symbolism in these three novels is so large and varied a subject that our demonstrations in this chapter have been necessarily limited. For this reason, we suggest two kinds of extended work. First, it will be worthwhile to pursue further one of the explorations we have started. Secondly, there are suggestions for other investigations into **structure** and **symbolism**, that you can start and pursue for yourself.

Furthering investigations begun in this chapter

In *Sons and Lovers*, you can pursue the presentation of industry in a rural landscape by studying the opening of Chapter I (p. 9), going as far as the paragraph on p. 10 ending '. . . and the kitchens opened onto that nasty alley of ash-pits'. The ambivalence of neatness and prettiness in colliery and housing development is set within a landscape filled with names from a past era.

In *The Rainbow*, our work on the moon symbol can be developed by studying the final sexual encounter between Ursula and Skrebensky, starting on p. 443 at the paragraph beginning 'Suddenly, cresting the heavy, sandy pass, Ursula lifted her head . . .' and continuing as far as the paragraph ending 'She trailed her dead body to the house, to her room, where she lay down, inert', on p. 445.

In *Women in Love*, carry out further exploration of the water symbol by studying two passages which relate to Gerald and Gudrun rather than Ursula and Birkin. Look at the description of Gerald swimming and Gudrun's response, beginning on p. 46 at 'Suddenly, from the boat-house, a white figure ran out . . .' and continuing to the paragraph ending '. . . she felt herself as if damned, out there on the high-road' on p. 47. Then turn to the 'Water-Party' chapter and look at the passage beginning 'He came again, and Birkin leaned to help him in to the boat' on p. 182, studying as far as Gerald's speech ending 'Goodnight, and thank you. Thank you very much' on p. 184. Here, the effect of immersion on Gerald is expressed in animal imagery, and his description of the world beneath the surface makes a revealing study.

Other suggested work

First, it would be worthwhile to list and think about the main journeys and settings, and the characters' occupations, in both *Sons and Lovers* and *Women in Love*, following the method for studying the structural 'framework' of a novel that was demonstrated on *The Rainbow* in this chapter. Secondly, choose from the following suggestions for investigations into symbolism:

In *Sons and Lovers*, look at the significance of trees and nature in the relationship of Paul and Miriam. You could begin your exploration with the occasion when Miriam takes him to see a wild-rose bush (p. 195, from 'She wanted to show him a certain wild-rose bush' to the paragraph ending 'The dusk came like smoke around, and still did not put out the roses'), and continue by looking at the function of the natural background when Paul and Miriam have their first sexual encounter, starting on p. 328 where a paragraph begins 'There was a great crop of cherries at the farm' and continuing as far as the paragraph ending 'He was tender and beautiful', on p. 330. Then follow the method shown in this chapter, to identify and study further passages.

In *The Rainbow*, look at the symbolism of arches and spires. You can begin this exploration by looking at Will and Anna's visit to Lincoln, beginning at 'They had passed through the gate' on page 186 and studying as far as 'She always had a sense of being roofed in' on p. 189. A further passage for study would be that on pp. 105–6, when Will Brangwen's passion for church architecture is described, but many other incidental details of church scenes will further enhance this vein of meaning.

In *Women in Love*, study the symbolic setting of the snowy peaks where the two couples spend their final weeks before splitting up, and Gerald's death. You can begin with a very short extract such as the two paragraphs on p. 460, beginning 'But he felt something icy gathering at his heart' and ending 'or a sheath of pure ice'. A further passage you will be led to is their first arrival at Hohenhausen, roughly from the beginning of Chapter XXX to p. 402. Finally, of course, your investigation of this utter and final landscape must include the account of Gerald's suicidal climb on pp. 472–4.

6

Conclusions to Part 1

We have attacked the study of Lawrence from several different angles. We have pursued his characterisation, his search for an ideal sexual relationship, how the novels present class and society, and imagery and symbolism. Each chapter has brought us some enlightenment about its particular focus; and at the same time we have found that the conclusions we reach build upon each other, or cross-reference, so that a little more light is shed onto the 'whole' works with each different analytical incursion. Can we draw together our different insights? What can we now say about the nature of these three novels, and Lawrence's achievement in them?

The first time you read a novel by D.H. Lawrence, you know that you are in the presence of a highly individual effect: his writing has a distinct and powerful personality which forces itself on your attention. Each detailed analysis of a passage has added to our understanding of many different ways in which this effect is achieved. We do not want to revisit these points in the present chapter, however: rather, we are looking for larger correspondences and connections, generalisations that will bring the details of analytical work together and enhance our 'overview' of what Lawrence has created.

Thinking back over the work we have done, we can pick out three 'patterns' which are consistently present. These 'patterns' are something between the conventional idea of a *theme*, and something else we can call a *process* or a *way of thinking*. Broadly, they are Lawrence's pursuit of **individualism**; the prevalence of two-sided concepts and themes, or **dualisms** in his novels; and the process of **progress**

through conflict which continually occurs. We will therefore pursue our conclusions under these three headings.

Individualism

All three novels represent a search, journey, battle, call it what you will, aiming towards a state in which the individual is both intact and independent, on the one hand, and fulfilled.

Broadly, the **struggle to remain intact** is presented as a battle in which the individual has to fight against virtually everything else in the world. The novels present a bewildering variety of external influences which threaten to constrain or enslave the individual. We remember the prisons of social class which tempt and threaten both Paul Morel and Rupert Birkin in different ways (Paul struggles to come to terms with being a misfit among both 'my common people' and 'the middle class'; Birkin has to fight to escape from his subjection to Hermione's controlling, 'spiritual' will and the middle-class pretension her house-party entails); the enslavement to 'duty' in the army, into which Skrebensky sinks as into a death; the great industrial 'machine', which rules Ursula's uncle Tom in Wiggiston and Gerald Crich the owner-manager, dominates the unfree, sado-masochistic aestheticism of Loerke in *Women in Love*, and threatens Paul Morel as the economic necessity of labour; the invitations of religious mysticism which tempt both Will Brangwen and Ursula in *The Rainbow*, and so on.

In addition to these external influences, the individual faces a threat of annihilation in love. Possession in love, and submission to the other partner's will, is vividly presented throughout the novels. We remember Mrs Morel's excessive love for her son, which destroys Paul's ability to form a relationship for himself; Miriam's submissive self-sacrifice; Ursula's aggressive female will, which Skrebensky cannot counter; and the destructive power-struggle between Gudrun and Gerald in *Women in Love*.

The individual, then, is shown in a multi-faceted **struggle to remain intact**, assailed by multiple attacks, incursions, invitations and challenges. The crucial qualities the individual pursues are

freedom and **independence**. Lawrence's characters display a drive towards this individual survival at an unconscious level – like a primitive instinct – which is stronger in some, and is weaker and succumbs in others.

What is the point of this battle against all external forces? Lawrence shows its necessity in numerous contexts, but in itself it is not the whole story of **individualism**. We remember the quotation from the novella *The Captain's Doll*, mentioned in Chapters 2 and 3:

> We must all be *able* to be alone, otherwise we are just victims. But when we *are* able to be alone, then we realize that the only thing to do is to start a new relationship with another – or even the same – human being. That people should all be stuck up apart, like so many telegraph-poles, is nonsense.[1]

The struggle to become free and independent, to keep individuality intact, makes us 'able to be alone' and prevents us from becoming 'just victims'. However, all this leads to is a sterile isolation of the individual. Lawrence's image for this is being 'stuck up apart, like so many telegraph-poles'. He tells us that isolation is not creative, it will not lead to progress: it is a 'nonsense'. Therefore, the individual faces a further challenge – that of forming a relationship with some other person. In other words, the individual, having achieved **independence**, must then go on to seek **fulfilment**.

In our studies in Chapters 1-5, we have found Lawrence symbolising the individual's journey away from captivity, and towards fulfilment, as comparable to Moses leading the chosen people out of captivity in Egypt, through the wilderness and across the Red Sea to the Promised Land. It can be helpful for us to gain an overview of the three novels, with all their narrative detail, by thinking in these terms: the individual quest for fulfilment is like the biblical journey chronicled in Exodus. Also, Lawrence compares an individual who is special and more aware than the common run of people, to a combination of Moses and the Israelites: he or she is in some way a

---

[1] From 'The Captain's Doll' in D. H. Lawrence, *Three Novellas*, London (Penguin Books), 1960, p. 207.

prophet, with a higher understanding than others, and is, in this sense, 'chosen'.

The nearest that any of the couples in these novels approach to Lawrence's ideal of a relationship in which they are 'fulfilled' is found in the relationship of Ursula and Birkin in *Women in Love*, in the chapter entitled 'Excurse' and afterwards. They both lose and find themselves in their union. We have noticed features of annihilation and rebirth, and an outcome Lawrence calls the 'Two-in-One' in his 'Study of Thomas Hardy', in our analysis of this most successful relationship.

It is too simplified, however, to see only one couple's achievement. All three novels chronicle quests for this relationship, for a complete and balanced sexual and spiritual union. So, when we think about the individual's drive towards **fulfilment**, we should recognise that Paul Morel's self-hatred when he blindly responds to Miriam's self-sacrifice, Tom Brangwen's intellectual vagueness when he describes a married couple as 'two angels', and Ursula's repression when her will overwhelms Skrebensky, are all manifestations of this same drive towards fulfilment in a relationship.

Dualisms

'Dualism' is a word we use to describe a two-sided way of thinking. We have found a number of **dualisms** in a number of different contexts. For example, Paul Morel's difficulty with social class presented itself in terms of the non-intellectual, instinctive 'warmth' he enjoys with 'my common people', and the middle classes 'that exchange ideas' (see *Sons and Lovers*, p. 298, and Chapter 4 above). This presents a dualism between natural instinct, a non-intellectual and physical way of life, and education and intellect. We could simplify this into body v. mind, body v. soul, material v. spiritual (although each of these traditional dualisms slightly distorts the way Lawrence's characters respond to their experiences).

Lawrence repeatedly shows his characters being confronted with experience in a dualistic form, then. So, as well as Paul Morel's perception of a natural working class and an intellectual middle class, we have met Birkin's perception of Ursula offering 'emotional, phys-ical' love in contrast to Hermione's 'abstract spiritual' offer. In Chapter 3, we explored these dualisms, and we were led to Lawrence's dualistic philosophy which is developed in his 'Study of Thomas Hardy'. There, he proposes that all the different varieties and contexts where life presents a dualistic face to the individual, are really only part of two dominant principles which govern the whole of life, gender, culture and history: the two principles of 'Love' and the 'Law'. Lawrence's exposition of this theory, and our analysis of the novels, shows that each of these dominant principles is made up of numerous aspects, and manifests itself in a wide variety of ways. For example, Lawrence identifies his principle of 'Love' as a mascu-line force, and that of the 'Law' as feminine. Then he attaches 'Spirit' to masculinity and 'Love' and 'Emotion' to femininity and 'Law'.

It does not serve our present purpose to worry about whether we agree or disagree with Lawrence's philosophy: it does not matter whether we think of masculine and feminine in the same terms as he does, or whether we have completely different ideas. The point is that he consistently sees life in terms of dualism. There are always two separate sides, whatever they may be. So dualism is a consistent 'shape' or pattern in the way Lawrence thinks.

How does this affect the individual in his novels? Here, we can go further than just saying that he thinks two sidedly. We have noticed that all of the dualisms, when they first present themselves, seem to be opposites, seem to be mutually exclusive and in conflict. Therefore, we have repeatedly found that characters think they have to make a choice. They feel that they have to choose between two principles. So, Paul Morel tries to choose between working-class and middle-class, thinking that he has to be one or the other, and this leads him to say 'I belong to the common people' (*Sons and Lovers*, p. 298). Birkin is driven to fury when he feels forced to choose between Hermione's 'abstract spiritual' and Ursula's 'emotional phys-ical', because he feels that they are both 'horrible' and 'nauseous' (see *Women in Love*, p. 309). However, throughout the three novels, Lawrence shows that these choices are false and misleading. So Mrs Morel points out that Paul is wrong: he does not belong to either the 'common people' or the 'middle classes'; and Birkin fights to force Ursula to offer more – not just the 'emotional physical' love he finds so nauseous. The individual confronted by dualism must resolve the conflict, then: the purpose and movement of all the individuals who move towards fulfilment in these novels is to reconcile and balance two overriding principles. What Lawrence tells us is that these battling forces must be fused, accepted and made into a new whole. Only then can life become complete, and the individual be fulfilled. So, in symbolic terms, Ursula has to accept both the black and silver rivers Birkin describes in 'Water-Party' (see *Women in Love*, pp. 172–3, and the analysis of water symbolism in Chapter 5 above).

In conclusion, we can say that Lawrence's world presents experience in the form of apparently opposed principles which challenge the individual with a false choice. The individual must rise above 'choice', and accept and reconcile two dominant forces, joining them into a complete whole. Lawrence's term for this ultimate whole is 'Two-in-One'.

Progress through Conflict

In Chapter 1 we looked at the texture of Lawrence's narrative. One of the features we noticed was the confusing volatility of emotions: characters seem to love and hate by momentary turns; and they are flooded by sudden violent states of emotion which, on the surface, are not consistent or rational. In our opening two chapters we identified and explored conflicts within the characters, finding that these inner struggles often explain the extreme emotional swings they undergo. As we have continued to study, we have discovered more and more processes which are founded on conflict, both within a character, between characters, and between the individual and his or her environment. Multiple conflicts are going on all the time, in fact; and Lawrence's writing conveys them as utter, lethal battles.

Conflict is taken to extremes, then. Two examples we have met in our study underline this point. Remember the quarrel between Ursula and Birkin, in 'Excurse', from *Women in Love*. 'Quarrel' is too tame a word for this: it is a flaming row in which each of them hurls insults and contempt at the other, which seems to lead to an absolute breach between them as Ursula hurls the rings at Birkin. In the same way, the struggle for dominance between Ursula and Skrebensky, which we looked at when following moon symbolism, is described as a matter of life or death: he was 'sinking, settling upon her, overcoming her life and energy, making her inert' as if 'he would gain power over her, to bear her down'. Skrebensky wishes to have her 'in a net of shadows, caught'. As the struggle of wills swings, she becomes 'corrosive' and 'She seemed to be destroying him' (quotations are from *The Rainbow*, pp. 297–9).

The violence and extremity of these battles impresses us. There is no compromise, no quarter asked or given. The fight continues to the end, to a pitch of exhaustion that is likened to a death. These processes of **conflict** seem to be destructive, vicious, uncompromising. However, Lawrence shows that progress occurs through these battles: only out of an apparently destructive fight, an utter conflict in which neither side submits, will come a new whole which is made out of the broken remains, paradoxically born from the destruction. The clearest example of this whole process that we have looked at occurs between Birkin and Ursula in 'Excurse', where their quarrel leads to a reconciliation filled with overtones of newness and wonder (see Chapter 3, and our exploration of water symbolism in Chapter 5, for discussion of this episode). This is the outstanding example in the three novels because theirs is the one fulfilling relationship achieved between any of the couples. However, the principle, that **conflict leads to progress**, has to be understood as present in many other episodes and in different contexts.

Two examples that we have met will support this point. We know that the attempt at union between Ursula and Skrebensky fails; but we should not dismiss their conflict for this reason. In their battle of wills, Skrebensky is destroyed and becomes a 'nullity'; but Ursula eventually grows through this struggle. The power struggle with Skrebensky, which is also a struggle against herself, is a violent struggle which leaves her 'spent', 'unconscious' (p. 454) after her confrontation with the horses, and 'faint, dim, closed up' after parting from Skrebensky (p. 448). When Ursula recovers from this experience, however, her character and personality has grown and her insight is far greater than it was before. Now she accepts that she must wait for her mate, who will be 'a man created by God' and would 'come from the Infinite'; and she achieves her vision of the rainbow, which includes the renewal of all humanity into something 'new, clean, naked' in a 'new germination' at the end of the book.

The process of **progress through conflict** is a continuous dynamic throughout these three novels, then. It is a mystical idea which is presented as a paradox: through destruction a new beginning is born. Elsewhere, Lawrence has used the symbol of the Phoenix – a legendary bird consumed by fire, which rises from its own ashes – as an emblem of this process. We can also understand this as analogous to a number of traditional cultural ideas. For example, Lawrence often implies that the crucifixion and resurrection in the Christian story are relevant, as the destruction of consciousness means passing into and through a form of 'death'. Alternatively, we can think of the idea of 'testing to destruction', or being 'tempered' (strengthened) by experience and suffering.

Taken together, these three consistent features in the novels, of **individualism, dualisms,** and **progress through conflict** embody an uncompromising and rigorous vision of life. However, they do portray a vision, and therefore underpin the fundamental optimism of Lawrence's novels. Much of the excitement and exhilaration of reading Lawrence comes from this sense that people are on a journey, they are struggling forward and do have a goal, however distant that ideal haven may be and however riven with apparent contradictions current circumstances still are.

PART 2

THE CONTEXT
AND THE
CRITICS

7

D. H. Lawrence's Life and Works

Controversy

The first part of Lawrence's life is quite well represented in *Sons and Lovers*. His parents were Arthur and Lydia Lawrence, not Walter and Gertrude Morel. Miriam Leivers is modelled on Jessie Chambers, and Clara Dawes more loosely represents a Mrs Dax. There are some differences between the novel and Lawrence's own life in terms of timing and events (for example, Lawrence only worked at Haywood's – the model for Jordan's – for a few months, rather than the years of employment as 'spiral clerk' Paul Morel sustains in the novel), but the reader of *Sons and Lovers* gains an understanding of the actual social background, physical environment, and of Lawrence family relationships, which seems to be a fairly reliable guide. Also, the young Lawrence's involvements with Jessie Chambers and Mrs Dax are fully described – from his point of view – in the story of Miriam and Clara we are told in *Sons and Lovers*. The brief biographical sketch we have room for in this chapter cannot provide anything approaching the autobiographical detail of the novel.

There has been controversy about *Sons and Lovers*, however, centring on two particular aspects of the view it presents of Lawrence's youth. First, critics, biographers and friends, Lawrence's siblings and Lawrence himself came to the view that he had been unfair to his father in the book. Lydia Lawrence's self-righteous puritanism, and her possessive jealousy of her children, is now thought to be just as much to blame for the conflict in her marriage as her husband's boorishness and drinking. They were an ill-matched couple, and for most of his life Lawrence is thought to have underestimated his father's qualities, out of loyalty to his mother and her memory. Lawrence's sister Ada, in her memoir, wrote that their mother had turned the children against the father;[1] and in 1922 Lawrence apparently told Achsah Brewster that he had 'not done justice to his father' in *Sons and Lovers* and 'felt like re-writing it' because he had not valued his father's 'unquenchable fire and relish for living'. Speaking of his mother, he is reported to have added that 'the righteous woman martyred in her righteousness is a terrible thing and that all self-righteous women ought to be martyred'.[2]

Secondly, Jessie Chambers published her *D. H. Lawrence: A Personal Record by E.T.* in 1936. This work expressed bitterness about the way Miriam was portrayed in *Sons and Lovers*, asserting that Lawrence was the one who could not form a sexual relationship, due to his mother's dominance of him. Jessie Chambers clearly believed herself to have been ill used by Lawrence, both in life and in print. In the present day, this criticism has widened and burgeoned into a general hostility towards Lawrence's and Paul Morel's treatment of the women in that novel, suggesting that he (and Paul Morel) first used and then discarded them all – including his mother.

Appropriately, our account of Lawrence's life has begun by mentioning controversies. The more you read about his life, the more you will be struck by the enormous number of arguments he generated and promoted wherever he went, and the vast range of different perceptions of all his friendships and relationships that have continued to boil and simmer down the years, right up to the present day. This seems to be both because Lawrence himself was a difficult and argumentative man, subject to sudden bursts of violent temper

---

[1] Ada Lawrence and G. Stuart Gelder, *The Early Life of D. H. Lawrence*, London 1932.
[2] E. and A. Brewster, *D. H. Lawrence: Reminiscences and Correspondence*, London 1934, p. 254.

during most of his adult life; and because his views were shocking and provocative to other people. Much of the vitriol heaped on his head was stoked up by his habit of including recognisable portraits of his friends and acquaintances in the novels. So, Jessie Chambers was angry about the characterisation of Miriam; Lady Ottoline Morell took offence at the character of Hermione Roddice; and many others – rightly or wrongly – saw themselves depicted and traduced in print.

This creates a difficulty for the literary critic: many of the judgements which have stuck to Lawrence's novels have a personal element at the root of them. Some early reviewers of *Lady Chatterley's Lover*, for example, castigated Lawrence for describing sexual acts to compensate for his own sexual problems;[3] and modern psychoanalytical criticism fastens onto the author's sexual inadequacies, and alleged perversions, when tackling the interpretation of passages describing sex. We have to be very careful when studying Lawrence, therefore. We have to remember that the characters in these novels are imagined creations, so the question of whether they are true or false portraits of real people is irrelevant. A work of literature has its own standard of 'truth', and if the people are convincingly 'true' in the created world of the book, that is all we need to concern ourselves with. It is equally pointless to castigate Lawrence for giving his characters sexual prowess he could not match himself. Do we blame Ian Fleming for not equalling James Bond's seductive successes, or Homer for being less beautiful than Helen?

On the other hand, there are legitimate questions which affect our critical judgements about the novels; and there are legitimate questions about the sex scenes. Contrary to popular myth, the majority of these scenes are not explicit – they are metaphorically described; and the question of what the characters are actually doing does arise. Any reader of Lawrence has to face these concerns and reach his or her own understanding of how they modify the experience of reading. These controversies – for example, concerning the presenta-

---

[3] For example, an anonymous review in *John Bull* commented that Lawrence had a 'diseased mind', so that 'since he has failed to conquer his obsession [with sex], the obsession has conquered him'.

tion of homosexual feelings and anal intercourse in the novels – will be discussed in the next chapter. In the meantime, we will give an account of the author's life itself. This was a tortuous and restless life, but we will make our account as plain as possible.

Lawrence's Life

David Herbert Richards Lawrence was born in the mining village of Eastwood, Nottinghamshire, in 1885. He was the fourth child of Arthur Lawrence, a miner, and his wife Lydia, who had briefly been a school-teacher before her marriage. He was born at a house in Victoria Street. The family moved to a house in the Breach when he was two (this is the house in two rows of back-to-back miners' cottages described in *Sons and Lovers*, where the estate is called 'The Bottoms') and moved again to a house in Walker Street, when he was six. The Walker Street house was higher up and looked away from the town, out over woods and countryside. In 1902 the family moved yet again, this time to a house in Lynn Croft, just around the corner from Walker Street.

Lawrence had two brothers and two sisters. George, the eldest, was born in 1876 and moved to Nottingham when he was ten, so he was hardly in the home during Lawrence's childhood. He eventually became an engineer; but was never close to his celebrated younger brother. Ernest, the second child, was born in 1878. He was the pride of the family – and of his mother particularly. Ernest went to work as a clerk when he was twelve, but kept up his schooling at night school, learning shorthand, typewriting and languages. He worked at Coventry for a time, and then went to London when he was twenty-one. Ernest seemed to have a hopeful career ahead of him, but died at his lodgings in London from erysipelas and pneumonia at the age of twenty-three. He was the model for Paul's brother William in the novel *Sons and Lovers*. The third child was Emily, born in 1882. D. H. Lawrence was the fourth child, and his younger sister Ada was born two years later in 1887. Since George lived in Nottingham and Ernest went out to work from when little 'Bert' was five years old, then moved away to Coventry and London,

D. H. Lawrence grew up with his sisters. He remained close to both of them throughout his life, although the one who visited him abroad most often, and helped to care for him during his bouts of illness towards the end of his life, was his younger sister Ada.

Bert Lawrence was reportedly a weak and sickly baby, then a small and weak child. He suffered from bullying at the Beauvais Board School he attended up to the age of twelve, as well as from comparison with the clever and dashing Ernest, whose achievements were still remembered there. At the age of twelve he won a County Council Scholarship which enabled him to continue his education at Nottingham High School. Here he continued until he was sixteen, and he received as good an education as could be had anywhere at the time. However, sending Bert to the High School entailed a severe strain on the family finances – a sacrifice Mrs Lawrence willingly made, but which left the household economy very stretched – and a strain on Lawrence himself. He had to travel to school by train, leaving before seven in the morning and only returning at seven in the evening.

Towards the end of his time at the High School, in 1901, Lawrence met Jessie Chambers, the girl who became a close friend and lover, who admired and encouraged his poetry and writing, and who remained an important figure in his life for the next twelve years. She was the daughter of Edmund Chambers, tenant-farmer at the Haggs farm; and as Lawrence's friendship with the Chambers family grew over the next few years, he frequently visited the Haggs, talking with the family in the farmhouse, going for long walks with Jessie, and helping her brothers and father with the farm work.

When he left the High School in 1901, Lawrence took a job as 'spiral clerk' at Haywood's, a firm dealing in artificial limbs and surgical supplies, where he stayed for about three months. Ernest's sudden death occurred during this time and soon after this tragedy Lawrence suffered a serious bout of pneumonia which nearly killed him. His mother nursed him through the winter of 1901–2 and he survived, but he never returned to Haywood's.

Instead, in the autumn of 1902, he took a post as pupil-teacher at the British School in Eastwood and, together with teacher-training at a school in Ilkeston, he stayed working at this 'savage teaching' until 1906. The conditions in which Lawrence began work as a teacher are described among Ursula's experiences in the chapter of *The Rainbow* called 'The Man's World'. During these years Lawrence socialised with a group of his fellow teacher-training students who called themselves 'the pagans'. These included Jessie Chambers, who joined the training programme, and another young woman who was to become important in Lawrence's life and in his novels. Louisa (Louie) Burrows is regarded as the original of Ursula Brangwen, the central character of both *The Rainbow* and *Women in Love*, although Lawrence seems to have grafted a great deal of his own feelings and later experiences onto Louisa Burrows's background, upbringing and appearance.

In 1904 Lawrence took the King's Scholarship examination and was placed first in England and Wales; but when, in June 1905, he came to the London Matriculation examination which would admit him to a teacher-training college his result, in the second division, was comparatively disappointing. However, this did seal his place to train as a teacher at Nottingham University College. He continued to work as a pupil-teacher at Eastwood for another year, saving his wages towards the expenses of college.

Between 1906 and 1908 Lawrence studied for his Teacher's Certificate at Nottingham, and he was gradually disillusioned with the dry restrictiveness of academic work, much in the same way as Ursula's idealism turns to disillusion in *The Rainbow*. During all his time as pupil-teacher and at college, Lawrence's writing was beginning to gather pace. He was producing poems and writing his first novel, *The White Peacock*, as well as writing short stories. Some of these were entered in a competition in which one of them, 'A Prelude' (sent in under Louisa Burrows's name), won a prize.

In October 1908 Lawrence went to Croydon in South London to become a teacher at the Davidson Road School. The very complicated texture of his adult life then began in earnest, involving the friends of his childhood and youth in Nottinghamshire, and an increasing number of new friends as Lawrence moved among various groups of people he met in London, on the continent, and eventually around the world. He was an indefatigable correspondent, and seems to have surrounded himself with groups of people compulsively wherever he went. However, one of the strongest impressions gained from reading his biography is of a man who would never willingly let go of another person. As you follow his life through the war years and the twenties, moving restlessly from place to place, often impelled on his way by violent quarrels and 'final' breaches with his supposed friends, it is astonishing how often Lawrence re-contacted a hated enemy only a few months later, or continued writing regularly to people he reviled. Even when he broke from Jessie Chambers and, later, from Louisa Burrows, he seems to have wanted to keep them as friends, and contact with them only gradually died out.

Lawrence taught in the Davidson Road School, Croydon, from October 1908 until November 1911, when he became ill. These were busy years: he worked hard as a teacher, wrote compulsively, carried on an increasingly hectic social life in London and maintained his links with the midlands, frequently seeing his friends from the pupil-teacher programme and visiting his family. In 1909 Jessie Chambers sent some of Lawrence's work to the *English Review*, which published a series of his poems that year, and two further groups of poems in 1910. The editor was Ford Madox Hueffer (later Ford), who took Lawrence up and introduced him to London literary society.

Lawrence maintained involvements with several women friends. The relationship with Jessie continued to be as romantic-spiritual, and unsatisfactory, as ever; there was a sort of love affair and intimate friendship which produced a series of poems, with a woman called Helen Corke; it seems likely that Lawrence had an affair with his landlady, Mrs Jones; and he was engaged to be married to Louisa Burrows between October 1910 and February 1912.

During the Croydon years also, Mrs Lydia Lawrence died. Her cancer was diagnosed in August 1910, and she died in December of that year. The story of her final illness is strongly told in *Sons and Lovers*, with the difference that in the novel Paul Morel lives at home, whereas Lawrence could only be present during school holidays and for alternate weekends. The final scene of Mrs Morel's life in the novel, when Paul and his sister carry out euthanasia by giving their mother an overdose, may have occurred. Lawrence is reported to have told Aubrey and Lina Waterfield in 1914 that the story was true and he had set his mother free. Lina Waterfield was shocked because in the novel it is the son who cannot bear his suffering while his mother still struggles to live. Whatever the truth of her ending, the steady inexorable wasting away of Mrs Lawrence over four months must have been a harrowing experience for Lawrence. She had been his most powerful love, and the controlling influence on his character. Different commentators and biographers describe her importance in slightly differing ways (Jessie Chambers certainly thought that their relationship was more like that of lovers than between mother and son). However we interpret Lawrence's psychology, all agree that the void left by her death must have been enormous.

Lawrence continued teaching at Croydon for another year before he himself became seriously ill. His sister Ada came to London to nurse him, and he spent several weeks convalescing in Bournemouth at the beginning of 1912. As he regained his health that spring, he thought of going to Germany as a 'foreign teacher of the mother tongue' in a German university, believing that this work would be less stressful, and so less of a threat to his health, than teaching in England. While he was pursuing this idea, Lawrence arranged to visit his old instructor in French from Nottingham University, Professor Ernest Weekley. He went to Weekley's house for lunch on a day in April 1912, arrived early, and met the professor's German wife Frieda.

Frieda Weekley was born into the Von Richthofen family, an aristocratic family: she was a baroness in her own right. When Lawrence met her she had three children, was bored with life in a respectable suburb of Nottingham, and had already been through several affairs. In 1907 she had an affair with the Viennese psychoanalyst and follower of Freud and Nietzsche, Otto Gross; and this experience, together with the ultra-modern and permissive society in which she and her sister Else moved, on the continent, had developed and confirmed her dedication to the cause of sexual liberation and free sexual expression. She immediately began an affair with Lawrence (probably before lunch on the day of his first visit). For the next month they met repeatedly and arranged that their separate plans to travel to Germany should coincide. They left for the continent together on 3 May, without definite plans but determined to spend some time together away from England, and away from Frieda's husband and family.

The story of what happened next is complicated: Lawrence wrote a letter to Weekley, announcing his love for Frieda and hers for him; there was an incident when Lawrence was arrested as an English spy; the breach with Weekley fuelled arguments in the Von Richthofen family, then the couple were apart while Lawrence visited cousins in Waldbröl and during these weeks Frieda found a new, temporary lover at Metz. However, it seems that Lawrence's determination kept this wild and unpredictable series of events all moving in one direction, so that he and Frieda spent the final week of May in a Bavarian mountain village *Gasthaus*, on their 'honeymoon'. This was followed by the loan of a flat in Munich until, on 5 August, they left to walk across the Alps to Italy. Part of the journey was accomplished on foot, but they took the train for the final stage into Italy. Lawrence and Frieda then settled at Gargnano on the shores of Lake Garda.

From the temptestuous year of 1912 onwards, Lawrence spent the rest of his life with Frieda. Their relationship was always volatile, seemingly due to a number of factors. Frieda followed her liberated sexual crusade, had many lovers and often displayed open promiscuity. She was completely cut off from her children for many years, also; and even when some limited access was arranged she had to face Lawrence's black rages of jealousy: he had demanded that she should forget them completely and devote herself to him. As the war years turned into the 1920s, the quarrels they had from the very start turned violent. Lawrence would insult her in public, verbally abuse her, throw things at her and beat her. Their sex life was problematic and some of the enduring bond between them seems to have been founded on abandoning procreative sex for anal intercourse, where Lawrence could achieve a deeper satisfaction. This appears to have compensated for the female domination and victory he feared, and suffered, from his failure to satisfy Frieda in conventional intercourse. Lawrence longed for children but they did not produce any. Finally, from the mid-1920s his health was increasingly broken, until he was an invalid in the last stages of tuberculosis. Despite all these difficulties, and the fiery characters of both of them, they stayed committed to each other – in a way few of those who knew them could understand – until Lawrence's death in March 1930.

The Lawrences never settled anywhere for a very long time, and they had large numbers of friends with whom they stayed or who stayed with them. They lived in Italy, England, Germany, France, Mexico, New Mexico, Ceylon, Australia and California. We do not have the space here to follow each stage of Lawrence's progress through groups of friends, moving from place to place, offending people and being offended by them; nor can we chart the many twists and turns in his long love-battle with Frieda. We can only highlight the more enduring and significant elements in the rest of his life, with apologies that this account has to be so selective.

Before and during the war years 1914–18, the Lawrences lived in England. For a time they were part of fashionable literary society and it was in this period that Lawrence was taken up by Lady Ottoline Morrell, who became the model for Hermione Roddice in *Women in Love*. He also met the philosopher Bertrand Russell and a group of Cambridge intellectuals, but became disillusioned with their dry approach and social ideals. At this time Lawrence was trying to found a colony of liberated and like-minded people, who would find somewhere to live away from the polluted corruption of conventional society, an utopia to which he gave the name 'Rananim'; but he quickly realised that Russell and the socialist intellectuals could never be revolutionary in their individual selves: they were talking, not living, their new world.

During the war the Lawrences lived in a tiny cottage at Zennor, one of the last and smallest hamlets before Land's End in Cornwall. John Middleton Murry and Katherine Mansfield were their close friends, were witnesses when Lawrence and Frieda married in July 1914, and subsequently lived for a time in another cottage in Zennor. The two couples moved between intimate friendship and angry breaches, but Murry ranks as one of the most consistent figures in Lawrence's life. Years later he and Frieda had an affair, but he was also still close to Lawrence at the time of his death. Around this time Lawrence also formed a close friendship with a local farmer in Cornwall, William Henry Hocking. It seems probable that he and

Lawrence became homosexual lovers, albeit briefly and perhaps only once.

Between 1919 and 1922 the Lawrences lived at Taormina in Sicily, before a wealthy American widow and patron of the arts, Mabel Dodge Sterne, wrote inviting them to join a colony of artists at Taos in New Mexico. They accepted this invitation and travelled to America by way of Ceylon and Australia, arriving in September 1922. The colony in New Mexico dominated the Lawrences' lives for three years. They spent some months in England between 1923 and 1924; and they travelled in Mexico for a time – where Lawrence became seriously ill and suffered his first pulmonary haemorrhage, a continuous flow of blood from the mouth – but for most of those three years they were settled at Taos. While there Mabel Dodge Sterne (now Mrs Luhan, as she had married her much younger American-Indian lover) offered to sell them Kiowa Ranch, a remote house with land high on Lobo Mountain. It was against Lawrence's principles to own property, so Frieda bought the ranch and their third and most settled year in New Mexico was spent there. The Lawrences kept a cow and chickens and lived a rough frontier life, and they both longed to return to Kiowa Ranch during the final five years. That they did not do so was due partly to the lack of a clear opportunity as Lawrence's health gradually deteriorated, partly to the hostility some of his writings had awakened in America, and partly to Lawrence's fear of medical examination by American immigration, which might brand him 'consumptive' and deny him entry. Despite the obvious symptoms and recurring bouts of illness, as well as the clear opinions of doctors, Lawrence consistently denied that he was suffering from 'consumption' and talked of 'bronchial infections' instead.

In 1924 Lawrence acquired a sort of disciple in the painter Dorothy Brett. She was a morbidly shy woman who nonetheless went with them when they returned to Taos from England, lived with them at the ranch for periods of time and typed Lawrence's manuscripts. She and Frieda fought a running battle for the author's attention: Frieda being loud and abusive, and Brett quietly tenacious.

In September 1925 the Lawrences returned to Europe. During the remaining years of his life the only home which held them for any length of time was a villa near Florence, the Villa Mirenda, which they rented for a total of about two and a half years, initially as a base while Lawrence studied the Etruscan culture of the dead. However, their time at the Mirenda was punctuated by restless travelling around Europe, staying in Switzerland, France and Germany and in different parts of Italy, in a hopeless search for somewhere where Lawrence's health would improve. These years were also marred by Frieda's first long-term affair: in 1926 she met Angelino Ravagli, an Italian army officer, and she periodically disappeared in order to spend time with him, or arranged her visits to her family in Germany to include a week with her lover, from that point onwards. After Lawrence's death, Ravagli became Frieda's third husband.

By 1929 their restlessness, Lawrence's illness, and the rapid series of moves between places not very far apart (mostly in Switzerland and southern France), had all become desperate. Early in 1930, Lawrence was finally persuaded to enter a sanatorium at Vence, on medical advice. However, he quickly found the institutional atmosphere intolerable, and after only a fortnight's stay he took a villa instead, having a nurse to attend him. He was brought to the new villa on Saturday, 1 March 1930, and died there at ten o'clock in the evening on Sunday, 2 March.

We mentioned the possible homosexual affair between Lawrence and William Henry Hocking in 1917. In addition to this his name has been connected to several women with various degrees of likelihood. The best-founded accounts are of an affair Lawrence had with Rosalind Thornycroft Baynes while she was living at a villa near Florence and Frieda was visiting her family in Germany, in the summer of 1920; and an attempted affair with Dorothy Brett – which apparently failed due to Lawrence's impotence – in 1926. Frieda, on the other hand, had numerous affairs during the eighteen years she remained with Lawrence. Frieda found a lover in Metz in the period between running away from England with Lawrence and setting up to live with him for their 'honeymoon' in Bavaria. During their walk across the Alps that summer (1912) they were joined for part of the hike by two young friends, David Garnett and Harold Hobson. Frieda apparently found opportunities to offer herself to Garnett (who declined) and to have sex with Hobson.

Three of Frieda's affairs perhaps stand out from the others. First, she had a longer term affair with Cecil Gray, a young composer living just outside Zennor, in 1917, and the scandal of this, combined with her notorious German name, contributed towards the Lawrences being evicted from their Cornish cottage. Secondly, Frieda's affair with John Middleton Murry (during the winter of 1923–4) seems to have upset and disturbed Lawrence more than other affairs he knew about. Finally, her affair with the Italian army officer Ravagli was her only relationship, apart from that with Lawrence himself, which endured. In June 1931 she and Ravagli arrived in Taos and set up house together on Kiowa Ranch. They returned there in 1933 following Frieda's successful court case against the Lawrence family, which secured all the earnings from his books for herself; and Frieda lived the rest of her life – another twenty-three years – with Ravagli.

Who were the important people in Lawrence's adult life? There were so many friends and enemies around the Lawrences, in a constant succession of visitors and invitations, that it is difficult to single out those who were more significant. We will not attempt any survey here, beyond mentioning that Aldous and Maria Huxley, and Earl and Achsah Brewster, provided a great deal of loyalty, hospitality, company and care of the invalid Lawrence during his final years in Europe.

Frieda herself was of supreme importance. She recognised her 'Lorenzo' as a genius, and took it as her mission to nurture and encourage 'her' genius; and in her way she was loyal to this vocation until his death. She also held forceful neo-Freudian, neo-Nietzschean ideas which both complemented and challenged Lawrence's own uneasy combination of the revolutionary and the puritan; and she took the midlands miner's son abroad.

Frieda's creed of sexual liberation drew upon her own and her sister Else's connections with followers of Freud (we have already mentioned Frieda's affair with Otto Gross, and his influence). These ideas joined Lawrence's own developing philosophy and chimed with his conviction that there was a pressing need for society, and individuals, to become liberated and reborn into a new, uncorrupted world. However, Lawrence never accepted Freudian psychoanalysis

in its entirety. In 1914 he met Dr M. D. Eder, one of the founders
of the London Institute of Psycho-Analysis, and formed an enduring
friendship with him. Lawrence rejected Freud's view of the unconscious because he felt it to be degrading, and developed his own
theory that the unconscious is the seat of natural impulses, 'the well-
head, the fountain of real motivity'.[4] He discussed and argued
Freud's and his own psychoanalytical ideas at length with Eder, and
his friend and colleague Ernest Jones, hoping that Jones would persuade Freud himself to alter and develop his theory to accommodate
the new ideas.

Large numbers of the artists, journalists and writers of the period
met and knew Lawrence, and several of them were lifelong friends.
Many have left memoirs, letters and diaries recording their impressions of him and his opinions. Lawrence's sister Ada, Jessie
Chambers, and some other midlands friends, have also written reminiscences. In addition, Lawrence was not the only writer to use portraits of his friends in a fictional context: Aldous Huxley based the
young working-class writer Rampion and his wife on Lawrence and
Frieda, in his novel *Point Counter Point* (1928). A number of such
portraits, together with a choice of full-length biographies, are listed
in the Further Reading section at the end of this book, and I can
only recommend that those who wish to find out more about the
vicissitudes and intricacies of Lawrence's life should look up some of
these titles.

Lawrence's Works

D. H. Lawrence's literary output was prodigious: he wrote compulsively, working fast and turning out a large amount of work even
throughout the unruly events of his meeting and elopement with
Frieda in 1912. He has left a vast amount of journalism and essays,
theoretical, psychoanalytic and philosophical works and major contributions to literary criticism, a huge body of poetry, several plays, a

---

[4] From 'Psychoanalysis and the Unconscious' in *Fantasia of the Unconscious and Psychoanalysis
and the Unconscious*, Penguin, London, 1960, p. 207.

large number of short stories, an exquisite group of novellas, and a wide and fulsome correspondence. All of these are in addition to his ten full-length novels, three of which we focus on in this book.

Not only did Lawrence write a vast amount in his short life: he has also established himself as a standard author in several genres. Lawrence is regarded as a major poet of the twentieth century; some of his short stories are among the finest in the language; the novellas are widely admired and much studied; and his critical works, particularly those on Thomas Hardy, and Classic American Literature, are still highly thought of. There is so much and such variety in Lawrence's output that we cannot include a thorough survey of all of it here. Instead, we will only give a fuller account of the novels, and following this we will briefly discuss Lawrence's overall achievement, mentioning one or two of the most admired titles in each of the genres in which he engaged.

D. H. Lawrence wrote ten full-length novels, and most of another (*Mr Noon*) which was not completed and published during his life. *The White Peacock* (1911) is a story of failed love set in a Nottinghamshire valley, in which first the woman and then the man marry others. The final chapters tell of the gradual, inexorable onset of futility in their lives after these marriages, and the decline of George Saxton into a brutal, vulgar drunkard. *The Trespasser* (1912) is another story of a failed love affair. Siegmund is a middle-aged man, married to an unsympathetic wife, and he attempts to break from his sense of futility and frustration through an affair with a younger woman, Helena. However, the affair is sexually unsatisfying for Siegmund. Following a holiday with Helena, he returns to his wife and soon afterwards commits suicide. Helena then seeks 'mere rest and warmth' with the feeble Cyril who attempts to comfort her after the shock of her lover's suicide.

The next three novels are those we have focused on in this book. *Sons and Lovers* was published in 1913, *The Rainbow* in 1915 and *Women in Love* in 1920. The writing and revising of Lawrence's novels may need some explanation here. *Sons and Lovers* began life under the title 'Paul Morel' in about 1910, and during 1911 Lawrence sent parts of the manuscript to Jessie Chambers for her comments, as well as asking her to write accounts of their memories from her point of view. This followed his established pattern of working: *The White Peacock* was begun as early as 1906 and went through three or four versions before being published. Again, Jessie Chambers read episodes and versions, and talked with Lawrence about the developing book; and *The Trespasser* began under the title 'The Saga', being rewritten and retitled following Edward Garnett's advice, between acceptance and publication. It appears that Lawrence wrote fast, writing complete manuscript versions of his novels in a few months, then leaving them while he wrote other material, or becoming frustrated when he felt a 'block' and could not finish. When he returned to a story to revise it, however, Lawrence appears to have started from the beginning again and written the whole novel 'fresh', rather than polishing and adapting the manuscript he had already written. The final version of *Sons and Lovers*, then, was written in 1912, and finished quickly at Gargnano in Italy. By this time, Lawrence's literary sounding-board and mentor was Frieda. His habit of completely rewriting meant that each revision was, in effect, a new novel: it reflected his current attitudes and opinions, and his current interpretation of life and events. This may go a long way to explaining why Jessie Chambers was so shocked at the final characterisation of Miriam in *Sons and Lovers*, despite having seen – and contributed to – 'Paul Morel' during several of its previous incarnations.

The Rainbow and *Women in Love* were originally intended to be one book. Lawrence's working title for this was 'The Sisters', and he began writing it in 1913. The same project was then rewritten under the title 'The Wedding Ring' in 1914, but in the same year Lawrence began writing *The Rainbow* as the story of the sisters' family, beginning with their grandparents and ending when Ursula breaks off her engagement to Skrebensky. *The Rainbow* was completed in 1915 – the year in which it was published, suppressed, prosecuted and banned. *Women in Love*, the story of 'The Sisters' Ursula and Gudrun Brangwen, was written between April and October 1916, revised in 1917 but not published until 1920.

By 1920, Lawrence had written a further novel, *The Lost Girl* (1920), was beginning another called *Mr Noon* (which was not finished or published in his lifetime); and had been working intermittently on a third, *Aaron's Rod* (1922), which he began writing in 1917.

The Lost Girl was reworked from a story Lawrence originally wrote as 'The Insurrection of Miss Houghton' when he and Frieda were living at Gargnano in 1912: the manuscript of this unfinished novel had spent the war years in Bavaria in the care of Frieda's sister, Else Jaffe, who returned it to the author when he settled at Taormina in Sicily in March 1920.

Aaron's Rod (1922) is a picaresque story in which the protagonist, Aaron, leaves his wife and embarks on a typically Lawrentian search – for a relationship with a woman, for self-fulfilment, for meaning, for nature. The events include failed relationships as Aaron appears in London society, back with his wife, and in Italy, and a series of involved conversations between Aaron and another character, a writer called Rawdon Lilly, in which both of them argue and pursue their personal and spiritual quests.

In *Kangaroo* (1923) Lawrence drew on his stay in Australia, on the way to New Mexico. The story is of a couple who recognisably resemble Lawrence and Frieda. The husband, Richard Somers, needs to find some involvement in life outside his marriage: some activity which will make him feel connected to other men and their actions in the wider world. He becomes involved with two kinds of political organisation – one a secret group with a demagogic leader, the 'Kangaroo' of the title, the other a socialist labour organisation. The assassination of 'Kangaroo' precipitates events, and Somers's attempt at involving himself in a male world of plans and actions ends in failure.

The Plumed Serpent (1926) takes the twice-widowed forty-year-old Kate Leslie into the interior of Mexico on a journey of discovery of herself, and renewal. Briefly, she is confronted with a choice between two revolutionary leaders: Don Ramon, a spiritual leader who is reviving an ancient cult, and Don Cipriano, a general. Kate ends the novel as the wife of Don Cipriano.

For most of the years since his death, Lawrence's final full-length novel, *Lady Chatterley's Lover* (1928), has been his most celebrated and notorious work. It tells the story of Lady Constance Chatterley, who leaves her impotent (war-wounded and wheelchair-bound) husband Clifford to live a full sexual life with the gamekeeper, Mellors. The explicit scenes of intercourse in this novel made it internationally notorious, and it became the subject of one of the most famous and decisive obscenity trials in the twentieth century.

When Penguin brought out the first English edition, the publishers were prosecuted, and the trial which took place in 1960 drew many famous names from literature and the establishment into the witness box, to speak either against or in defence of Lawrence's work. The publishers won, *Lady Chatterley's Lover* was not suppressed, and this landmark ruling confirmed the strong shift towards freedom of speech and subject-matter, and towards permissiveness, of the 1950s and 1960s.

Lady Chatterley's Lover had already served a useful purpose for Lawrence before he died, however. He had the book printed at his own expense and was his own bookseller, making more money than he had ever managed to earn from his other novels, poems, stories and articles. He sold *Lady Chatterley* to customers all over the world by private subscription and mail order. In the final two years of his life, Lawrence was well off as a result of the novel's success; and he was able to feel that Frieda would be assured of a good income at his death.

Among the hundreds of poems Lawrence produced are a number of love poems written in his youth for or about Jessie Chambers, Louisa Burrows and Helen Corke, as well as nature poetry from his youth in Nottinghamshire and some poems recording his experiences as a teacher. Some of the school poems have become well known through being frequently anthologised and becoming favourites in schools and colleges. For example, thousands of students have come across 'Last Lesson of the Afternoon', 'Discipline' or 'The Punisher', which were first published in periodicals in 1909 and 1912. The poems to Helen Corke make a series which tell the story of their relationship. They appeared in the collections *Love Poems and Others* (1913) and *Amores* (1916). Of these, looking at 'The Appeal' from *Love Poems and Others*, and 'Excursion Train' and 'These Clever Women' from *Amores* will give a flavour of the series, with its accent on the woman's remoteness and the lover's anxiety about rejection. 'Dog-tired' (from *Love Poems and Others*),

'Monologue of a Mother' and 'Last Words to Miriam' (from *Amores*) may be of interest in relation to *Sons and Lovers*, also.

Lawrence published three major collections of his poems during the period of his mature output: *Look! We Have Come Through!* (1917) is a cycle of poems which focuses on Lawrence's state of dejection before he met Frieda, their love, and the first years of their life together. In his foreword, Lawrence advises that 'These poems should not be considered separately', because they are 'an essential story, or history, or confession' connected in 'organic development'.[5] This collection does indeed have a strong effect when read as a series: the viewpoint and circumstances may change between individual poems, but the cumulative depiction of Lawrence and Frieda's relationship reveals itself and accretes experiences and meaning when the poems are read in this way.

The next collection, *Birds, Beasts and Flowers* (1923) is divided into the sections 'Fruits', 'Trees', 'Flowers', 'The Evangelistic Beasts', 'Creatures', 'Reptiles', 'Birds', 'Animals' and 'Ghosts'. Here again Lawrence organises his poems in the form of series or groups; and this collection contains many of the best-known nature poems such as 'Snake', 'Bat' and 'Mountain Lion'. Finally, Lawrence published the collection *Pansies* in 1929. This time he explains that the poems are a 'little bunch of fragments' and *Pansies* is meant as an anglicised corruption of 'pensées', so they are 'a handful of thoughts'. He goes on:

> Each little piece is a thought; not a bare idea or an opinion or a didactic statement, but a true thought, which comes as much from the heart and the genitals as from the head. A thought, with its own blood of emotion and instinct running in it like the fire in a fire-opal . . .[6]

Among these late poems are some of Lawrence's most powerful and explicit statements, concerning society, industrialism and humanity's future. Look at 'How Beastly the Bourgeois Is', 'Two Performing

---

[5] V. de S. Pinto and Warren Roberts (eds), *The Complete Poems of D. H. Lawrence*, London, 1964, p. 191.
[6] Ibid., p. 417.

Elephants', 'The Noble Englishman' and 'Let us Be Men', to begin getting to know this collection. Additionally, *Pansies* contains a number of more personal poems where Lawrence seems to have achieved extraordinary brevity and intensity, expressing a complex moment's emotion in compressed form. In this connection try 'Leda', 'There is Rain in Me', 'The Sea, the Sea' and 'Spray', although there are many more exquisite miniatures to explore.

Lawrence's novellas, or short novels, have a singleness of theme and action which, it can be argued, gives them a more satisfying structure and a more tightly focused power than is achieved in the longer novels. The most widely read of these are *The Fox, The Ladybird* and *The Captain's Doll*, which were published together in 1923; *St Mawr*, published in 1925; *The Man Who Died* (published as 'The Escaped Cock' in 1929); and *The Virgin and the Gypsy* (1930). In each of these stories, Lawrence's expansive, incremental style is applied to a single relationship or love triangle and centres on a single experience. The result seems to be a tension between treatment and form which achieves a powerful effect. Similarly, some of the short stories achieve intensity and economy and are recognised as among the greatest examples of the genre. Lawrence wrote many stories, among which 'The Prussian Officer', 'Odour of Chrysanthemums' and 'The Rocking-Horse Winner' are all outstanding examples. 'Odour of Chrysanthemums' was also rewritten as a play, *The Widowing of Mrs Holroyd* (1914), which was twice produced – not very successfully – during Lawrence's life. He never attracted attention as a dramatist during his life but in 1968 the Royal Court Theatre in London staged three Lawrence plays, *A Collier's Friday Night, The Widowing of Mrs Holroyd* and *The Daughter-in-Law*, to critical acclaim.

Lawrence's literary criticism, and his essays, are idiosyncratic works in which he pursued his own philosophy with single-minded energy. When the subject-matter irritated him, Lawrence could allow his theoretical writing to degenerate into an angry rant; and there were times when he expressed extreme opinions which are disturbing for readers from the present politically correct age. For example, Lawrence seems to have shared some of the anti-Semitic feelings of his contemporaries; and he would consign the dull majority of human beings to richly deserved extinction when he was in an impatient frame of mind. However, both the continuity and a sometimes apparent discontinuity in the development of his thought are fascinating. We have quoted at length from the 'Study of Thomas Hardy', which was not published during Lawrence's lifetime, and there is also the *Studies in Classic American Literature* (1923). An important aspect of these theoretical writings is the contribution Lawrence made by trying to change public perceptions of the recently ended Victorian age, and calling for both freedom from censorship and the liberation and renewal of the 'natural' individual. Powerful examples of Lawrence's expository writings are 'Pornography and Obscenity' (1929), 'A Propos of *Lady Chatterley*' (1930), and the essays in *Psychoanalysis and the Unconscious* (1921). Lawrence's essential optimism, his belief in the underlying potential of human beings, is particularly apparent when he differentiates between his psychological ideas and those of Freud.

Finally, Lawrence is recognised as a great travel writer, not only capable of vivid descriptive writing, of unusual evocative power, but also able to capture the features of a strange culture in sharp discussion and anecdotes of his personal experiences. *Twilight in Italy* (1916), *Sea and Sardinia* (1921), *Mornings in Mexico* (1927) belong in this genre.

Lawrence was the son of a miner from a small Nottinghamshire mining village. His health was always weak and he probably contracted consumption before he was thirty. He was only forty-four when he died. To have left such an enormous legacy of work, and to have scaled such heights as novelist, novellist, travel writer, poet and short-story writer, is an extraordinary achievement.

8

Lawrence's Place in the Development of the Novel

Lawrence's place in the development of prose fiction is at once easy to explain in a general sense and perennially controversial in relation to particular strands among the cultural movements which were taking place during his writing life. His novels are ultimately unique and his own, the product of his powerful personality, and they defy easy definition.

We have already recognised, in Part 1 of this book, that Lawrence's novels incessantly use the fictional creation to argue his own feelings: he is a highly visible and idiosyncratic author on every page. When Lawrence saw a group label coming, or if he felt the insidious approach of a label, he usually responded by delivering a literary punch on the jaw to lay the label out flat, and so assert his individualism, his difference. Later in this chapter we will briefly discuss how Lawrence's works continue to evade any settled critical judgement: it is as if he is still alive, still provoking arguments and delivering counterblows to the defining critical 'schools'.

In the broadest terms, however, we can place Lawrence's works among the 'modernist' experiments in fiction of his time, alongside the works of James Joyce, Virginia Woolf and others. There is no doubt that Lawrence's novels took part in what Virginia Woolf called the 'smashing and the crashing',[1] the tearing down of literary con-

---

[1] Virginia Woolf, 'Mr Bennett and Mrs Brown', from Rachel Bowlby (ed.), *A Woman's Essays: Selected Essays, Vol. 1*, Penguin, London, 1992, p. 84.

ventions and destruction of accepted forms that many artists in different media were engaged in at the same time.

Modernism

During the nineteenth century, the novel form established itself as a major means of literary expression. If you were living at the turn of the century and looking back through literary history, it was not difficult to analyse the history of the novel and recognise several established 'genres' within the overall form of prose narrative fiction. So, for example, autobiographical novels such as Dickens's *David Copperfield* could be seen as descendants from early examples such as Defoe's *Robinson Crusoe*. Similarly, Emily Brontë's *Wuthering Heights*, with its emphasis on dreams and visions and its tragic intensity of emotion, inherited the gothic-romantic tradition from Mary Shelley's *Frankenstein* and Mrs Radcliffe's *Udolpho*. It was also clear that the novel had begun to respond to the cultural shocks of rationalism in the second half of the century. Hardy's novels, for example, confront the rationalist's experience of atheism after Darwin. Dickens in England and, even more, Émile Zola in France, had written damning indictments of industrial exploitation, using the novel form to campaign for social justice and reform; and Dostoevsky's *Crime and Punishment* had appeared in 1866. At the end of the nineteenth century, then, it was relatively easy to see what novels had achieved; but it was also clear that the conventional novel form was having difficulty in containing a radically new outlook on the world.

When we say that novelists had begun to respond to the shocks of rationalism, this is a simplification. The subject-matter chosen by novelists such as Dostoevsky, Hardy, Dickens and Zola took account of the revolution in ideas that was taking place; but one effect of this was to place greater strain on the conventional novel form. A sequential prose narrative, centring on a structured plot, struggled to express a radically new, and much more unsettled, experience of life. So, for example, Dickens's later novels are increasingly allegorical, filled with symbolism and grotesques; and Thomas Hardy's description of nature becomes increasingly visionary rather than naturalistic in his later tragedies, *Tess of the D'Urbervilles* (1891) and *Jude the Obscure* (1896). To grasp the scale of the intellectual upheaval that was taking place during Lawrence's childhood and youth, we must appreciate how completely humanity's outlook on the world had been changed.

If we imagine that the combined ideas of Marx, Darwin and Freud, and many other thinkers of about the same time, are like a vast axe that chopped away the supports on which the Victorian world-view was built, we can appreciate the shock and new challenge felt by individuals in their attempt to confront life. It must have been both frightening and stimulating. In a context of atheism, disturbing news from the unconscious, an unjustifiable, crumbling social structure and a ruinous war, the 'new' individual had to search for a meaning and a purpose – the individual had to start from scratch and find a reason for living.

In this process, many writers began to tear down the old certainties not only about the nature and purpose of life, but also about the novel form. New, experimental approaches to representing life experience in prose were tried; and old conventional types of novel were reinvented, being undermined and subversively distorted to give expression to the new chaos, the new uncertainties. James Joyce in *A Portrait of the Artist as a Young Man* (1916) and *Ulysses* (1922), and Virginia Woolf in *Mrs Dalloway* (1925) and *To the Lighthouse* (1927), developed the form of narrative called 'stream of consciousness' writing, an attempt to represent mental experience at the interface between consciousness and the unconscious. These novels are virtually without plot in the conventional sense: external events tend to be trivial and appear accidental, mere triggers for inner events in the psychology of the character. *Mrs Dalloway*, for example, is an exploration of memory, in which the eponymous heroine realises the significance of events which took place twenty years before the single day of the novel's narrative. At the same time, E. M. Forster adopted an apparently conventional form for his *A Passage to India* (1924) but undermined this sequential narrative of events, characters and relationships by building his novel around a crucial event that is impossible to explain or describe. In effect, Forster wrote a conventional novel and deliberately placed an empty hole right in the middle of it.

The three novels we are studying in this book, *Sons and Lovers* (1913), *The Rainbow* (1915) and *Women in Love* (1920), all show signs of both 'modernist' approaches – the search for a new narrative mode, and the subversive 're-invention' of conventional form. A brief discussion of each text will clarify the nature of Lawrence's innovations.

Sons and Lovers shares many characteristics with the 'autobiographical' novels of the nineteenth century such as *David Copperfield* or *Great Expectations*. It tells the story of a single protagonist from his birth to the point where he enters adulthood. It is a novel of growing up and many of its plot features mirror those in the earlier novels of growing up, by Dickens. For example, Paul Morel's first day at work could be closely compared to David Copperfield's arrival at Murdstone and Grinby's in *David Copperfield*; his move to the grammar school in Nottingham has a parallel in Pip's arrival at Mr Pocket's in *Great Expectations*. In short, the plot of *Sons and Lovers* takes us through all the normal first experiences of a boy growing up, just as Dickens's novels do. On the other hand, *Sons and Lovers* is completely unlike these novels. The story of Paul Morel is of a boy whose development is crippled by his mother's excessive love. He is weak and effeminate, and so emotionally damaged that he fails in his attempts at courtship and is unable to establish a romantic relationship. Eventually, Paul is left adrift, without profession or mate. On the final page of the novel, he struggles to overcome suicidal thoughts and just about manages to turn towards life – but there is neither certainty, attraction or hope in his victory, only an impression of fatalistic determination. The accent on the final page is on the infinite and incomprehensible universe in which Paul is an insignificant speck:

> Stars and sun, a few bright grains, went spinning round for terror and holding each other in embrace, there in a darkness that outpassed them all and left them tiny and daunted. So much, and himself, infinitesimal, at the core a nothingness, and yet not nothing.
>
> (*Sons and Lovers*, p. 464)

Paul's ending reflects a distinctively 'modernist' consciousness: he considers the riddle of his own existence and cannot understand it, and he views the cosmos as empty and frightened. He determines to live, but has no idea why. We can think of Paul as an 'anti-hero', then, and *Sons and Lovers* as an 'anti-autobiography': a parody of the traditional genre, in which the protagonist achieves and discovers nothing except his isolation and lack of purpose in life.

In *The Rainbow* Lawrence adopts the overall form of a family saga, so this novel craves comparison with, for example, Galsworthy's *The Forsyte Saga* (1906–21) or even Emily Brontë's *Wuthering Heights* (1847). The steady movement of members of the Brangwen family out of farming and up towards the professional middle class, as well as their progressive adoption of higher and higher educational goals, echoes the conventional theme of such novels. On the other hand, Lawrence's novel subverts this theme at the same time. He undermines the social, professional and academic values so that each achievement is also a disillusionment (see, for example, Ursula's pyrrhic victory over her pupils in Chapter XIII, 'The Man's World'; or her disillusion with academia described on pp. 402–4). At the end of *The Rainbow*, Lawrence again denies the traditional 'courtship' resolution: the last chapter relates the final breakdown of Ursula's romantic connection, a miscarriage and a nervous collapse. As with Paul Morel, the main protagonist at the end of *The Rainbow* is left exhausted, struggling to banish her despairing and disgusted vision of the world, and her sense of futility. She does so, but only just.

Women in Love is, in form, a double courtship novel. Astonishingly, it begs a close comparison with Jane Austen's *Pride and Prejudice* (1813) in which two pairs of lovers court and marry. The parallels between the two plots are amusing to rehearse: both Ursula's and Elizabeth Bennet's marriages are a romantic 'rags-to-riches' story; both Birkin and Darcy have to endure being humbled and rejected, and both of them have to overcome aspects of their own personalities before they deserve to be successful in love. We can imagine Birkin admitting to Ursula, in Darcy's words: 'You showed me how insufficient were all my pretensions to please a woman worthy of being pleased' (*Pride and Prejudice*, Penguin, London, 1996, p. 297).

These parallels are startling, however, only because of the over-whelming contrast between the two novels. Lawrence introduces a number of subversive elements into his plot: one courtship leads to death, and the other ends in an unfinished disagreement. Where Elizabeth Bennet steadily progresses towards the idealised 'family circle' in an English country house, Pemberley, the two couples in *Women in Love* move inexorably further and further away from Breadalby and Shortlands, and out into an empty desolation, a final landscape of remote peaks, ice and snow; and Breadalby and Shortlands are both subversive parodies of the Austen ideal.

The second 'modernist' trait we mentioned is the search for a new narrative mode, and Lawrence is distinctively 'modernist' in his style. The conclusions we reached in the first chapter of Part 1 are suffi-cient to show this. The real 'story' of a Lawrence novel lies at a level of emotion and pre-conscious impulse in characters, so that external events and much of the conversation seem less significant. Lawrence's writing is not quite 'stream-of-consciousness', but it can be described as 'stream of metaphors and emotion' and is radically different from any conventional narrative modes to be found in the nineteenth century, with the possible exception of certain passages from *Wuthering Heights*.

We should also notice that the way in which the reader receives understanding from Lawrence is much less dependent on plot, action, thought and speech than was the convention at the time. What Virginia Woolf called the 'scaffolding' of a conventional novel hardly matters in Lawrence, as a brief example will make clear.

In Chapter XIX of *Women in Love*, called 'Moony', Birkin throws stones at the moon's reflection in the mill-pond. This is merely a compulsive activity, 'Like a madness'. In the external world of deci-sions, actions and events it is entirely irrelevant. Birkin's attack on the moon's reflection has a profound effect on his and Ursula's emo-tions – but if we question this episode it is all unrealistic nonsense. Does Birkin know that Lawrence is writing a book about him, and that the author has decided to make the moon a hostile symbol of dominant femininity? The question is absurd – yet the reader must accept that author and characters share the same response to metaphors and symbols, otherwise the actions and meaning of the book fall apart. In this sense, a created structure of symbolism plays an active part in Lawrence, taking the place of conventionally significant elements such as proposals, marriages, births, deaths, battles and disputes. Birkin must sense *what he is really doing* when he stones the moon, otherwise why would he do it? Ursula must sense it as well, otherwise why would she be 'afraid' of him starting again? (see *Women in Love*, p. 248). The overriding point is that the novel would hardly mean anything if we did not accord some almost magical reality to its metaphoric and symbolic structures. It is characteristic of 'modernism' that 'even while depicting disorder in their works, modernists also injected order by creating patterns of **allusion**, **symbol**, and **myth**'.[2]

Lawrence's Influence

In his own way, Lawrence contributed to innumerable developments and changes that were taking place in the literary world of his time; and our analysis, in Part 1, of the three novels which are the focus of this book shows them to be full and complex works of literature which can be approached from many angles. However, Lawrence's most public contribution – the one which contributed most to his fame and had the most shocking or liberating effect on his contemporaries and imitators – was his lifelong effort to dis-taboo sex in literature, to treat sexual experience as a legitimate and important subject which should be portrayed as honestly as any other aspect of life. It is for this reason that *The Times* reported, during the 1970s, that Lawrence was 'still regarded in local parlance [in Eastwood] as "That mucky man"'.[3] Edward Garnett, one of Lawrence's earliest editors, clearly looked forward to the final accomplishment of this campaign, telling Lawrence that he would like to see a book which explicitly describes 'the whole act'. Eventually, he received a free

---

[2] Ross Murfin and Supryia M. Ray, *The Bedford Glossary of Critical and Literary Terms*, Boston and New York, 1997, p. 221.

[3] Quoted in Harry T. Moore, *The Priest of Love: A Biography of D. H. Lawrence*, revised edn, Penguin, London, 1976, p. 45.

copy of *Lady Chatterley's Lover* from the author, which satisfied this ambition.

Lawrence was far from being the only writer trying to demystify sex in literature at the time: Joyce was another, and many contemporaries benefited from the new explicitness (see, for example, the frankness Aldous Huxley could include in his *Brave New World*, 1932). However, thanks to the scandal of his elopement with Frieda, in which he gloried, and the outspoken manner in which he publicised his views on sexuality, Lawrence became the most notorious shocker of the establishment in this respect, during his life. The partly fortuitous choice of *Lady Chatterley's Lover* as a legal test case, which redefined obscenity law in England in 1960, has cemented this aspect of Lawrence's reputation firmly in the public consciousness: his championing of the sexual act is now a part of twentieth-century history.

Lawrence's writings on the subject of censorship, and attitudes to sexuality, go further than merely to substantiate the popular perception. As we have seen in our study of his novels, Lawrence did not advocate free love, and his long search for completeness and balance in the relation between man and woman is predominantly a monogamous quest, the very opposite of permissiveness. Whenever an establishment is threatened, it tends to demonise its antagonist as a bogeyman who will destroy all security and values; Lawrence suffered some of this effect just as communists did in the McCarthyite USA, or Jews did in Nazi Germany. His reputation as a 'mucky' man was encouraged by the prurient reaction of those who wished to preserve the Victorian taboo, who thought that any mention of sex was 'dirty'.

Lawrence campaigned to transform attitudes. He wanted sexual love to be recognised as beautiful and clean, the highest expression of union between male and female, and he complained bitterly about the Victorian age, taking part in the modernists' attack on that era with gusto. In *Pornography and Obscenity* (1929), Lawrence attacked taboos, saying that 'The whole question of pornography seems to me a question of secrecy'.[4] His theory, which seems obvious

---

[4] All quotations in the following discussion of Lawrence's theories about obscenity are taken from his essay 'Pornography and Obscenity', as reprinted in Anthony Beal (ed.), *D. H. Lawrence, Selected Literary Criticism*, London, 1967, pp. 32–51.

to us in the present day, is that sex only seemed 'dirty' because people thought it was 'dirty' and would not talk about it. The remedy is to talk about it: 'the way to treat the disease is to come out into the open with sex and sex stimulus'. Lawrence regarded the dirtying of sex as a terrible mistake, which was unique to the Victorian period and its aftermath. He called it 'the catastrophe of our civilisation' because 'no other civilisation has driven sex into the underworld'.

All of this could now be part of an accepted history of social attitudes. But Lawrence developed his campaign in a vitriolic and contemptuous style which was, of course, inflammatory. In addition, he theorised about the origin of puritan attitudes, identifying them with perversions, masturbation and an obsession with excrement. The 'grey Puritan is a sick man, soul and body sick', and the common people are 'the great pornographical class' who 'tell dirty stories, carry indecent picture postcards' and 'have as great a hate and contempt of sex as the greyest Puritan'. Lawrence accuses his enemies of hypocrisy. They decry sex in public, and are secretly perverted: 'They have the grey disease of sex-hatred, coupled with the yellow disease of dirt-lust'. Becoming more specific about the secret perversions of the moral majority, Lawrence explains 'Sex is a creative flow, the excrementory flow is towards dissolution, de-creation':

> But in the degraded human being the deep instincts have gone dead, and then the two flows become identical. *This* is the secret of really vulgar and of pornographical people: the sex flow and the excrement flow is the same to them. It happens when the psyche deteriorates, and the profound controlling instincts collapse. Then sex is dirt and dirt is sex, and sexual excitement becomes a playing with dirt, and any sign of sex in a woman becomes a show of her dirt. This is the condition of the common, vulgar human being whose name is legion, and who lifts his voice and it is the *Vox populi, vox Dei*. And this is the source of all pornography.

Lawrence does not stop there. He points out that in sexual intercourse there is 'give and take', but in masturbation there is only sterile 'futility', so that 'masturbation is certainly the most dangerous sexual vice that a society can be afflicted with'. Masturbation is so prevalent in his own time, Lawrence argues, that it has affected everything, including literature:

> The only positive effect of masturbation is that it seems to release a certain mental energy, in some people . . . The sentimentalism and the niggling analysis, often self-analysis, of most of our modern literature, is a sign of self-abuse.

It is no wonder that Lawrence made enemies, when he accused the writers of 'self-analysis', those 'modern' authors who might otherwise have been his natural allies, of being masturbators!

Lawrence then turns his fire upon the nineteenth century, saying that 'the real masturbation of Englishmen began only in the nineteenth century', and that therefore that century was 'the eunuch century, the century of the mealy-mouthed lie, the century that has tried to destroy humanity' and was ruled by the 'dirty little secret'. Finally, his prescription is a stirring call:

> Away with the secret! No more secrecy! The only way to stop the terrible mental itch about sex is to come out quite simply and naturally into the open with it.

All individuals must 'fight the sentimental lie of purity and the dirty little secret wherever you meet it, inside yourself or in the world outside'. This is a call to battle against the 'grey' puritans left over from the last century, whom Lawrence characterises as old, perverted, impotent and oppressive. However, Lawrence also warns against a dispassionately scientific liberal attitude – like that of Dr Marie Stopes, and the progressive 'bohemians'. This, he tells us, sets sex free from censorship, but also dehumanises it until we see it only as a 'mechanism'. On the contrary, he writes, openly accepting one's own sexuality will bring true liberation:

> We have to be sufficiently conscious, and self-conscious, to know our own limits and to be aware of the greater urge within us and beyond us. Then we cease to be primarily interested in ourselves. Then we learn to leave ourselves alone, in all the affective centres: not to force our feelings in any way, and never to force our sex. Then we make the

great onslaught on to the outside lie, the inside lie being settled. And that is freedom and the fight for freedom.

Lawrence carried on this 'fight for freedom' in his novels throughout his life. Our study of the novels in Part 1 of this book has brought out numerous instances where characters struggle with 'self-con-sciousness', and fight to overcome the many temptations leading them to 'force' their feelings, or sex. For example, remember Paul Morel's surrender to a macho rite of passage, forcing his desires and making himself go through with sex with Miriam, in *Sons and Lovers*; or Birkin, arguing against the forced notion of 'love' until he was satisfied that Ursula's offer of 'love' did not mean a forced, imprisoning relationship, in *Women in Love*; or Ursula, forcing her consciousness into a sentimental contemplation of Skrebensky after his departure, unable to settle what Lawrence calls 'the inside lie' at that point in *The Rainbow*.

In the final two years of his life, Lawrence published *Lady Chatterley's Lover*, in which explicit descriptions of sexual intercourse, celebrating the love between Constance and Mellors, appeared. In addition, Lawrence made free use of words which are still considered 'dirty' in these descriptions. The notoriety and gradual acceptance of this one novel, together with the history of its famous trial, makes a suitable postscript to the author's lifelong battle against prurient cen-sorship: a battle his novel eventually won, thirty years after his death.

Before we leave this subject, we should note that many critics regard Lawrence himself as his most persistent censor. In particular, his treatment of homosexual love, and of anal intercourse, appears to have been 'encoded' into allusion and uneasy symbolism in his novels.[5] This growing body of opinion has pointed out that there were areas of sexuality Lawrence himself found so personal and dis-

---

[5] See, for example, John Sparrow, '*Lady Chatterley's Lover*: An Undisclosed Element in the Case' from *Encounter*, 1962. Sparrow argued that Lawrence was not only evasive in his writing about Constance's and Mellors's sixth sexual encounter, but that the subliminal message of the book is a one of 'reckless, shameless sensuality', not the celebration of sexual love which was its overt message. Feminist critics have also argued that Mellors uses Constance like a sex-slave in this scene, so the coded message of the book is not liberating at all, but the old oppressive message of male sexual domination.

turbing, that he was unable to write about them with his vaunted frankness.

Continuing Controversy

Lawrence himself seemed to provoke arguments wherever he went, and this has remained a characteristic of his works since his death. The consensus is now well established, that Lawrence's works belong in the canon of 'great literature': they have won their place among permanently available and critically studied works. There is still a minority which regards Lawrence with distaste, but it is unlikely that his writings will now be dislodged from syllabuses, book lists and shops. However, at that point all agreement ends.

First, there is a continuing argument over which works should be included in the canon of 'great literature'. F. R. Leavis's influential book *D. H. Lawrence: Novelist* (1955) set the general opinion during the Lawrence revival of the late 1950s and following the *Chatterley* trial, proposing that there were four great novels – the three studied in the present book, and *Lady Chatterley's Lover*. Leavis dismissed the novels of the mid-1920s, regarding them as experiments which do not achieve artistic success, and a strong (and rather patronising) body of opinion has grown up that Lawrence more or less went off the rails in or around 1920. Since that time, however, many critics have argued either that Lawrence's highest achievement lies in the symbolist novels, including *The Plumed Serpent*, *Aaron's Rod* and *Kangaroo*, or that the semi-symbolic tales commonly called 'novellas' have been wrongly ignored and are both artistically more satisfying, and a more advanced formal achievement, than the rather diffuse and flawed longer novels favoured by Leavis. These commentators admire *The Fox*, *The Ladybird*, *The Virgin and the Gypsy*, *The Captain's Doll* and *St Mawr* as well as some of the more symbolic short stories – *The Man Who Died* and 'The Rocking-Horse Winner', for example. They tend to divide Lawrence's output at around 1920, and argue about the merits or demerits of the novels of Lawrence's final decade.

Secondly, Lawrence has caused terrible problems – which have led to many separate controversies – for feminist and Marxist/cultural critical schools. Feminism has considerable difficulty, and a brief reminder of the novels we have studied will quickly show why. It is clear that Lawrence wrote about women with uncommon sensitivity and understanding: there are episodes in his novels which depict the oppression of women, and a female struggle for liberation and self-articulation, with great success. We need only think of Ursula's experiences as a school-teacher in the chapter of *The Rainbow* called 'The Man's World' to understand that feminism has reason to claim Lawrence as a male writer of powerful and sympathetic insight. On the other hand, Lawrence offends feminism just as quickly as he elicits its admiration. As we have mentioned in connection with *Lady Chatterley's Lover*, there is the view that Lawrence's campaign for sexual liberation was only another cover for oppressive male domination, celebrating phallic tyranny and the degradation of women. This case particularly applies to scenes of anal intercourse, where the man initiates a perverted act in the name of 'liberation'. In this connection, students of *Women in Love* can recall the scene on pp. 412 and 413, and Ursula's response to Birkin's 'repulsively attractive' licentiousness:

> How could anything that gave one satisfaction be excluded? What was degrading? – Who cared? Degrading things were real, with a different reality. And he was so unabashed and unrestrained. Wasn't it rather horrible . . .
>
> (*Women in Love*, p. 413)

Underpinning such scenes in his fiction are Lawrence's theories of maleness and femaleness (see Chapter 3 in Part 1, above), and his development of a symbolic language which many see as an unjustifiable glorification of his own sexual peculiarity – notably the 'river of darkness' which is the 'excremental flow' and is an essential part of the symbolic structure of *Women in Love*.

Many critics have tried to confront the apparent contradictions which run through Lawrence's works, but these efforts merely give rise to continuing arguments. Lawrence's treatment of women is certainly a contentious area, and his novels do not help us towards any clear resolution. For example, in *The Rainbow*, the emphasis at the start of the book, and as far as Anna's capitulation to child-bearing, seems to propose a patronising view of women. They 'look out' and see 'the activity of man in the world at large' (p. 11), admiring the squire and the vicar; then they decide to live through their children, giving them 'this education, this higher form of being' which would enable the next generation to take part in a life where 'men moved dominant and creative' (p. 11). Throughout the first part of the novel this strain persists, until Anna conceives of herself as a 'threshold' (p. 182) for her children, and gives up her individual journey to become what feminism would call a 'breeding-machine'.

The contradiction of these gender stereotypes is implicitly present from the start; for the Brangwen men are not like squire and vicar and have a 'feminine' intimacy with what Lawrence would elsewhere have called the female principle of 'the Law'. They live with 'their senses full fed' and 'their faces always turned to the heat of the blood, . . . the source of generation' (p. 11). This contradiction comes out into the open and, in the view of many, splits the gender politics of the novel wide open, when Ursula is introduced. In summary, Ursula's struggles towards independence, education and out towards the 'widening circle' of experience, are given to the wrong sex. In short, Lawrence sets out an admiring concept of maleness, then gives it to his female character! Meanwhile, in the second half of the novel, the male protagonist (Skrebensky) fails abjectly to 'move dominant and creative' in the outside world, becoming a mere cipher of the army machine, a 'nullity'.

In this book we have focused on the three novels, and we do not have the space to range through Lawrence's writings very widely. So, we have not come across some of Lawrence's more extreme and offensive gender diatribes, or some of the opinions which have deeply antagonised many feminists. However, even in the scope of this book, we have met enough volatility, contradiction and confusion in his sexual politics to justify the virulence of continuing arguments.

Finally, there has been a similar long-standing discussion among those who are interested in Lawrence and society. He was initially taken up by London literary society, as a 'working-class' writer; and sensitive modern ears detect a strong element of condescension in accounts of him which survive from Ford Madox Hueffer, Ottoline Morrell, and others among the middle-class literati who met him in the pre-war and war years. Lawrence apparently played up to this form of celebrity somewhat, laughing about it at the same time; several biographers agree that he was snobbishly proud of Frieda's aristocratic pedigree.

More importantly, Lawrence appeared to champion the quality of 'warmth' he describes as typically working class, an essential vitality he finds lacking in the middle classes. There is much in the novels· we have studied to support this view of Lawrence, as a progressive analyst of a sick society. For example, we remember Paul Morel's discussion with his mother in which he declares that he 'belongs' among the common people (*Sons and Lovers*, pp. 298–9); the careful charting of social and educational progress throughout *The Rainbow*; and the devastating satire of middle-class sterility in the 'Breadalby' chapter of *Women in Love*. This strand in Lawrence's novels has also had a powerful influence on other fiction. Post-war English 'working-class' novelists such as Alan Sillitoe and Keith Waterhouse owe an acknowledged debt to Lawrence.

On the other hand, Marxist criticism, and its more recent incarnation as cultural materialism, have continued to argue over Lawrence's work. It is accepted that he brought class and social issues to the fore in his novels, but many such critics regard the ultimate effect of his work as culturally retrograde. Lawrence's split with Bertrand Russell and the 'socialists' seems to be the crux of this dispute, because he could not commit himself to thinking in terms of groups and classes, and to pursuing the improvement of society by means of group or political action. Instead, Lawrence is accused of advocating an isolated, negative 'individualism' – a retreat from social responsibility in the bourgeois-liberal tradition.

In addition, we must acknowledge that Lawrence's opinions on society were often wild and extreme. He was capable of gross anti-Semitism; his 'aristocratic' ideal was not always expressed in the metaphorical terms which make it more acceptable in *The Rainbow*, but sometimes appeared in the form of a raw elitism; and he was attracted by demagogic ideals of 'leadership' during the 1920s. In this argument, many critics decry Lawrence as 'proto-fascist'.

The feminist and Marxist arguments continue, and there is no sign that they will go away. These controversies are deeply relevant to Lawrence's work and must be taken seriously. Without wishing to sidestep these issues, however, it is important to remember why they arise and persist. Lawrence would have been mere anathema to both feminists and Marxists if his works were simply opposed to their causes. Instead, his position on these issues remains impossible to resolve. There are contradictory statements in his writings, and apparently contradictory fictions in his novels. And yet, irrespective of his opinions and theoretical views, Lawrence the fictional writer exhibited an intuitive sympathy. In many places in his novels he displays a powerful, intimate and moving insight into social and industrial oppression. From descriptions of blackened men trailing home from the pit in *Sons and Lovers*, and the felt horror of Wiggiston in *The Rainbow*, to the inhumane subjection of Gerald and his workers in 'The Industrial Magnate' chapter of *Women in Love*, social oppression is vividly presented to the reader. Fear, anger and horror at injustice and wasted humanity are movingly communicated by these writings.

With regard to feminism, we have already mentioned Lawrence's uncannily sensitive portrayal of female experience in 'The Man's World' chapter of *The Rainbow*. However, his characterisation often has an intuitive 'truth' which counters the effect of his more dogmatic writings.[6] Notice, for example, his perceptive characterisation of Miriam – a victim of her upbringing who can only 'sacrifice' herself to a man and is suppressed by Paul. With sensitive 'truth', Lawrence shows the oppressive power of her background: even when she agrees with Paul's modern attitudes, she cannot enact them in her heart. In the novel, we are in no doubt that Lawrence creates this as a tragic shame.

This reminder of Lawrence's idiosyncracies does not claim to settle the arguments. However, it does bring back into focus his

---

[6] The instinctive 'truth' of his characterisations even counters the effect of his narrative in the same novel, as Diane S. Bonds argues in her article discussed in Chapter 9 below (see Diane S. Bonds, 'Narrative Evasion in *Sons and Lovers*: A Metaphysical Unsettling', from Rick Rylance (ed.), *New Casebooks: Sons and Lovers*, Macmillan, London, 1996).

creative 'gift' as a novelist, which ensures that his fascination – and his potential for further controversy – will endure.

9

A Sample of Critical Views

Hundreds of books and articles have been written about D. H. Lawrence by academic critics, and many more are published each year. They are often written in a kind of specialised jargon, or in an over-complicated style: academics are just as fond of showing off as anybody else. It is important to remember that you have read and studied Lawrence's novels, so your ideas are just as valid as theirs. It is also worth remembering that Lawrence is a particularly self-contradictory writer: his novels have remained obstinately insoluble, resisting any accepted critical resolution. Your attempt to grasp a 'whole' out of Lawrence's conjoined creations, is likely to be as coherent as anyone else's.

Always be sceptical in approaching the critics' ideas: you are not under an obligation to agree with them. Your mind can be stimulated by discussing the text with your teachers and lecturers, or in a class. Treat the critics in the same way: it is stimulating to debate Lawrence by reading critical books and articles, challenging your ideas and theirs. This is the spirit in which you should read 'the critics'.

In this chapter we look at four different critics' reactions to the novels, but without any pretence that they are 'representative'. Those who are interested in the varieties of critical theory and approach should go on to read from the suggestions in the Further Reading section following this chapter, and make use of further bibliographies in the critical works themselves to pursue their research. Such reading will reveal that there are several very different strands of each of feminist, psychoanalytical, Marxist/cultural, structuralist and post-structuralist criticisms, as well as a wealth of other critics who have no single theoretical approach but borrow their concerns and techniques eclectically. The virtue of the four critics we discuss here, then, is simply that they are stimulating, and different from each other.

H. M. DALESKI

The first critic we consider is H. M. Daleski. His book, *The Forked Flame: A Study of D. H. Lawrence*, was published in 1965, five years after the celebrated trial of *Lady Chatterley's Lover*, and Daleski frequently refers to other critics who participated in the growth of Lawrence studies during the late 1950s and early 1960s. Daleski's full-length study is particularly written in the context of Leavis's *D. H. Lawrence: Novelist* (London, 1955) and Graham Hough's *The Dark Sun* (London, 1956).

Daleski's title is a quotation from Mellors's letter to Connie at the end of *Lady Chatterley's Lover*: 'So I believe in the little flame between us. For me now, it's the only thing in the world . . . it's my Pentecost, the forked flame between me and you'.[1] He uses the image of a 'forked' flame as the emblem of an essential duality between spirit and body which he regards as the central crux of Lawrence's novels throughout his life. Daleski makes extensive use of the 'Study of Thomas Hardy', which he regards as a central expository text among Lawrence's writings, to show that this duality between male and female principles is embodied throughout the novels:

> It is my contention that Lawrence, though believing intensely in himself as a male, was fundamentally identified with the female principle as he himself defines it in the essay on Hardy. The consequent breach in his nature made it imperative for him to try to reconcile the opposed elements within himself, and I have viewed his work as a life-long attempt to effect such a reconciliation.[2]

---

[1] D. H. Lawrence, *Lady Chatterley's Lover*, Modern Library Edn, New York, 1993, p. 455.

[2] H. M. Daleski, *The Forked Flame: A Study of D. H. Lawrence*, London, 1965, p. 13. Further quotations from Daleski in this chapter will be followed by the abbreviation *FF* and the relevant page-number, in brackets.

Daleski does not suggest that studying male/female conflict in Lawrence will 'explain' his novels; however, he makes a claim similar to the one we made for our 'axioms' of male/female relationship, in our second chapter (see Part 1): that a knowledge of Lawrence's duality, his concepts of male and female and the conflict between them, will help us to interpret Lawrence's symbolism and to understand 'obscure' passages in the novels (*FF*, 14). Yet, Daleski is also engaging in criticism which argues a relation between Lawrence's own psycho-sexual make-up, and the struggle for reconciliation between male and female which is expressed in his novels.

Daleski begins by analysing the principles Lawrence identified as 'male' and 'female' in the 'Study of Thomas Hardy'. Aware of the confusions that can arise from Lawrence's habit of continually adding to or changing the terms of the debate, Daleski has constructed a table of the qualities that Lawrence attributes to each principle at various different stages of his argument (see *FF*, 30–1). From looking at this table and thinking about it in relation to Lawrence's biography, and the novels, Daleski comes to the conclusion that Lawrence is fundamentally identified with the qualities he regards as female:

> The male principle is almost exactly coextensive with all that Lawrence spent most of his life fighting against: abstraction, idealism, what he called, generically, the 'mental consciousness'; and conversely . . . the female principle comes close to subsuming what he termed the 'phallic consciousness', which he fiercely espoused.
>
> (*FF*, 35)

Daleski refers to the *Studies in Classic American Literature* to further the biographical part of his argument, pointing out that Lawrence identifies his father closely with 'blood-consciousness', and qualities which are undoubtedly related to the 'female' principle; while his mother was identified with 'mind-consciousness' and maleness. According to Daleski, this paradoxical problem in Lawrence's psycho-sexual development led to a deep division within himself and a heightened perception of duality, as well as an increased drive towards the attempt to reconcile that duality or conflict. In the course of developing this part of his theory, Daleski also broadens his point to include the experiences of 'fusion' and 'separateness' as part of the duality Lawrence sought to reconcile, pointing out that Lawrence hoped for the sex act to be a union between man and woman, but not a fusion, with no loss of each one's individual identity. This kind of act, Lawrence hoped, would lead to the partners becoming pure male and pure female.

Daleski divides Lawrence's writing life into four approximate 'periods'. The first period covers his early novels and stories and culminates in *Sons and Lovers*. In his analysis of the early life of Mr and Mrs Morel, Daleski points out that the actual depiction of scenes of conflict between them gives an equivocal impression, where we could allocate equal blame to the man and the woman for the failure of their marriage. For example, although Morel is 'factually responsible' for attacking his wife, she 'goads him into fury'. On the other hand, he criticises Lawrence for some narrative comments which appear to be more partisan and blame the father, saying that it is 'very much as if Lawrence shirks the conclusions of his own art' (*FF*, 47). Later in the novel, however, Daleski points out that Lawrence's treatment of mother and father continues oddly disjointed from the author's comments. The scene in which Mrs Morel tells Paul how attractive her husband used to be (*Sons and Lovers*, p. 236), for example, shows 'that the Morels are – at the least – equally responsible for the failure of their marriage' (*FF*, 48), yet the narrative has Morel contemplating 'the ruin he had made' of it. Daleski refutes the common criticism that Lawrence depicted Miriam dishonestly, because he was unaware of how his mother's possessive love prevented him from forming other relationships. On the contrary, Daleski cites scenes in which Mrs Morel is pathetically jealous of Miriam, and Paul's clear reply to her statement that he has not yet met the right woman ('And I never shall meet the right woman while you live', *Sons and Lovers*, p. 395), to support his contention that Lawrence understands the nature of Paul's love for his mother and to 'refute the criticism that in *Sons and Lovers* Lawrence capitulates to his mother' (*FF*, 55). This criticism is imputed to an acceptance of the egoistical complaints of Jessie Chambers, whereas Daleski contends that the character of Paul is portrayed objectively and honestly in the novel. Even the failure of his relationship with Miriam is fairly treated. Daleski points out that there are frequent acknowledgements of Paul's responsibility for the failure of the relationship with Miriam. The form of the novel as a whole tells the story of Paul's gradual realisation of his own inadequacies, and the effects on him of his mother's excessive love.

Instead of criticising this novel on grounds of flawed autobiography, Daleski emphasises the achievement of self-knowledge *Sons and Lovers* represents, and sees it as a necessary stage in Lawrence recognising an underlying duality, and identifying this duality as a central subject of his concern.

> Both Miriam and Clara, therefore, are vital to Paul's development; Miriam is his intellectual threshing-floor and Clara is his sexual testing-ground. But what they give him is not sufficient. 'We are creatures of two halves,' Lawrence wrote later, 'spiritual and sensual – and each half is as important as the other'.
>
> (*FF*, 73)

Sons and Lovers, then, was a 'catharsis' which set Lawrence free from his young manhood, to develop as a writer. It left him with an abiding sense of duality, and he strove to reconcile the divisions of which he was so acutely aware. This led him to consider the poles which he called 'male' and 'female' in the expository writings – notably in the 'Study of Thomas Hardy' – and duality also became a central concern of his novels:

> In his fiction he set himself the task of seeking the 'Holy Ghost' in a dualistic universe. This, in *The Rainbow* and *Women in Love*, is characteristically expressed as an attempt to balance the male and female principles.
>
> (*FF*, 73)

When Daleski turns his attention to the second period of *The Rainbow* and *Women in Love*, he finds Lawrence's attention firmly fixed upon the nature of the duality, male and female, Love and the Law; and upon the attempt to find a reconciliation between these two principles in the form of a relationship between male and female. Lawrence is also fully concerned with the paradox of union without fusion: a union which brings about a new 'accession into being' for both individuals.

Daleski commentates on the two couples who are the first two generations of *The Rainbow* in some detail; and he is often particularly enlightening when he detects elements that are failures from a specifically Lawrentian point of view, in these experiences of relationship, so that the extent of the couples' successes and the measure of their failure is clearly defined. So, for example, he comments that the 'rainbow' symbol's appearance in Will's and Anna's dispute at Lincoln Cathedral is 'artificial, a compound projection of the cathedral arch and of the "jewelled gloom"; and what it symbolizes is not unity in diversity, the union of a separate heaven and earth, but the attainment of a "oneness" that obliterates all distinction' (*FF*, 102). At the same time, the mention of the rainbow symbol at the end of the chapter called 'Anna Victrix' is of a future promise beyond her reach because it is 'a long way off . . . a shadow-door', so that Anna herself is to blame for turning away from her life's journey. Daleski points out many ways in which Anna has consistently resisted the unknown. This analysis charts the gradual development towards what he sees as the finally successful story of Ursula.

Daleski's conclusions about *The Rainbow* are based on his interpretation of the episode with the horses (pp. 450–4) as a symbolic passage which retrospectively relates the story of Ursula's struggles towards achieving her final 'spiritual rebirth' or her creation of 'a consummated self' (*FF*, 125). He sees her first awareness of the horses (see *The Rainbow*, pp. 451–2), when their power seems to almost overwhelm her, as emblematic of 'Ursula's sudden, overwhelming, adolescent experience of sexual passion, . . . the time of her frantic consummation under the moon at the age of sixteen. The "lightning of knowledge" that travels through her then is forked'. On the one hand, she becomes aware of passion, 'the value of her physical being' as a 'fire' that 'can never be put out'; on the other hand, she realises that 'the sort of assertion to which she resorts with Skrebensky is . . . a dead end' and will not lead to 'the fullness of being she is seeking' (all from *FF*, 123). Daleski then turns to the second approach of the horses, and Ursula's escape, and comments that this passage is crucial because it dramatises a 'crisis' which is not created elsewhere in the novel. The 'pressing' of the horses drives Ursula near to exhaustion, but 'shuddering, with limbs like water, dreading every moment to fall' (*The Rainbow*, p. 453), Ursula nonetheless manages to surmount this challenge to her separate self, by climbing the tree and escaping over the hedge.

Because Ursula finally sees the horses restrained by the hedge and 'almost pathetic, now', Daleski argues that she has not merely escaped them but brought them into a 'new relation with herself'. Therefore, her vision of the rainbow on the novel's final page is not achieved by an obliteration of the self, as some have argued. Instead, it is 'a vision of wholeness which springs from the realignment in a unified self of hitherto violently contending forces, forces which Lawrence symbolizes by the tiger and the lamb or the lion and the unicorn in the expository writings, and which are represented in the scene on the common by the horses and the high-road' (*FF*, 124).

Daleski argues, then, that Ursula's final experience with Skrebensky, and the emblematic passage of her encounter with the horses, represent her achievement of a full 'spiritual rebirth' which leaves her ready to meet and accept, 'to recognize a man created by God' – who will be Birkin in *Women in Love*. Daleski does, however, have reservations about the vision on the final page, since he finds the leap from Ursula being 'made new herself' to the rejuvenation of the whole world, 'facile' and 'a weakness in the book' (*FF*, 125).

Turning to *Women in Love*, Daleski views this work as written from a very different mood. Lawrence wrote this novel during the war years and it is 'a sustained dramatization of his belief in a personal immunity amid the public disaster' (*FF*, 127). This accounts for the apparent double 'motion' of the book:

> On the one hand . . . there is a continuation of the search, begun in *The Rainbow*, for a lasting relation between the sexes, a search for the 'two in one'. The marriage of Birkin and Ursula . . . is presented as an achieved relation of this kind, and its significance is heightened by the contrasted destructive passion of Gerald and Gudrun. But at the same time, . . . both couples are shown to be on board a ship which is rapidly heading for destruction.
>
> (*FF*, 127)

Daleski sees Lawrence depicting more than a contrast between successful and failed relationships, however. He sees Birkin and Ursula
affirming a desire for life which leads them to 'abandon ship'; while
Gerald and Gudrun evince a desire for death which prefigures the
wreck of everything, and in themselves are examples of the destructive human condition which is bringing about that disaster.

Briefly, Daleski argues that *Women in Love* seriously qualifies
Lawrence's quest for a full relation between man and woman, since
as soon as Birkin and Ursula achieve their 'accession into being' they
resolve to withdraw from the world. He points out that earlier male
characters were castigated for their failure in the wider, 'creative'
world of work. So, Tom and Will and Skrebensky were in a novel
where 'the realization of "man-being" was seen to be dependent on
effective "utterance" in the "man's world",' and they were con-
demned for their failure to achieve this. In *Women in Love*, on the
other hand, Gerald's work and Gudrun's art are both associated with
the disintegration and dissolution of the world; and this appears to
be a reversal of Lawrence's views that spreads into the characterisation of his protagonist, Birkin. Daleski relates Birkin's qualities to
those attributed to the opposed principles in the 'Study of Thomas
Hardy'. He emphasises Birkin's insistence on separateness of being as
a primary condition of the relationship he establishes with Ursula,
and points out that it is in order to maintain this that Birkin urges
their withdrawal from their jobs and the world:

> 'Doing', 'Public Good', and 'Community' are typical attributes of the
> male principle as opposed to female 'Being' and 'Self-Establishment'.
> It is therefore on essentially female terms, though in the name of a
> clear and determined manhood, that Birkin is set to live his life with
> Ursula.
>
> (*FF*, 182)

Daleski contrasts Birkin's approach to Ursula with his approach to
Gerald, pointing out that there are repeated references to a desire
for oneness with the other man, such as that they should be 'of one
blood' and 'given to each other, organically'. His conclusion about
the novel as a whole rests largely on this perception, further devel-

oped by his analysis of two passages which he regards as being parallel to each other. The first of these is the description of the establishment of 'two-in-one' between Ursula and Birkin, in the public parlour at the inn (see the chapter entitled 'Excurse'), which establishes the proper relation between them and leads both to their 'accession into being' and their consummation through intercourse in the forest later the same night. The second passage Daleski looks at in detail is the description of Birkin and Gerald wrestling (see the chapter entitled 'Gladiatorial'). Daleski finds the first passage unsatisfactory, calling it an 'expedient' which uses a bombastic and high-flown style, and heavy repetitions which do not convey sufficient meaning, in order to reconcile the contradictions which are inherent in the characterisation of Birkin. The second passage, on the other hand, is clear; and, although Daleski does not read it as a neo-homosexual encounter, it is 'evidence of the pronounced feminine component in his [Lawrence's] make-up, of a latent or repressed homosexual tendency' (*FF*, 185). Highlighting the emphasis on separateness he finds in the relation between Birkin and Ursula, and the tendency towards fusion he sees in Birkin's relation to Gerald, Daleski concludes by referring to the unfinished discussion between the married couple with which the novel ends:

> The 'two kinds of love' which Birkin says he wanted should not be distinguished simply as love for a woman and love for a man: what is involved, as I have tried to show, is a need on his part both for firm singleness and for melting union.
>
> (*FF*, 187)

The ambivalent final words of the novel indicate that Lawrence continued to believe in the possibility of reconciling these two principles. The remainder of Daleski's study concerns the novels of the 1920s, which he divides into two further 'periods', although this classification merely amounts to separating *Lady Chatterley's Lover* from the rest. His conclusions on this, final, novel complete the case he has been arguing throughout, which is that Lawrence ultimately fails to reconcile the male/female duality he has been concerned with in all his fiction. The reason for this Daleski ascribes to the author's own unresolved sexual identity, suggesting that Lawrence consistently failed to acknowledge his own greater sympathy with the 'female' principle. Daleski argues that this failure to recognise his own femaleness led, first, to novels where the predominant action contradicts the theoretical gender identities the author proposes (we have previously remarked that Ursula's role in the second half of *The Rainbow* appears to be that ascribed to 'men' in the opening pages of the same novel); and secondly, led Lawrence to insert inferior passages of masculine assertion, as a compensation, which are artistic weaknesses where they arise.

Daleski's study is a fascinating and illuminating work. It contains much brilliant analysis, and there is no doubt that the application of the 'Study of Thomas Hardy' to the novels of the same period throws a welcome light of definition over those passages which describe the consummation of various loves. We certainly gain understanding about where the individual characters succeed, and to what extent they are seen to fail in Lawrentian terms. At the same time, Daleski is an example of the criticism of his time, in two significant respects: first, he focuses on the inner story of the individual character, and on the continuing quest for both intact individuality and a successful relation between the sexes. In doing so, Daleski pays scant attention to the socio-historical content of the novels, the extrapolation of Lawrence's dualistic 'principles' into society, the class system, history and culture. Secondly, Daleski moves towards the psychoanalysis of Lawrence. His theory, that Lawrence could not acknowledge his own fundamentally female nature, is adumbrated on the basis of literary analysis (i.e. he perceives a contradiction between fictional creation and explicit authorial comment); but it does, typically for that period in Lawrence studies, seek explanations for the unresolvable elements in the novels by turning to the problematic personality of their author.

R. E. PRITCHARD

We will follow this road and look briefly at a slightly later product in the progressive psychoanalysis of Lawrence himself. The second critic we sample in this chapter is R. E. Pritchard, whose *D. H.*

Lawrence: Body of Darkness appeared in 1971.[3] Pritchard takes theories of the author's Oedipal childhood and repressed homosexuality further than they go in Daleski's text-derived study. I say we will look at this study briefly because a few passages quoted from the introductory first chapter, 'The Buried Self', will serve to demonstrate Pritchard's theory quite clearly, while the remainder of the study marshals the evidence for this interpretation from analysis (largely of imagery and symbol) of Lawrence's works. The study as a whole is quite convincing: our reservations are not about whether Lawrence's psychological make-up was really as Pritchard says. The final problem remains that we are unsure what the book's conclusions add up to, or why Lawrence is studied in this way: whether it is to illuminate his art, undermine his artistic achievement, excuse the man, excuse the books, or simply as a case study relating to Lawrence's life in a crux of personal development which was also a crux of cultural and historical development.

Pritchard begins with the standard analysis of Lawrence's childhood, for his mother 'reciprocated [his] loves abnormally'. Pritchard then moves on from this first fact – which is both self-evident and self-acknowledged in *Sons and Lovers* – through the sexual difficulties, many of which Lawrence was also aware of, to consequences which appear to have remained unconscious throughout the author's life. So, Lawrence's physical being 'had to be suppressed. Normally such desires would be displaced on to other women, but in so far as these women were only surrogate mothers, he still felt guilt in his sexual relations, which inhibited him from achieving full satisfaction. It seemed to Lawrence that women possessed him, exploiting him for their own satisfaction . . . this produced the image of the winged, beaked harpy gnawing on his body' (*BD*, 22).

He had grown up fearing his father's passionate nature, and 'confusing violence with sexuality (that seemed to threaten both his mother and himself). His inability to achieve the necessary relationship and identification with his father led – as is common in such

---

[3] R. E. Pritchard, *D. H. Lawrence: Body of Darkness*, Hutchinson, London, 1971. Further quotations from this work will be followed by the abbreviation *BD* and the relevant page number, in brackets.

cases – to a homosexual desire to submit to and be possessed by father-figures of male potency' (*BD*, 23). As a result, Lawrence feared women, feared his own homosexuality and feared phallic violence.

Pritchard discusses various responses to this situation:

> Woman as the 'Magna Mater' . . . seemed to dominate and dispossess his masculinity; the resentful reaction produced a furtive subversive quality . . . and perverse sexual self-assertion, associated with images of rat, seal, weasel and bat . . . one reaction was to sacrifice [women] and their values to brutal male power. Yet when his feminine self, or anima, identified him with the woman, he again saw subjection to phallicism as a terrifying sacrifice of his own civilised self. Another impulse was to gain power by frustratingly withdrawing from sexual engagement. In so far as the erect phallus embodied a potency that was exhausted by sexual activity, non-involvement ensured the retention of potency.
>
> (*BD*, 24)

Pritchard explores other elements in this hopeless set of responses to a hopeless situation, then moves on, making a crucial link between the absolute frustration he shows Lawrence experiencing in relation to sexual experience with women, and the next stage of his argument which he represents as a means of escape or diversion from that intolerable situation:

> In reaction against the demands and frustrations of sexuality, he returned to another aspect – and the most denied and guilt-ridden – of the physical being: the anal and excremental. In infant psychology, excretion is pleasurable and a form of creation; furthermore, it does not require – as does sexual intercourse – another person for its satisfaction. Awareness of the anal-excremental emphasises the physical reality of the body, as suppressed by consciousness, and the independence of the individual.
>
> (*BD*, 24)

Thus, Pritchard proposes that Lawrence's phrase 'the body of darkness', which stands for the buried self or 'dark sun', could include several desires and concepts: the unconscious self suppressed by self-conscious existence; 'non-human' life in the womb, which is like death and of which ordinary living is the negation; and the 'primary, pre-conscious forces in nature, of which the sexual forces were the most obvious, but even more suppressed and "therefore" more fundamental and real was the anal-excretory complex' (*BD*, 26).

The remainder of Pritchard's study of Lawrence applies these insights to the writings, often in an illuminating way, and gradually builds the sense of an artist who explored this 'body of darkness' with as much truth and determination as he could muster (although Pritchard does, in psychoanalytic manner, identify areas Lawrence himself could not perceive), throughout his life. Lawrence is seen as an artist who saw anal possession of a woman as 'liberation from shame of the body and basic childish pleasures' (*BD*, 25), and for whom Pritchard makes this final claim:

> He strove for an acceptance of the totality of man's being, as the only liberation from the dehumanising inhibitions of modern civilisation. His effort was to produce a spirit not of exploitation but of respect for the free play of living energy, whether within oneself or others or the natural world, to create a greater sympathy and sense of wholeness.
>
> (*BD*, 208)

Pritchard considers, in his conclusion, that Lawrence's 'courageous exploration of his own nature' gave him an insight also into the agony or malaise of the world around him, so that he became 'a profound . . . analyst and interpreter of the crisis in the culture of his own times' (*BD*, 208).

GRAHAM HOLDERNESS

In the second half of this chapter we turn to more recent criticism, much of which has adopted either a cultural/historical perspective as Marxist studies of literature have evolved, or an approach which highlights the sexual politics of literature. The next critic we sample, Graham Holderness, would reject Pritchard's suggestion that Lawrence was 'an interpreter of the crisis in the culture of his own time'. On the contrary, Holderness argues that, in *The Rainbow* at least, Lawrence denied, suppressed and avoided that crisis, creating an ideological myth to take its place. We will sample the chapter on

The Rainbow from Holderness's *D. H. Lawrence: History, Ideology and Fiction.*[4]

Holderness begins by taking issue with Terry Eagleton, who had suggested that *The Rainbow* 'explodes realism in its letter, even as it preserves it in the "totalising" organicism of its evolving generational structure'.[5] On the contrary, Holderness writes, 'Ideology is not, in *The Rainbow*, set into conflictual relationship with history; ideology is, simply, offered as an alternative to history' (*GH*, 50).

The Rainbow is a very different kind of novel from *Sons and Lovers*. Lawrence adopted a more 'analytical' technique in order to represent a deeper layer in the experience of the characters than a realist novel could achieve, so inevitably the external features – 'social existence and relationships, morals and manners' – recede into the background. On the other hand, the form of the novel with its three generations and background of social change seems, on the surface, built around history in a very thorough way. Holderness confronts the challenge of the apparent social reality described in the second half of the novel, beginning with the wry comment that the establishment critical view (that it is less artistically successful than the first half) is probably a response to its onslaught on bourgeois-capitalist society:

> Ursula develops a profound dissatisfaction with the ethics of bourgeois democracy, imperialism and war; teaching in a school, she finds a 'hard, malevolent system' which reproduces the general relations of society; at college she discovers education to be 'a warehouse of dead unreality', a 'little side-show to the factories of the town'. Her major decision, made as the novel closes, involves the rejection of a bourgeois marriage. At the very heart of this system is industrial capitalism, and the primary image of that civilisation is a colliery town, Wiggiston.
>
> (*GH*, 52)

---

[4] Graham Holderness, *D. H. Lawrence: History, Ideology and Fiction*, Dublin, 1982. The extracts included here are taken from the chapter reprinted in Peter Widdowson (ed.), *D. H. Lawrence*, Longman Critical Readers, London and New York, 1992, pp. 49–61. Quotations are followed by the author's initials *GH* and the relevant page-number in the reprinted version, in brackets.

[5] Holderness quotes this from Eagleton's *Criticism and Ideology*, London, 1978, p. 160.

Holderness then analyses the 'description' of Wiggiston, which he says is not a description in realist terms at all. The colliery town is seen from Tom Brangwen's and Ursula's points of view, that is, from outside; and this is completely different from the inside perspective of *Sons and Lovers*. Furthermore, the episode is rich in abstractions, so Wiggiston is called 'amorphous' and 'mathematical', for example; and the style presents the town in terms of an apparition or dream as it 'appears' and is inhabited by 'spectres'. In the middle of Wiggiston is a wide empty space, and Holderness suggests that 'It is from that empty space, that social and human absence in the centre of industrial society, that the myth of pre-industrial society – the myth of Marsh Farm – is generated' (*GH*, 53).

Ursula rejects Wiggiston, and with it the whole of industrial capitalism (although she acknowledges that it has a perverse attraction). She therefore excludes herself from the 'social totality'. However, Holderness's point is that the change in narrative presentation between *Sons and Lovers* and *The Rainbow* is more significant than simply a development in the novelist's technique. It makes Wiggiston different from the Eastwood depicted in the earlier novel, because Wiggiston is only Ursula's perception: it is 'not a social reality, but a bad dream. And, of course, from a dream one can always awake' (*GH*, 53). The fact that Ursula sees the whole of society as a bad dream, means that she has a choice: she can, by conscious effort and decision, wake up from the nightmare, deny her social reality, resist being connected to that society. Holderness sees this development as a 'fracture' and a 'contradiction' which leaves a 'blank space' between the living subject and an alien, 'reified' society. Lawrence has filled that blank space by creating a myth and ideology – the myth of pre-industrial rural society:

> I am proposing that we read *The Rainbow* backwards, from Wiggiston to Marsh Farm, rather than the other way round. We should see the novel not as a record of historical process, with Wiggiston as the culmination of a real history of social decline, but as mythology, where the 'history' is deduced from the present and cast backwards into the past. Marsh Farm is a myth created to fill that blank space in the centre of Wiggiston, that human absence at the heart of the modern community; a myth created to seal the painful breach between indi-

vidual and community so clearly revealed in Ursula's vision of
Wiggiston.

(*GH*, 54)

Holderness now turns his attention to this 'myth' of Marsh Farm.
First, he remarks that the opening pages are self-presented as a poem
rather than a historical narrative, and continually refer to such words
as 'epic' and 'Odyssey', underlining the myth-like quality of the
passage. Secondly, Holderness asserts that the community depicted
in these pages is complete in itself: the women look towards something beyond the life of the farm and their men, but their lives and
aspirations are completed and fulfilled by vicar, squire and squire's
lady. The lady of the Hall performed this function for the Brangwen
women: 'In her they lived imaginatively . . . they had their own
Odyssey enacting itself'. This, according to Holderness:

> . . . is a myth in the strictly philosophical sense: an ideological har-
> monising and resolution of real social contradictions. There is no con-
> flict between individual and community, because the Brangwen race is
> an unindividualised, collective entity; there is no conflict between
> 'society' and 'nature', because human life and the natural world are
> mediated by agricultural labour.

(*GH*, 55)

Holderness continues to analyse the opening pages, moving on to
the historical chronicle which begins by mentioning the building of
a canal. He shows that these developments do not create a rural
community at all; they simply leave the Marsh Farm as one isolated
family; and as the narrative proceeds, we reach the point where the
only Brangwen left on the farm is Tom. In the remainder of the
novel, farm labourers, servants, agricultural work and business, are
all more or less ignored, so that the 'myth' only really encompasses
one nuclear family living alone. As a result, 'the novel's narrative
technique works to confirm this abstraction of individual and family
from community' (*GH*, 57).

Holderness finally looks at the vision of a transformed society
which concludes the novel, which he treats as 'simply a substitution
of pastoral dream for the myth of industrial nightmare' (*GH*, 59).

Noting that the arch and rainbow images are inherent in the values of the Marsh Farm, and that Ursula carries these with her as the 'organic descendant of the Marsh Farm myth', he comments on the return of this over-arching and containing image on the final page. The rainbow – symbol of this ideological myth – has been 'unmolested by real history':

> A completely unqualified ideology of individualism replaces the imagery of social harmony which was the pastoral ideology of Marsh Farm; the individualising, historically suppressive manner of the novel achieves, by an extraordinary ideological *tour de force*, a synthesis of those utterly contradictory structures: if the individual cannot be at one with society, then society will be incorporated into the individual and reproduced in her image.
>
> (*GH*, 59–60)

Holderness points out that the novel was written at a time when social tragedy would have been an appropriate formal response, during the First World War. Even the progress of the story, from 'organic past to industrial present', is the stuff of tragedy. However, the characters follow a separate evolution and so evade this historical reality. In this sense, the ending is not optimism 'tacked on' to the novel (Leavis's opinion), but should be seen as 'the true consummation of the novel's form, the symbol for its explicit refusal of historical tragedy' (*GH*, 60).

This analysis of *The Rainbow* is implicitly, and at several points, critical of Lawrence. The novel is treated as an evasion of the truth, and as creating a myth – an unreal and unconvincing solution to real problems – in order to cover the author's impossible attempt to deny and exclude himself from external realities of society and history. Holderness writes of Lawrence's 'refusal' and how he allows his characters to 'evade'; and points out that the function of ideology is to 'deny' contradictions. The critic's belief that history and society are inescapable, and his suspicion of bourgeois-romantic individualism as a palliative lie, are plain in the pejorative force of these comments. On the other hand, he acknowledges that Lawrence provided a damning critique of bourgeois-capitalist society in the second half of the novel.

Just as Marxist critics have subjected Lawrence's novels to critical scrutiny from a cultural/historical perspective, so feminists have studied his works on the basis that, in the battles of gender, there is no such thing as neutrality. Kate Millett's influential *Sexual Politics*[6] analyses Paul Morel's role in *Sons and Lovers* as that of a male egoist who uses and abuses the women in his life, and discards them when he no longer needs them: first murdering his mother, then ditching Miriam and finally, with extraordinary cheek, handing Clara back to her husband with the conceited idea that she was better for having had an affair with him! Millett's evidence is compelling, and is assembled from the text of *Sons and Lovers*. However, this approach to reading Lawrence does raise the question of how such a radically alternative interpretation of the main character can exist within the same text which expresses consistent sympathy for Paul. More recently, feminist criticism has examined the nature of this text more fully in order to explore this question, and our fourth critic, Diane S. Bonds, looks closely at the role of the narrator in *Sons and Lovers*.

DIANE S. BONDS

We will examine part of Diane S. Bonds's *Language and the Self in D. H. Lawrence*,[7] which analyses what she calls 'Narrative Evasion in *Sons and Lovers*'. She is particularly concerned with the way Paul Morel's relationship with Miriam, and Miriam's character, are presented in two apparently contradictory ways within the novel. Her thesis is that there is a discrepancy between the actual relationship that is created, and which we meet in the events, scenes and dialogues involving these two characters, on the one hand, and the narrator's commentary on Miriam, which tells a different and biased story.

Bonds begins by highlighting Paul's explanation of his painting, a speech he delivers to Miriam. Here is the passage she quotes:

---

[6] Kate Millett, *Sexual Politics*, London, 1971.

[7] Diane S. Bonds, *Language and the Self in D. H. Lawrence*, UMI Research Press, 1988. The part of her argument summarised here is reprinted as an essay in Rick Rylance (ed.), *New Casebooks: Sons and Lovers*, Macmillan, London, 1996. Page references to the *New Casebook* are given in brackets after quotations, preceded by the abbreviation *NE* for 'Narrative Evasion', the title of the essay referred to here.

'It's because – it's because there is scarcely any shadow in it – it's more shimmery – as if I'd painted the shimmering protoplasm in the leaves and everywhere, and not the stiffness of the shape. That seems dead to me. Only this shimmeriness is the real living. The shape is a dead crust. The shimmer is inside, really.'

(Sons and Lovers, p. 183)

Bonds points out the opposition this explanation describes, between an outer dead 'crust' and inner vitality. What Paul describes as the 'shimmering protoplasm' is an inner essence, and *Sons and Lovers* uses imagery of light, warmth and glowing colour to keep this idea of an inner vitality in front of the reader throughout the book. This is related to Walter Morel's 'sensuous flame of life, that flowed off his flesh like the flame from a candle' and to a number of scenes of domestic life featuring both Mr and Mrs Morel, which centre around the fire, such as that describing the father's breakfast routine (p. 37), and the cutting of William's hair (p. 23). Bonds comments on the effect of this imagery of heat and light, that its use binds together the different aspects of narrative, so that:

. . . the coalescence of sensory detail and emotional import, of concrete and abstract, further endorses the values communicated through the imagery of heat and light: the values of immediacy, spontaneity, and presence. Now it is important to recognise that this stylistic trait corresponds to a belief in the symbolic nature of language: a belief in the possibility of a seamless unity of language and truth, image and idea, signifier and signified. Such a belief appears to animate those earnest, 'struggling, abstract speeches' of the adolescent Paul Morel. But when he talks to Miriam about his painting, he does so in a context where the light imagery makes significant counterstatements to the implications of his speech.

(NE, 92)

Bonds now looks at the scene of Paul explaining to Miriam in closer detail. The clear narrative commentary tells us that Paul 'apprehends things directly . . . he sees into the heart of things' *(NE*, 93) and Miriam needs his 'struggling' explanation because this enables her to come 'distinctly at her beloved objects'. Bonds picks out that Miriam is described using two powerful images of light – her eyes are 'alight like water that shakes with a stream of gold in the dark', and she gives him 'dazzled looks' which are 'close, intimate'. These images locate the vital essence (the 'shimmering protoplasm' of life) in Miriam herself rather than in the painting, and this counters the narrator's claim that she received contact with the essence of things through Paul's 'struggling' speeches. Furthermore, the narrator says that Paul's words gave her a feeling of life 'again'. There are, says Bonds, two possibilities: first, that she needs Paul's words in order to contact the flame of life there is within her, or to have it 'kindled'. Secondly, that Paul's clumsy abstract speeches actually damp down her intuitively vital response to the painting, and she rekindles this flame after he has finished talking, by her own imaginative effort ('She managed to find some meaning in his struggling, abstract speeches').

A second contradiction in the scene is between Paul's behaviour and his speech: we note that he 'shrank' from her 'close, intimate, dazzled looks', which contradicts the value his speech places on inner life and vitality, and in doing so contradicts 'values endorsed by much of the imagery of the novel' (*NE*, 94). Bonds points out:

> On the one hand, the verbal relations of the characters in the novel suggest the power of language to create meaning and unity: the power of language for communication and communion. On the other hand, they also dramatise the ways in which language can be used to subvert communication and prevent intimacy.
>
> (*NE*, 94)

Paul uses words to avoid intimacy with Miriam, in fact, rather than to contact her. Bonds borrows from psychoanalytical criticism the truism about Paul's Oedipal problem, that 'A clinical view of [his] requirements is likely to conclude that Paul needs Miriam to remain non-sexual, virginal' (*NE*, 95), and proceeds to analyse a number of the scenes between them which show various ways in which his conversation has the effect of keeping Miriam at a distance, and protecting himself from contact with her enkindled sexual attraction. The narrator uses the brutal and utilitarian image of Miriam as

Paul's 'threshing-floor on which he threshed out all his beliefs', yet the scene where Paul cannot bring himself to read one passage from the Bible reveals a sexual discomfort, not an intellectual one.

However, 'Paul's most characteristic strategy for avoiding intimacy is not . . . to discuss religion, but rather to make pronouncements about Miriam's personality and feelings' (*NE*, 96). Bonds suggests that there is a clear pattern in the way Paul 'labels' Miriam. First, he gives names to her character and feelings; then, she attempts to contradict him, to tell him that she is not really like that; next, Paul insists that she is wrong and he is right. Following this, she becomes intimidated, frustrated and confused, and cannot speak. Finally, Paul easily diverts the subject by making a trivial remark or starting to talk about something else. The example Bonds analyses perfectly fits this pattern: it is the scene when Paul castigates Miriam for never laughing (see *Sons and Lovers*, p. 226). The end of their exchange is Paul's inconsequential remark 'But there, it's autumn . . . and everybody feels like a disembodied spirit then'. A similar scene, a few pages later, ends when Paul 'got up and began to talk trivialities' (p. 233). Bonds comments: 'How remarkable are the deadness and automatism with which he persists in his notions about Miriam, and then his willingness to give up his pursuit of truth as soon as she threatens, with her questions, to spoil his illusions about her!' (*NE*, 98).

Bonds next turns her attention to the narrator's pose as an authority who commentates Miriam's character. She particularly treats the first two paragraphs of Part II (see *Sons and Lovers*, pp. 173–4), which purport to be an objective description of Miriam. Here she is seen as over-religious, over-romantic, over-sensitive, out of touch with reality and living in a facile fantasy, as well as discontented as a farm-girl and unable to get on with others. This passage prefigures a number of the accusations the character Paul levels at Miriam in later scenes; and Bonds believes that the reader is more likely to accept Paul's opinions – however unjustified they may seem to be in relation to the girl he 'labels' – because we have previously read these opinions from the pen of the supposedly objective narrator. In short, the power of the narrator is added to Paul's side of the debate.

This also happens in terms of characteristic 'voice' or discourse.

Bonds has already drawn our attention to the habit of inadequate, inconsequential diversion Paul has, when he dismisses their disagreements and changes the subject after insisting on his own point of view. Bonds finds the same inadequacy of discourse in, for example, the narrator's commentary after Paul points out some celandines to Miriam:

> Anthropomorphic as she was, she stimulated him into appreciating things thus, and then they lived for her. She seemed to need things kindling in her imagination or in her soul, before she felt she had them. And she was cut off from ordinary life, by her religious intensity, which made the world for her either a nunnery garden, or a Paradise where sin and knowledge were not, or else an ugly, cruel thing.
>   So it was in this atmosphere of subtle intimacy, this meeting in their common feeling for some thing in nature, that their love started.
>   (*Sons and Lovers*, p. 179)

The narrator's sentences beginning 'And' and 'So' give a false impression of causality, whereas in fact each one merely intensifies the effect of categorising Miriam and repeating accusations that she is over-religious and out of touch with reality – we can hear Paul's strident voice in the narrator's commentary. Finally, the inadequate generalisation about how 'their love started' reminds us of Paul's 'But there . . . it's autumn' – an escape from, and shelving of, the subject.

Additionally, the narrator often abets Paul in changing the subject at uncomfortable moments. One such moment is when he feels 'a strange, roused sensation', a 'strange stimulant' when he is in the middle of catechising her, because she 'got so near him' (see *Sons and Lovers*, p. 183). The narrative suddenly veers off on a new tack at this moment, with 'Then sometimes he hated her', and enters a new scene of her smothering her younger brother with love:

> By means of this pose of authority the narrator of *Sons and Lovers* attempts to shape the reader's view of Miriam as much as Paul, in his conversations with her, attempts to shape her view of herself . . . To the extent that Miriam allows herself to assent to this view, she allows herself to be victimised by Paul. And to the extent that readers allow

this view to command their unquestioning assent, they allow themselves to be victimised by the narrator of *Sons and Lovers*.

(*NE*, 105)

Bonds goes on to suggest that the narrative is comparable to a psychological 'game', and that in such games there are only three roles: 'victim, persecutor, and rescuer'. Lawrence critics have played all three roles. Mark Schorer, for example, was playing the role of persecutor when he wrote that 'The handling of the girl, Miriam, if viewed closely, is pathetic in what it signifies for Lawrence, both as man and artist'. Several critics have argued that the presentation of Miriam is successful, because it conveys Paul's ambivalence, and in doing so have attempted to 'rescue' the novel with the claim that, whatever the contradictions, 'it works'. However, Bonds argues that these responses to the contradictions of the text are all founded on concepts of the novel's 'form' and 'technique'. In relying on these concepts, the critics stretch ideas of form and technique far beyond any rational limits and distort them out of recognition. Instead, she concludes, it is possible to look at *Sons and Lovers* 'in epistemological terms':

> . . . the text may be seen as one in which the point of view reflects a belief in the possibility of truth and in the power of language to uncover the truth; at the same time, however, the narrative 'facts' presented in the text undermine those beliefs. That is, the story the narrator undertakes to tell deconstructs the belief in an unambiguous relation between language and truth. Like Paul's story, the narrator's quest for truth dramatises an exile from a world of clarity, immediacy, and presence to one of obscurity, deferment, and absence.
>
> (*NE*, 107)

Diane Bonds appears to have been walking a tightrope throughout this analysis of *Sons and Lovers*. The charge against the novel, of evasion, denial and refusal reminds us of that levelled by Graham Holderness; but there is a difference.

Holderness effectively judges the novel against a basic truth in which he believes: this truth is part of the doctrine he brings with him to the novel, and as readers we are challenged to decide whether we agree or disagree with him. Put simply, he does not believe it is possible to cut one's self off from society and history, and he regards the bourgeois-romantic ideal of individualism as a retrogressive illusion. In this, he asserts that he knows the world better than Lawrence; there is a 'true' history of the Brangwens, but *The Rainbow* suppresses it and creates a false mythology in its place. He acknowledges that this creation is a Lawrentian 'tour de force', but in all other respects his analysis suggests that the novel is a retreat, and a defeat for those of us who wish to confront the real world as it necessarily is.

This kind of criticism is very enlightening and challenging: we are provoked to make up our minds not only about the novel but also about our fundamental assumptions about literature and its role in society's struggles and development. Additionally, Holderness's analysis of the 'social history' element in *The Rainbow* illuminates something that is certainly present in Lawrence's creation – the peculiarly selective and elegiac creation of the Brangwens's rural origins.

Diane Bonds might appear, at first glance, to be engaging in a similar form of criticism, as she appears to know a 'real' Miriam who is not recognised by either Paul – the protagonist – or the narrator. If this were the case, Bonds would simply be guilty of the same fallacy as Jessie Chambers, whose *D. H. Lawrence: A Personal Record* (1965) complains that Miriam is not the same 'real' person as herself. This is not, however, what Bonds proposes. Instead, she is careful to point out that the 'different' Miriam she sees is alive *on the pages of the novel*, and the contradiction exists between narrator and the narrative itself, just as it exists between Paul the character and the scenes and relationships in which he is more or less confusedly involved.

There are deep disagreements between the four critics we have sampled in this chapter. The reader may be struck by the very different attitudes they bring to the reading of Lawrence, which lead them to focus on such different aspects of the texts they analyse, that the kinds of novels they are reading and the kinds of lives they consider appear to be almost unrecognisable to each other. However, all four of these critics are honestly concerned with illuminating the text, and we can reread the novels with a sense of recognition. What we recognise on returning to the texts is that Lawrence's writing has created all four of the very different responses sampled in this chapter. Certainly, preoccupations and attitudes have moved on a great deal between 1965, when Daleski was writing, and 1988, when Diane Bonds's study was published. It is salutary to recognise that we bring ourselves to the reading of literature, so that reinterpretation is a constant and continuing process. At the same time, this critical richness and variety reminds us that Lawrence's novels are complex, vital and unresolved texts, which will continue to fascinate and challenge their readers.

Further Reading

Your first job is to study the text. There is no substitute for the work of detailed analysis: that is how you gain the close familiarity with the text, and the fully developed understanding of its content, which make the essays you write both personal and convincing. For this reason I recommend that you take it as a rule not to read any other books around or about the text you are studying until you have finished studying it for yourself.

Once you are familiar with the text, you may wish to read around and about it. This brief chapter is only intended to set you off: there are hundreds of relevant books and we can only mention a few. However, most good editions, and critical works, have suggestions for further reading or a bibliography of their own. Once you have begun to read beyond your text, you can use these and a good library to follow up your particular interests. This chapter is divided into **Reading around the text**, which lists other works by D. H. Lawrence, and some by other writers; **Biography**, which includes both memoirs by people who knew Lawrence, and some more recent works about his life; and **Criticism**, which contains a selection of suggested titles that will introduce you to the varieties of opinion among professional critics.

Reading around the text

Lawrence wrote ten novels. The three we focus on in this book are

Sons and Lovers (1913), *The Rainbow* (1915) and *Women in Love* (1920). The next novel to read, in order to build your knowledge of Lawrence's novels, is the notorious *Lady Chatterley's Lover* (1928). This novel is regarded as Lawrence's best work by some critics and it arguably completes the quest for a complete sexual relationship, begun in the three texts we have studied. Following this, it will be worthwhile to read an early novel, and one from the middle period. Lawrence's first novel, *The White Peacock* (1911), together with *Kangaroo* (1923), are both interesting and very different from each other. The rest of the novels are *The Trespasser* (1912), *The Lost Girl* (1920), *Aaron's Rod* (1922), and *The Plumed Serpent* (1926). Another novel, *Mr Noon*, was published from Lawrence's manuscript papers after his death.

Lawrence wrote many short stories, and you can begin by reading 'The Prussian Officer', 'Odour of Chrysanthemums' and 'The Rocking-Horse Winner'. Among the novellas, read *The Virgin and the Gypsy*, then *The Fox*, *The Ladybird* and *The Captain's Doll* which are available together as *Three Novellas* in Penguin. The more explicitly symbolic *St Mawr* and *The Man Who Died* are also short novels, for Lawrence enthusiasts.

The poetry is now collected and published as *The Complete Poems of D. H. Lawrence*, edited by Vivian de Sola Pinto and Warren Roberts, in two volumes (Heinemann, London, 1964). There are suggestions for particular titles to try, to begin familiarising yourself with Lawrence's poetry, in Chapter 7 above.

Among Lawrence's other works, it is well worth reading his 'Study of Thomas Hardy' in connection with his novels; and 'Pornography and Obscenity' is a short essay which gives a sample of the writings against censorship. *Psychoanalysis and the Unconscious* is of interest to those who wish to understand where Lawrence's views differed from those of Freud. However, for pleasure, it is also worth looking at the travel writing, *Twilight in Italy*, *Sea and Sardinia* and *Mornings in Mexico*.

Choosing novels analogous to Lawrence's, to read as a literary context for his work, is difficult. As we remarked in earlier chapters, he is idiosyncratic; and although he undoubtedly participated in experiments in the novel form along with others of his time, he is not 'like' anyone else. This said, it is useful to look at some 'modernist' fiction. Try James Joyce's *Portrait of the Artist as a Young Man* (1915) and Virginia Woolf's *To the Lighthouse* (1927); and it may be interesting to look at Aldous Huxley's *Point Counter Point* (1928), in which the character Rampion is a portrait of D. H. Lawrence. It is worth understanding the strains which were appearing in the novel form before Lawrence's time, as writers sought to confront new ideas and discoveries. In this connection, look at Thomas Hardy's tragic novel *Jude the Obscure* (1896). A good example of a 1950s 'working-class novel' written in the wake of Lawrence, is Allan Sillitoe's *Saturday Night and Sunday Morning*.

Biography

There is a great deal of published material about Lawrence's life to choose from. I shall suggest two full-length biographies. First, there is Harry T. Moore's *The Priest of Love: A Life of D. H. Lawrence* (a revised version of the biography first published under the title *The Intelligent Heart*), London, 1974. Harry T. Moore has researched the Lawrence ancestors and provides much incidental detail of Eastwood and the surrounding area: he is full of information about the conditions and environment in which Lawrence spent his childhood and youth. The other biography I suggest takes a different emphasis. *The Married Man: A Life of D. H. Lawrence*, by Brenda Maddox (London, 1994) does narrate Lawrence's background and youth, but takes the meeting with Frieda in 1912 as the starting-point for its detailed treatment of their life together.

These are full-length biographies; but the reader interested in Lawrence's personality, his character, opinions and behaviour, may find the many memoirs written by people who knew him, more fruitful. Edward Nehls's *D. H. Lawrence: A Composite Biography* (University of Wisconsin Press, 1957) is a three-volume compilation of recollections and portraits of Lawrence, written by those who knew him, and dipping into this work in a good library is a fascinating occupation.

Some particular memoirs are worthy of remark, also. *D. H.*

Lawrence: A Personal Record by E. T., by Jessie Chambers (New York, 1936, reprinted Cambridge, 1980) commands attention because of the writer's relationship with Lawrence, and her involvement with the writing of the first novels, stories and poems. Not merely for the sake of balance, but because her feelings should also be heard, Frieda Lawrence's *Not I, But the Wind* (New Mexico, 1934; London, 1935) is also noteworthy.

Other memoirs of note are J. Middleton Murry's *Reminiscences of D. H. Lawrence* and *Son of Woman: The Story of D. H. Lawrence* (both London, 1931); Earl and Achsah Brewster's *D. H. Lawrence: Reminiscences and Correspondence* (London, 1934); and Ada Lawrence (with G. Stuart Gelder): *The Early Life of D. H. Lawrence* (London, 1932). However, these suggestions merely scratch the surface of a vast amount of material. Many of the people Lawrence knew – such as, for example, Ernest Jones, the psychoanalyst; and Bertrand Russell, the philosopher – have written their own autobiographies, recording their friendships and quarrels with Lawrence. A good cross-referenced subject catalogue in the library will turn up many of these.

Finally, Lawrence's letters cause further problems. Cambridge University Press has put together a seven-volume collection (*The Letters of D. H. Lawrence*), which has been published part by part between 1979 and 1993, most of the volumes edited by James T. Boulton with others. However, a large number of the letters are more readily available in *The Collected Letters of D. H. Lawrence*, in two volumes, edited by Harry T. Moore (New York, 1962). Collecting Lawrence's correspondence has been a lengthy and difficult task, because many of his friends who had collections of letters at his death, were unwilling to part with their 'batch' of letters, and published their own separate collections of correspondence alongside their own memoirs of him.

Criticism

The critical works sampled in Chapter 9 are: H. M. Daleski, *The Forked Flame: A Study of D. H. Lawrence* (London, 1965); R. E.

Pritchard, *D. H. Lawrence: Body of Darkness* (London, 1971);
Graham Holderness, *D. H. Lawrence: History, Ideology and Fiction*
(Dublin, 1982); and Diane S. Bonds, *Language and the Self in D. H.
Lawrence* (Ann Arbor, MI, 1988).

Anthologies of critical essays and articles are a good way to sample
the critics. You can then go on to read the full-length books written
by those critics whose ideas and approaches you find stimulating.
The New Casebooks series (general editors John Peck and Martin
Coyle), published by Macmillan, collects a variety of critical articles
together and provides an introduction which discusses the critical
history of the text. The volume on *Sons and Lovers* is edited by Rick
Rylance (1996). A Macmillan 'Casebook' is available on *The
Rainbow* and *Women in Love*, edited by Colin C. Clarke (London,
Macmillan, 1969). *D. H. Lawrence*, edited by Peter Widdowson in
the Longman Critical Readers series (London, 1992) is a challenging
collection of essays and articles, focusing on feminist, Marxist, post-
structuralist and post-modernist contributions to the reading of
Lawrence. *The Spirit of D. H. Lawrence: Centenary Studies*, edited by
Gamini Salgado and G. K. Das (London, Macmillan, 1988) is
another stimulating collection of critical essays.

The following full-length critical works may also be of interest
and should be stimulating whether you agree or disagree with the
writer's analysis. F. R. Leavis, *D. H. Lawrence: Novelist* (London,
1955) and Graham Hough, *The Dark Sun: A Study of D. H.
Lawrence* (London, 1956) both contributed to the revival of
Lawrence studies and the establishment of Lawrence's work as 'litera-
ture', which continued through the 1960 trial of *Lady Chatterley's
Lover*, and provide much of the critical context in which H. M.
Daleski's *The Forked Flame* appeared. The chapter on Lawrence in
Raymond Williams's *The English Novel from Dickens to Lawrence*
(London, 1970) was influential, leading on to the chapter in Terry
Eagleton's *Criticism and Ideology: A Study in Marxist Literary Theory*
(London, 1976) and Peter Sheckner's full-length study *Class, Politics
and the Individual: A Study of the Major Works of D. H. Lawrence*
(London, 1985). Graham Holderness's *D. H. Lawrence: History,
Ideology and Fiction*, part of which we have sampled in Chapter 9
above, is another full-length reading of the novels, as is Allan

Ingram's *The Language of D. H. Lawrence* (London, Macmillan, 1990).

Feminist readings of D. H. Lawrence might begin with Kate Millett's *Sexual Politics* (London, 1977). Carol Dix, *D. H. Lawrence and Women* (London, 1980) defends Lawrence's characterisation of women; and Judith Ruderman, *D. H. Lawrence and the Devouring Mother: The Search for a Patriarchal Ideal of Leadership* (Durham, NC., 1984), as its title suggests, puts forward a different argument.

Some of the most influential criticisms of D. H. Lawrence have appeared within critical works with a wider scope than the one author (like the works by Terry Eagleton, Raymond Williams or Kate Millett, already mentioned in this section), or as articles in anthologies or periodicals. In this connection, it is worthwhile to use the subject index in a library, and references and bibliographies which appear in the critical works you try first, both of which will point you towards many valuable contributions to the critical debate, and the many different critical approaches such as Marxism, feminism, psychoanalysis, structuralism, post-structuralism, and so on.

Index